"Just as the writer Virgil sent Aeneas into the underworld with the Sibyl of Cumae by his side, if you're going to Hell, you should always have a guide who knows the territory. In *Dispatches from the House of Death*, our guide Bill Conroy takes us down into one of the darkest places on earth, the nightmare world of Mexican drug smuggling — with its unending violence, constantly mutating alliances and corruption so deep that U.S. officials protected an informant who participated in murder after murder at The House of Death." — ***Richard Bell, investigative reporter, editor and co-author of Nukespeak: The Selling of Nuclear Technology from the Manhattan Project to Fukushima***

DISPATCHES FROM THE HOUSE OF DEATH

Bill Conroy

Moonshine Cove Publishing, LLC

Abbeville, South Carolina U.S.A.

First Moonshine Cove Edition Aug 2023

DEA commander and House of Death whistleblower Sandalio Gonzalez said to me when I first started reporting on this drug-war horror story.... "If this had been a city on the Canadian border, these murders would not have happened. Our government would not allow Canadian citizens to be tortured and murdered. But, in the House of Death case, they did let it happen, because it was El Paso and Juarez and a bunch of Mexicans that they don't give a shit about."

Dispatches from the House of Death tells the all-too true story of how and why a U.S.-paid Immigration and Customs Enforcement (ICE) informant, who had a leading role with the infamous Juarez Cartel, was allowed to participate in mass murder in Mexico — with the knowledge of his U.S. law enforcement handlers and prosecutors. In the course of the carnage, a DEA agent operating in Juarez as well as his family are nearly assassinated, resulting in the evacuation of all DEA personnel from Juarez. When a DEA supervisor seeks to expose the informant's role in the bloodshed, he is silenced by his superiors while an effort is launched by ICE to deport the informant back to Mexico and certain death. In the end, the entire bloody affair is whitewashed away in a coverup born of callous self-interest and indifference that reaches to the highest levels of the U.S. government.

Editorial Reviews

"This book reads like a murder mystery because it is. The mystery, which Bill Conroy explores with great determination, is why the U.S. government allowed murders implicating law enforcement to go unrepented and unpunished." — **Bill Lueders, journalist and author, former editor of The Progressive**

"Bill Conroy for years has launched himself at this story without fear. He did not shy away from the sword (the government). He is like 'el mesquite verde, no se raja.' He went above and beyond his call of duty." — ***Cele Castillo, former DEA agent, author and Chicano artist***

"Bill Conroy's book, *Dispatches from the House of Death,* explores the shocking and unbelievable true story of an informant on ICE's payroll who was involved in mass murder in Juarez, Mexico, with the knowledge and sanction of officials from ICE and DOJ. Conroy expertly unpacks the subsequent coverup and follows the trail of victims, perpetrators and law enforcers involved in the heinous crimes. As someone who has lived, researched and knows Mexico inside out, I found Conroy's account both gripping and enlightening. I couldn't put this book down!" — ***Nati del Paso, author of Women of Fire and Snow, and the Jaguar's Calling***

"Bill Conroy's exposing the truth about the so-called war on drugs placed his life and family in jeopardy —not to mention the government's use of intimidation in an attempt to control his reporting. His honestly in reporting impressed me. In my tenure of almost 30 years in federal law enforcement, I have never met a reporter who was more interested in the truth than enhancing his career." — ***Ruben Gonzalez, former Associate Special Agent in Charge, U. S. Department of Homeland Security/Office of Investigations, Houston***

"The so-called 'War on Drugs' is the longest and yet least understood conflict in the Americas and veteran journalist Bill Conroy is one of the most incisive reporters to tackle this crucial subject. His groundbreaking reporting on the 'House of Death' scandal is a must-read for anyone seeking to understand both the hypocrisy at the root of U.S. policy in Mexico and the absolute horror of its consequences south of the border." — ***Nicholas Schou, veteran investigative reporter; former editor in chief at OC Weekly; and author of Kill the Messenger, Orange Sunshine, The Weed Runners and Spooked***

"The struggle for justice is universally considered a lofty, worthwhile goal to be pursued ethically and morally in service of the rule of law. Bill Conroy's *Dispatches from the House of Death* exposes the murderous underbelly of America's war on drugs, where ambition corrupts the rule of law and the American officials charged with pursuing it. It takes integrity of the kind Bill Conroy exercises to shine the light of truth on a failed policy and its devastating impacts." — ***Vito De la Cruz, civil rights attorney***

"Bill Conroy exists in that rarified air of those individuals who are willing to do whatever it takes to follow the truth wherever it leads. This book is not just a bombshell of a story, it is also a timely reminder that investigative journalism is vital to any nation that seeks to hold itself accountable." — *Heather McCuen, writer and social strategist*

"Bill Conroy is among the highly valued investigative journalists. His diligence, integrity and insight come through in this book." — *Richard Berg, past president of Chicago Teamster Local 743 and host of the Fight Back! Radio podcast*

"Bill Conroy is a true investigative journalist in the tradition of Charles Bowden and Gary Webb — a man of courage, insight, persistence and eloquence. Dispatches from the House of Death tells a gripping and meticulously documented story about the violence and corruption at the heart of the "war on drugs" in the United States and Mexico. It is vital and deeply unsettling reading for anyone who wants to understand the realities and consequences of our nation's drug policies and border policies." — *Sean Padraig O'Donoghue, writer, teacher and author of The Forest Reminds Us of Who We Are and Courting the Wild Queen*

"For Bill Conroy of narconews.com, who stood his watch when others turned away and pretended none of this had happened." — *author and journalist Charles Bowden, a dedication from his book Dreamland: The Way Out of Juarez*

"Bill Conroy is an indefatigable journalist, a reporter pit bull who, once he gets his teeth into a story, refuses to let go until the truth comes out. He literally does know where the bodies are buried because he has doggedly reported on the United States' failed drug policy for two decades, and now he brings it all together in this important book." — *Megan Kamerick, KUNM public radio news director; independent producer*

"Bill Conroy meticulously presents a grizzly scene, the House of Death, that shows the war on drugs is like most wars: forged by people who seek to gain political or monetary capital and who do not care about those who perish as a result. In this heart-wrenching portrait of American indifference, Conroy asks and answers the questions that those who should have cared refused to." — ***R.V. Gundur, author of Trying to Make it: The Enterprises, Gangs, and People of the American Drug Trade***

"Absolutely no one captures the folly of the decades-long War on Drugs as thoroughly as Bill Conroy. The story of The House of Death has to be read to be believed. It's also a master class on investigative journalism and why the world still needs it." — ***Gregory Berger, journalist, comedian and Mexican TV personality***

"Bill Conroy's book urges all human beings to take a stand against the corruption spread by the drug trade and a failed war on drugs. The book is going to light fires under all good men and women, law enforcement agencies and policymakers to wake up and play their responsible roles and reverse this cancerous societal problem. The book is definitely a gift to humanity." — ***Mkhuseli "Khusta" Jack, deputy executive mayor of Nelson Mandela Bay Municipality and a past leader in South Africa's anti-apartheid movement***

"In his book *Dispatches from the House of Death*, Bill Conroy tells the story of an ICE informant who assisted a drug cartel with torture and murders at the 'House of Death' — and how the U.S. government sought to whitewash that truth. Conroy brings the reader with him to that time and place and provides a clear view not only of the local dynamics on both sides of the border but also demonstrates how an exemplary journalist operates in the field. Conroy's years of experience covering U.S. operatives in Latin America have made him a keen analyst. His book reveals why the U.S.-led war on drugs is such an abysmal failure: racism." — ***Natalia Viana, executive director of Agencia Publica, Brazil's largest investigative journalism outlet***

"It is a giant of a story. There is simply no way to understand the 'war on drugs' without reading this book." — ***Al Giordano, author, journalist, and the founder and publisher of The Narco News Bulletin [narconews.com]***

ISBN: 9781952439636

Library of Congress LCCN: 2023913548

© Copyright 2023 by Bill Conroy

All rights reserved. No part of this book may be reproduced in whole or in part without written permission from the publisher except by reviewers who may quote brief excerpts in connection with a review in a newspaper, magazine or electronic publication; nor may any part of this book be reproduced, stored in a retrieval system or transmitted in any form or by any means electronic, mechanical, photocopying, recording or any other means, without written permission from the publisher.

This book shall not be lent, resold, hired out or otherwise circulated without the publisher's prior consent in any form of binding or cover other than that in which it is published. For information about permission to reproduce selections from this book, write to Moonshine Cove Publishing, 150 Willow Pt, Abbeville, SC 29620

Cover illustration by Mark Marshall — New York-based digital artist and designer, expert soundman and musician extraordinaire; interior design by Moonshine Cove staff.

About the Author

Journalist Bill Conroy has covered the "war on drugs" since the 1980s in America's cities, along the U.S.-Mexico border and beyond. His journalism career has focused heavily on investigative reporting — as an editor-in-chief, managing editor and reporter. Conroy's work has been published online and in print for a range of publications, including daily newspapers; alternative and business weeklies; magazines; and national and international online publications — such as *The Narco News Bulletin*, the *Daily Beast*, *Agencia Publica* in Brazil and *HousingWire*. His coverage of the war on drugs also has been cited in some three dozen nonfiction books since 2001.

Conroy has been featured in investigative documentaries aired by major TV networks, including the BBC, the History Channel and Al Jazeera, that are available through streaming services, such as Prime Video and Apple TV. He also has appeared on-air for the following local TV and radio stations: KLRN and WOAI [a public TV station and the NBC affiliate, respectively, in San Antonio, Texas]; *Radio* — WBAI [New York City], WNUR [Chicago], CKUT [Montreal], WZBC [Boston], among others, including numerous podcast shows.

https://houseofdeath.org/home

Credits and Dedication

This book would not have been possible without the eagle eyes and great patience of the stellar group of editors who spent hours of their precious time helping me to get this tome in shape through several intensive rewrites. They include my wife of 34 years, the brilliant Teddi Beam-Conroy, Ph.D.; and Victor Whitman, the definition of a journalist's journalist; and the eagle-eye editors at Moonshine Cove Publishing.

I also am indebted to my long-time compadre in adventure and authentic journalism, Al Giordano, founder, publisher and editor of the nonprofit *Narco News Bulletin* — where the original versions of the dispatches that inform this book were published (many edited by Al). During the final proofing process for this book, Al passed away after battling a series of chronic health issues. Al lived life on his own terms, speaking his truth to power and working to organize other people to do the same, so that an even bigger truth rises. His work will live on far past his critics' last gasps.

I'd also like to extend a special thanks to documentarian, film professor and former *Narco News* TV producer Greg Berger, aka Joe T. Hodo, and to all the other loyal compadres of the *Narco News* team who over the years helped to edit, translate, promote, offer insights and otherwise ensure my journalism remained in the public eye. And to those who have or will read my journalism, I extend a special thank you.

This book is dedicated to all the victims and disappeared in the cruel, ongoing "war on drugs."

Books Citing Bill Conroy's Journalism Work

• *Bolivia's Border System: Globalization of Illegal Markets*
By José Blanes Jiménez; Edited by Daniela Salinas — 2023
• *Trying to Make It: The Enterprises, Gangs, and People of the American Drug Trade*
By R.V. Gundur — 2022
• *El futuro de Mexico al 2035*
By Manuel Perio and Silvia Incian — 2022
• *Drug Wars and Covert Netherworlds: The Transformation of Mexico's Narco Cartels*
By James H. Creechan — 2021
• *Mexican Drug Violence: Hybrid Warfare, Predatory Capitalism and the Logic of Cruelty*
By Teun Voeten — 2020
• *Conspiracy Theories and the People Who Believe Them*
Edited by Joseph E. Uscinski — 2019
• *Borderland Beat: Reporting on the Mexican Cartel Drug War*
By Alejandro Marentes — 2019
• *Field of Battle*
By Sergio Gonzalez Rodriguez — 2019
• *La Situacion de la Violencia Relacionada con las Drogas en Mexico del 2006 al 2017 ¿Es un Conflicto Armado No Internacional?*
By Universiteit Leiden, Grotius Centre for International Legal Studies — 2019
• *The Rise of the Narcostate*
By John P. Sullivan — 2018
• *Cain's Crime: The Proliferation of Weapons and the Targeting of Civilians in Contemporary War*
By Thomas Trzyna — 2018
• *Addicted to Christ: Remaking Men in Puerto Rican Pentecostal Drug Ministries —*
By Helena Hansen — 2018
• *Modern Mexican Culture: Critical Foundations*
Edited by Stuart A. Day — 2017
• *Sexual Homicide of Women on the U.S.-Mexican Border*
By Sara Schatz — 2017

- *The American Drug Culture*
By Thomas S. Weinberg, Gerhard Falk and Ursula Adler Falk — 2017
- *Zero Zero Zero*
By Roberto Saviano — 2016
- *The CIA as Organized Crime: How Illegal Operations Corrupts America and the World*
By Douglas Vallentine — 2016
- *Mexico's Illicit Drug Networks and the State Reaction*
By Nathan P. Jones — 2016
- *Sexual Homicide of Women on the U.S.-Mexican Border*
By Sara Schatz — 2016
- *Eclipse of the Assassins: The CIA, Imperial Politics and the Slaying of Mexican Journalist Manuel Buendia*
By Russell H. Bartley and Sylvia Erickson Bartley — 2015
- *Drug War Capitalism*
By Dawn Paley — 2014
- *The Death of a Giant: The End of the Illegal Drug Industry*
By David Duncan Sr. — 2014
- *Crime Wars and Narco Terrorism in the Americas: A Small Wars Journal/El Centro Anthology*
Edited by Robert J. Bunker and John P. Sullivan — 2014
- *The Black History of the White House*
By Clarence Lusane — 2013
- *The Fight to Save Juarez: Life in the Heart of Mexico's Drug War*
By Ricardo C. Ainslie — 2013
- *A War that Can't Be Won: Binational Perspectives on the War on Drugs*
By Z. Anthony Kruszewski — 2013
- *Criminal Insurgencies in Mexico and the Americas: The Gangs and Cartels Wage War*
Edited by Robert J. Bunker — 2013
- *The Impact of President Felipe Calderon's War on Drugs in the Armed Forces*
By George W. Grayson, The Strategic Studies Institute — 2013
- *The Executioner's Men: Los Zetas, Rogue Soldiers, Criminal Entrepreneurs*
By George W. Grayson, Samuel Logan — 2012

- *The Femicide Machine*
By Sergio González Rodríguez — 2012
- *Censored 2012: The Top Censored Stories and Media Analysis of 2010-2011*
By Mickey Huff and Project Censored — 2011
- *Dreamland: The Way Out of Juarez*
By Charles Bowden (Author), Alice Leora Briggs (Artist) — 2011
- *Gun Trafficking and the Southwest Border*
By Vivian S. Chu — 2010
- *Empire's New Clothes: Barack Obama in the Real World of Power*
By Paul Street — 2010
- *Come Hell or High Water: Hurricane Katrina and the Color of Disaster*
By Michael Eric Dyson — 2010
- *In Confidence: When to Protect Secrecy and When to Require Disclosure*
By Ronald Goldfarb — 2009
- *To Kill a Country*
By Pamela J. Ray — 2006
- *Guanajuato, Mexico: Your Expat, Study Abroad, and Vacation Survival Manual in the Land of Frogs*
By Doug and Cindi Bower — 2006
- *U.S Customs: Badge of Dishonor*
By Darlene Fitzgerald — 2001

CONTENTS

PART I

MASS MURDER

Dispatch 1
April 22, 2008...
Pages 19-30

Dispatch 2
April 22, 2004...
Pages 31-41

Dispatch 3
December 30, 2004..
Pages 42-50

THE WHISTLEBLOWER

Dispatch 4
February 18, 2005...
Pages 51-62

Dispatch 5
March 26, 2005...
Pages 63-71

Dispatch 6
September 12, 2005..
Pages 72-86

Dispatch 7
September 30, 2006..
Pages 87-93

THE VICTIMS

Dispatch 8
November 6, 2006..
Pages 94-104

Dispatch 9
August 25, 2007..
Pages 105-123

Dispatch 10
August 13, 2007..
Pages 124-130

PART II

DEPORTATION BATTLE

Dispatch 11
June 28, 2009..
Pages 131-140

Dispatch 12
October 11, 2007..
Pages 141-142

Dispatch 13
March 13, 2009..
Pages 143-145

Dispatch 14
August 4, 2009...
Pages 146-147

Dispatch 15
April 8, 2010..
Pages 148-150

STONEWALL

Dispatch 16
May 7, 2006..
Pages 151-160

Dispatch 17
May 6, 2008..
Pages 161-167

BLOOD IN THE STREETS

Dispatch 18
December 15, 2006....................................
Pages 168-181

Dispatch 19
January 30, 2012.......................................
Pages 182-194

THE INFORMANT INTERVIEWS

Dispatch 20
June 4, 2009...
Pages 195-199

Dispatch 21
August 18, 2008..
Pages 200-206

Dispatch 22
October 12, 2006......................................
Pages 207-213

Dispatch 23
July 6, 2009..
Pages 214-234

PART III

CAREER CONSEQUENCES

Dispatch 24
December 6, 2006..
Pages 235-257

Dispatch 25
March 31, 2007...
Pages 258-277

Dispatch 26
October 23, 2007...
Pages 278-283

Dispatch 27
May 17, 2009..
Pages 284-291

Dispatch 28
June 1, 2013...
Pages 292-304

THE PRODIGAL SON

Dispatch 29
September 3, 2014...
Pages 305-318

Dispatch 30
July 9, 2020..
Pages 319-331

CLOSING THE DOOR

Dispatch 31
The Past is Always Present...
Pages 332-337

References: A bibliography listing the source references for the book is available online at **https://houseofdeath.org** — along with other content related to the book. Questions and comments can be directed to **warfordrugs@gmail.com**.

Part I

Mass Murder

Dispatch 1
April 22, 2008

I was headed to Ciudad Juarez, despite the U.S. State Department warnings urging U.S. citizens to avoid this Mexican border town because it is too dangerous.

Juarez was engulfed in bloodshed due to a violent turf war being waged by rival narco-trafficking groups. The bloodshed was extreme — some 200-plus murders over the first several months of 2008. (That figure would rise to more than 1,600 by year's end in a city of 1.3 million). As a consequence, Mexican President Felipe Calderon deployed hundreds of federal police and military troops to the city.

Juarez is immediately south of a slender strip of dark Rio Grande water. The placid West Texas city of El Paso, with some 614,000 souls, is sprawled over rocky foothills on the far edge of the U.S. Empire and has the high ground overlooking the Mexican border town. El Paso was to be my first stop, before venturing into the badlands of Juarez.

My paranoia over this trip is enhanced further by the fact that my major goal is to seek out and find the House of Death — the site of a series of gruesome murders some four years earlier. The murders at the house were carried out by Mexican cops working for a narco-trafficker named Heriberto Santillan Tabares, who was part of the Vicente Carrillo Fuentes criminal organization, better known as the "Juarez Cartel." The notorious criminal syndicate is led by Vicente Carrillo Fuentes, who took over the reins of the Juarez Cartel after his brother Amado's demise in 1997 — in the aftermath of a deadly face-changing underground surgery.

Participating in the murder spree (a dozen bodies were found buried in the backyard of this house on Parsioneros Street in Juarez) was Santillan's right-hand man, a former Mexican highway cop who used the alias Jesus Contreras or, at times, was known simply by the Spanish nickname for Edward, "Lalo." It turns out Contreras was, in fact, working for the U.S. government as a paid informant even as he assisted the Juarez Cartel in carrying out mass murder.

Even though it is the prevalent term in the media, the word "cartel" is a completely inaccurate word for describing Mexican criminal organizations, given it implies a far more rigid and monopolistic structure exists within that world than is the reality. The fact that there are many competing, and sometimes cooperating, criminal syndicates in Mexico — actually their reach is international in some cases — is proof that a single cartel in the sense of the Organization of Oil Producing Countries, or OPEC, simply does not exist. Still, cartel is the word many have come to associate with Mexico's various criminal syndicates: i.e., The Tijuana Cartel, the Gulf Cartel, the Sinaloa Cartel, the Juarez Cartel. And new iterations of these criminal organization rise and fall over the decades with each new generation of leaders.

Joining me for the trip into the heart of Juarez Cartel territory on this bright, sauna-like day in April is a Peruvian freelance TV producer named Fernando Lucena — who lived and worked in London and was freelancing for Al Jazeera's European network. Fernando, too, was interested in locating the House of Death. Our guide for this journey is an El Paso resident named Mary, who knows the backstreets of Juarez well from the time she has spent there advocating for women's rights. Mary's fire for justice has been lit as a result of the infamous Juarez femicides. That was a name assigned to the unsolved cases of the hundreds of poor young women who had been disappeared or abducted, raped, tortured and then murdered — their lifeless, mutilated bodies later dumped in desolate sites along the dusty high-desert backroads of Juarez.

So, it was with a mixed sense of foreboding and loathing that I set off for Juarez in search of the now-infamous House of Death *narcofosa* (the latter a Spanish term for a mass-homicide grave, essentially). Before heading into Juarez, we spent some time in El Paso. Fernando and I had lunch with a professor of public policy named Bill Weaver at a sub sandwich shop near the University of Texas at El Paso.

Weaver, whom I first met several years earlier, had lived in the El Paso/Juarez area for quite some time and was more than a little experienced in researching the drug war. His areas of academic specialty are government abuse, secrecy and intelligence. Weaver is far from the stereotypical academic type lacking in real-world experience — having served as an intelligence analyst for years with the U.S. military prior to his university gig and more recently as an expert witness on the United Nations Convention Against Torture as applied to drug trafficking-related court cases.

Weaver relayed to me that his contacts (including "cartel" sources — some of whom do their business in Juarez but live in El Paso) tell him that the current Mexican federal police/military onslaught in Juarez plays right into the hands of the business interests of the dominate Juarez narco-trafficking organization, the so-called Juarez Cartel, which in recent years, he says, has been facing increased competition from "independent operators." Whether Mexican President Calderon intends this or not, Weaver insists that the Juarez organization is taking advantage of the situation and its corrupt reach within the Mexican feds and military to take out the competition.

Weaver says the cops that have been killed in Juarez in recent months had, for the most part, lined up with the independent operators. Basically, most of the murders in Juarez' ongoing bloody turf war have been part of this effort by the existing dominate narco-trafficking organization (the Juarez Cartel) to consolidate power by eliminating the competition with the help of corrupt elements of Mexican federal law enforcement and the military.

Weaver says the Juarez organization is now one of the largest, if not the largest, narco-trafficking businesses in the world — a type of Coca-Cola of the narco-trafficking industry. He says his sources claim the Juarez organization has been favored by the Mexican government, at least under the past administration of Vicente Fox — and possibly even now, in 2008, under President Felipe Calderon, who replaced Fox in 2006. Both are members of Mexico's National Action Party, or PAN.

"The Juarez organization is going to emerge from this [current bloodbath] stronger," Weaver explains. It could well become a monopoly, a true "cartel," as a result of Calderon's decision to bring federal law enforcers and the military into Juarez.

As I munched on my sub, I couldn't help but think that regardless of whether Weaver's prediction was correct, he was talking about the bigger forces at play, and he left out all the cartoon characters (the El Chapos and El Mayos) that mark so many mainstream media stories on the drug war. And in that moment, Weaver may have been right, and the Juarez Cartel might have had the upper hand. But the truth is, no one really knew for sure at the time what larger forces were at play and who was "winning" what. Bullets don't come with names.

As it turned out, history has revealed to those willing to check their theories against it that Weaver was not totally on the money when it came to the cops in Juarez, or the dominance of the Juarez Cartel. Much of the bloodshed there, it was later learned, was spilled in turf-war gun battles and assassinations sparked by an invading enemy, and not by unaligned independent operators seeking to expand their turf in Juarez — though they are a factor as well.

The invading enemy was determined to wage a war against criminal cells loyal to the Juarez Cartel and its turf, including local cops and politicians on the Juarez Cartel's payroll. Their goal was to take over the lucrative Juarez plaza, or distribution hub, and the drug routes converging there. That enemy was the Sinaloa Cartel (a separate organized crime syndicate with cells/gangs loyal to it or recruited to it), plus corrupt elements of the Mexican military and federal police, which had been sent into Juarez in 2008 in large numbers — ostensibly to provide public security. Some even suspected that the Sinaloa marauders had the clandestine support of the Mexican government, and possibility the U.S. government — as part of a divide-and-conquer strategy common to military counter-insurgency efforts, in which the enemy of your enemy becomes a friend of convenience.

Even that analysis, backed by many facts and events supporting it, offers only a partial glimpse of the dynamics in the war for drugs playing out in Juarez the day I arrived on the scene in April 2008, and into the future.

I sipped my Pepsi to wash down the sub sandwich and noticed that the people at the table across from us seemed a bit uneasy, like maybe we were talking too loudly — or about a subject that is taboo in a fast-food joint. After all, such matters are best left to the two-dimensional drug-war coverage of the commercial media, where cartoon characters remain trapped safely on the page — to be enjoyed at a distance over expensive lattes.

We crossed the border from El Paso into Juarez in the early afternoon on Saturday, April 19. Fernando, who had flown in from London to film a story centered on Juarez, was in the backseat of Mary's four-passenger pick-up truck. I was planted in the front passenger seat. Mary was at the wheel because she knew her way around the city.

We got the green light to proceed at the border crossing — a stroke of luck because that meant we would not be pulled over by Mexican Customs and have to explain why Fernando was packing a $10,000 professional camera for a short "tourist" visit involving no visas. Earlier we had plotted our route to the House of Death on a map. The directions seemed simple enough — head south on Panamericana (a major boulevard in Juarez) to Ramon Rivera Lara and hang a left; then go right on Acequia Mayor, which runs right into Calle Parsioneros (a dead-end street, or calle, where the House of Death is located at the address 3633).

We soon found ourselves negotiating the traffic on Panamericana. The sun is hot in the clear sky and the exhaust from the hundreds of buzzing vehicles is particularly aromatic, which might explain why I was less than alert when a backfiring car jolted me to attention. Moments later, a large Mexican Army HUMVEE pulled in front of us. The vehicle's flatbed was packed with eight or nine soldiers sporting assault rifles. We came to a stop at a traffic light behind the HUMVEE. I notice that one of the soldiers is holding his weapon across his knee, with the muzzle pointing in the general direction of my face. He cracked a smile. I knew it was going to be all right, then — if only the traffic light changed soon (and the gun's safety was switched on).

The House of Death is located several blocks off Panamericana, near a large, seemingly new hotel. We pulled to a stop in front of a house on the short U-shaped Parsioneros Street. All the houses on the street are similar in appearance. But I knew what this house looked like. It had been in my dreams more than once over the past four years of covering the House of Death murders.

From the street, the house, located in Juarez's Las Acequias neighborhood, looks unassuming — a yellowish brown two-story cinder-block home with a tall wrought-iron fence standing guard in the front yard. The fence gate is secured with a chain. The white paint coating the fence is beginning to chip away in spots, revealing flecks of rusted iron beneath. The house abuts the neighboring home to the left as you face it, almost like a row house, but it stands alone — with a closer look revealing that the two homes are separated by a high wall between their front yards that is topped with rolls of barbed wire.

Fernando and I got out of the truck, him with his camera and me with a chill up my spine. This was it, the house that had consumed so much of my life's energy, the house where 12 corpses were found buried in the backyard; the house where human beings were tortured and murdered by Mexican cops on the payroll of a narco-trafficker, all with the help of a U.S. government informant, all to make a drug case that never went to trial; the house that spawned a major coverup by the U.S. government.

It seemed too small to be that big.

The house was locked down when we arrived, the windows covered from the inside with cardboard and framed by metal bars on the outside — with ghouls and ghosts seemingly peeking through the bars securing the front door. Although we could not enter the house this day, I had seen photos of the interior previously, at least of the living room, where the executions were carried out — by strangulation, suffocation or occasionally by bullets fired through guns equipped with silencers. The interior of the home is dimly lit, the living-room floor covered with a grimy grey carpet accented by dingy white walls. The room is sparsely furnished, with a rumpled suede-fabric recliner positioned near a wall facing the front door, where a metal folding chair stands guard. Sheets of discarded plastic are seen near the recliner, and a black cord, possibly an electrical cord of some kind, is partially coiled up in the center of the room like a slithering snake.

Fernando was done filming. The people walking on the nearby street were beginning to take notice of our presence.

It was time to leave.

We packed back into Mary's truck, joking about our paranoia but all hoping that no one had copied down our license plate. I had previously discovered, after plotting out addresses found in news stories to a map, that two other mass graves discovered in early 2008 by Mexican law enforcers in Juarez were both located along a line that intersects Panamericana — with the Parsioneros House of Death at its center.

One of those houses, on Cocoyoc Street (where nine bodies were discovered) is less than a mile to the west of Parsioneros Street, right off of Panamericana. The second house, located on Pedregal Street, is about three miles to the east of Parsioneros.

Spanish news agency EFE reported at the time that the corpses found at the homes were the handiwork of Juarez Cartel assassins. U.S. Immigration and Customs Enforcement sources told me that the bodies found at the Cocoyoc and Pedregal houses in 2008 — most of them skeletons, in the ground four to five years — are linked to the House of Death case, though they could not provide any details beyond that.

The U.S. government informant "Jesus Contreras," via a previous interview conducted by e-mail and vetted through his attorney at the time, also told me the following when asked if he was aware of any other mass graves in Juarez:

> Me: Were there other similar operations in that neighborhood [of the Parsioneros house], or in the Juarez area in general, that you were involved with or had knowledge of? If so, could you provide some details on those operations?

> The Informant Contreras: From 2001, which was when they gave me the authorization to infiltrate the VCF [the Vicente Carrillo Fuentes criminal organization, also known as the "Juarez Cartel"], I reported various incidents similar to this, and I stated unconditionally the highest of risk that I was running given that this organization and its members do not hesitate to kill, and they laugh at their murders.

* * *

We entered the Camino Real Highway on the West Side of Juarez passing a cement plant. It's a four-lane highway divided by a guardrail, and it cuts a path through the center of a mountain of rock, literally, some of which tends to fall onto the road from time to time.

We stopped about halfway along this barren highway and pulled into a scenic overlook featuring strange cement arches, blocks of pavement that don't quite line up, two port-a-potties and a large parking lot beneath the elevated overlook. This "tourist draw" overlooks the city of Juarez, offering a panoramic view that was ideal for Fernando's film project. He set up his camera near a railing overlooking the smog line of Juarez. As he was filming, we saw two Juarez cops on motorcycles speeding by on the Camino Real below.

"This is perfect," Fernando exclaimed, referring to the view.

After Fernando had spent 15 or 20 minutes adjusting his camera and filming under the hot sun, we all decided to head back to Mary's truck in the parking lot below the overlook. As Mary was starting the truck, we notice a Juarez municipal police car, with lights flashing, blocking one side of the only exit out of the parking lot.

All of us became instantly focused.

This was a moment, I realized, where making the wrong choice could change your life — maybe even end it. It was clear to me the cop expected us to stop. We were expected to fear that if we drove past him — and onto the road through the parking lot's entrance lane — we would be breaking a traffic law that would justify him pulling over our vehicle, Texas plates and all, and making our life very difficult.

But my thoughts were more immediate, more about being trapped in that parking lot with a Juarez cop and whoever else might show up to assist him. At a minimum, I expected the cop would want to know what Fernando was filming and to explain what he (a Peruvian living in London) was doing in Juarez. That led down an ugly path for us — even a possible trip to the nick (British slang for a jail) that I did not relish experiencing as part of this odyssey.

"Go around him," I said.

Without hesitating, Mary did just that, pulling onto the Camino Real Highway and hitting the gas.

"Where's the next exit?" I asked.

"There is only one exit," Mary replied, "at the end of the freeway."

Seconds later, Fernando pointed out that the cop had pulled out of the overlook's parking lot.

"He's following us," Mary said, with a note of dark concern.

"His lights are off now," Fernando added — a fact that offered none of us much relief.

Oh, well, I thought ... from the frying pan into the fire. I feared we would soon be cut off up the road by some more of Juarez' finest, trapped on this moonscape highway surrounded by 100-foot-high rock bluffs on either side with only our wits to defend against a dire outcome.

The crosses painted on the utility poles along the highway flashed by us, one after another, as we sped down the highway. Those black crosses encased in pink backgrounds, Mary had explained on a previous journey, were memorials to the hundreds of women who were victims of the Juarez femicides. You see, the Camino Real's only exit along the patch of land we found ourselves traversing — where the borders of Mexico, New Mexico and Texas converge — forks in two directions. One of those puts you on a path to the New Mexico border and the Lomas del Poleo community — a desperately impoverished neighborhood that was home to a number of the disappeared women.

Lomas del Poleo also is the site of another Juarez tragedy, an ongoing siege of a small neighborhood cobbled together with modest materials atop a mesa overlooking the other meager homes of Lomas. Unfortunately for the residents of that mesa community, the land on which they built their homes, some as long ago as the 1970s, had now become prime real estate for development as part of a grand plan to exploit nearby border crossings. Those included the existing Santa Theresa, New Mexico, border crossing as well as a proposed new border crossing that would connect Sunland Park, New Mexico, and Puerto de Anapra, Mexico. All of that economic-development bulldozing was now headed toward the mesa dweller's humble abodes.

In fact, the whole point of the Camino Real highway is to serve as a fast, modern roadway for moving goods and people between Juarez and the future Sunland Park crossing as well as the Santa Theresa international port (slated then to become the nexus for master-planned border sister cities). And the downtrodden Lomas community, in general, seems to be an impediment to the smooth enactment of these development plans being pursued by wealthy interests on both sides of the border. So, it seems no accident that Lomas outsiders have erected high concrete posts strung with sharp barbed-wire around the impoverished mesa community. Private security Pinkertons and slightly underfed dogs guard the only entrance to the community, a gate through which only the residents are allowed to pass — no food deliveries allowed.

This service has been provided to the resident of the mesa not for their protection, but rather to make life very difficult for them in hopes of running them off the land to expedite future development plans. The strategy has been successful to an extent, as many of the mesa dwellers have moved on with little more than the clothes on their backs. In one case, Mary recounted, a widow with nine kids was visiting her dying child in the hospital only to return to the mesa community to find her house bulldozed. The community, she adds, has now been reduced to a hardcore group of about a 120 families — maybe fewer by now. (A March 2008 report by The North American Human Rights Delegation estimated that the number of homes still standing at the site was 92.)

I suspect this may have been the true source of the Juarez cops' concern, that Fernando might bring the lens of his TV camera to this concentration camp on the mesa. Mary insisted later that "cartel hawks" are everywhere in Juarez, and that we likely got too close to the recently discovered narcofosas for our own comfort. We continued down the canyon highway, passing a dirt road to our right that led into a small enclave of shacks and partially walled stucco structures. Out of the corner of my eye, I noticed two Mexican motorcycle cops poised on their bikes at the end of that road. The cop in the squad car was still tailing us, though he was now a ways back, a flicker of an image in the rearview mirror.

Mary soon came to the end of the highway. She veered off onto the exit — a traffic circle that shot you onto another road heading west to the Lomas de Poleo neighborhood, or toward the only other way out — east into a broken neighborhood on the far northwest side of Juarez that caresses the Texas/Mexico border. We chose the latter route and were greeted once again by more crosses, a dead dog on the side of the road, and row after row of squalid homes, junk cars and people tending to their business — oblivious to our recent highway journey.

We didn't stop.

To my relief, the cops, by now, had disappeared from sight, perhaps content that we were not headed for the concentration camp on the mesa. Or, if Mary's read was correct, perhaps the cops only intended to scare us away from the narcofosas, including the House of Death, and make it convenient for us to exit the city. The truth is we'll never know for sure.

As we drove through the hardscrabble streets of Juarez, snuggled up against the border, I could see the modern, neatly spaced homes and shiny officer towers of El Paso across the tiny sliver of the Rio Grande and the bustling lanes of U.S. Interstate 10 just beyond that murky river. Those barriers kept me in Juarez for now, but I knew I was going home later that day because I had a U.S. passport — and more than a bit of Irish luck it seems. For the people of Lomas and this poverty-burdened neighborhood on Juarez' northwestern edge, however, there was no escape from a harsh daily reality. Juarez was their world, with all its ugly warts and tragedy; it was their home; it was their community.

Juarez exists in many dimensions along this border between what is and what can't be retrieved. In this case, if anyone was the cartoon in this media narrative, it was me, playing the part of the gringo reporter — the Scooby Doo character with no clue who was now hightailing it out of town, back to the enchanted land across the border where all the drug-war cartoon characters are manufactured.

Dispatch 2

April 22, 2004

Mexican state police commander Miguel Loya Gallegos disappeared in January 2004. Several of his associates disappeared at the same time, too, vexing law enforcement agents, who said their mysterious disappearance — and consequent unavailability as potential witnesses to multiple murders — would prove very convenient to U.S. prosecutors and a confidential informant under their protection.

U.S. law enforcement agents, coming forward on the condition of anonymity, explained that the *comandante* was witness to and participated in multiple murders along with a confidential informant while that informant was on the payroll of U.S. Immigration and Customs Enforcement. The same law enforcement sources did not know if Loya was dead or alive, but they feared he was probably dead: If he were alive, they said, the *comandante*'s testimony linking the informant to the murders would likely have derailed two high-profile, priority cases that were then being prosecuted by the U.S. Attorney's Office.

Just prior to disappearing, the commander was last seen in the Mexican city of Juarez, across from El Paso, Texas. But he and his assistants are now nowhere to be found. The disappearance of these potential witnesses raises just some of the troubling unanswered questions involving the bizarre case then pending against 49-year-old Heriberto Santillan Tabares, who, U.S. prosecutors allege is a top lieutenant in the Juarez Cartel, headed by Vicente Carrillo Fuentes.

Santillan in January 2004 was sitting in prison in El Paso, Texas, after being charged with drug smuggling and five counts of murder allegedly carried out as part of a continuing criminal enterprise. The confidential informant — known by several names, including Lalo — played a critical role in snaring Santillan.

The same informant, according to law enforcement sources, also played a crucial role in a separate case that resulted in a 92-count federal indictment against 19 people allegedly involved in a scheme to smuggle $37 million worth of black-market cigarettes into the United States. The supposed ringleader of that racket, according to a federal indictment unsealed in late January 2004, was 34-year-old Jorge Abraham of Sunland Park, New Mexico — a quadriplegic who also faced federal charges for marijuana smuggling.

"This informant was key to making both of these cases," one law enforcement official said.

At stake in this tale of treachery and murder were not only the Santillan and Abraham legal cases, but also the moral convictions of multiple law enforcement sources. They came forward at the time to tell this story to me, a correspondent for the online newspaper *Narco News*, as a matter of conscience, they said.

The informant, under guidance of U.S. officials, over the course of several years had wormed his way into a high standing with Santillan's operation and the Juarez Cartel itself. During all this time — from roughly 2001 when the Santillan investigation was launched to early 2004 when he was arrested — the law enforcement sources explained, Lalo was on the U.S. government payroll. He would be contacted whenever Santillan determined there was a need to "open up the house" in Juarez where bodies were to be buried in the backyard after the victims were tortured and murdered.

The informant, the law enforcement whistleblowers alleged, even brought the tape to bind victims and the lime used to help dispose of the bodies. Most of those killed were allegedly Mexican drug runners or unfortunate witnesses to cartel misdeeds. At least one individual was a U.S. resident — "some kid from Socorro, Texas, just south of El Paso," said one law enforcement source. That kid's name was Luis Padilla — 29 years old at the time of his death.

The Santillan organization, law enforcers said, used the house as a chamber of horrors to extract information from people through torture.

The victims included competing smugglers who made the mistake of trying to run drugs through Juarez, or Santillan underlings suspected of stealing from the boss, or others outside the business who ended up in the wrong place at the wrong time. These individuals would be brought to the house and tortured in retaliation for betraying Santillan, whether that was true or not. In other cases, they were tortured until they gave up the locations of stash houses where they kept their drugs, mainly marijuana. The victims would then be killed and buried in the back yard of the House of Death on Parsionaros Street in Juarez.

The informant, the law enforcement sources claimed, participated in many of the murders — on at least one occasion tape-recording the murder for his U.S. law enforcement handlers at U.S. Immigration and Customs Enforcement (ICE). But they believe that the key executioner at the House of Death was then 35-year-old Miguel Loya Gallegos, a night-shift *comandante* with the state police of Chihuahua, Mexico — an indicted (on drug trafficking charges), but disappeared, co-defendant in the Santillan case.

The law enforcement sources contend that Loya and what they called "his death squad" of a dozen or more Mexican state police agents were on Santillan's payroll. His men ran the murder machine, using their cover as law-enforcement officials, their badges, to pull people into the House of Death. The informant — also known as Jesus Contreras, a cover name — was the middleman for Santillan. He opened the House of Death when needed and was, they explained, the go-between for providing payments to the killers, including commander Loya, and various gravediggers. During all this, the informant also was passing information onto his ICE handlers — federal agents based in El Paso, Texas.

The informant had been on the payroll of ICE (and its predecessor agency, the U.S. Customs Service) since 2000. The informant also worked for the U.S. Drug Enforcement Administration (DEA) for a short time but was "deactivated" by the agency in July 2003 — after he was caught trying to run 100 pounds of weed across the border. That bust never showed up on his record, though, as drug trafficking charges were conveniently not pursued by U.S. prosecutors, allowing the informant to continue working for ICE.

The informant's handlers at ICE in El Paso became aware of the House of Death at least by August of 2003, when the informant told his handlers that he had participated in a murder there, a murder that was memorialized on tape because, again, the informant was wearing a recording device that day. At that point, DEA officials, who were clued into the ICE operation, wanted to make Mexican officials aware of the murder and to pull in the ropes on Santillan and the ICE case being built against him. Officials with ICE and the U.S. Attorney's Office, however, refused to shut the investigation down. The reason, according to multiple sources, was that exposing the informant's participation in the House of Death murder would have crashed not only the Santillan narco-trafficking case, but also the Abraham cigarette-smuggling case — because the same informant, Lalo, was a key player in making both cases stick. The refusal to close down the Santillan investigation and inform the Mexican government of the informant's role in the murder did not sit well with a number of U.S. law-enforcement officials familiar with the case.

"What's more important, murder or a cigarette case?" one source asks. "Where do they draw the line?" From the time of that first House of Death murder in August 2003 until mid-January 2004, as many as 11 more people were tortured, killed and buried in the backyard of the house, and the informant assisted with and reported to his ICE handlers many of those additional murders.

"After all this happened, the U.S. Attorney's office issued a superseding indictment against Santillan (in mid-February 2004) charging him with five murders," one source points out. "Four of those murders didn't have to happen." Santillan faced the ultimate penalty in the United States because a murder carried out as part of a continuing criminal enterprise, such as drug smuggling, carries the federal death penalty.

On January 14, 2004, three people were tortured and murdered, but not before one of them gave up an address to a stash house in Juarez. Santillan's operatives went to the house and banged on the door. No one answered.

In fact, the occupants, a mother and her children, were inside, in fear of the strangers at the door. The mother managed to contact her husband, who returned to the house. The entire family then got in the car and left the house.

The bad guys were watching, though. The car was pulled over a short time later by a marked municipal police vehicle. Some of Loya's state police henchmen also were present at the traffic stop. The occupants of the car were likely in store for a trip to the House of Death.

Loya's underlings were not sure who the driver was, however, so they contacted their boss. Santillan in turn contacted the informant, who allegedly had bragged in the past that he was well-connected on the U.S. side of the border. Santillan wanted the informant to check out the driver, to see who he was.

In the meantime, the driver stayed in his car and put out a call from his cell phone. Soon, another car arrived. Around the same time, the informant's ICE handlers ran their check and figured out the identity of the driver.

The driver pulled out a consular ID, as did the individual who had come to his assistance.

They were both DEA agents.

The lid was blown off of Santillan's House of Death, as was the fact that some officials with ICE and the U.S. Attorney's Office, in their zeal to make a criminal case, had allowed up to 12 murders to occur under their watch and now had nearly cost the lives of two DEA agents — and put the family of one of those U.S. law enforcers in grave danger.

The threatening traffic stop led DEA to evacuate all of its agents and their families from Juarez as a safety precaution. The Mexican government also dispatched some 80 federal agents to Juarez to investigate the situation. More than a dozen of Loya's state police gang, along with some low-level soldiers and gravediggers, were taken into custody.

* * *

How many murders allegedly occurred under the reign of terror by Loya and his henchman is not known. One law enforcement source contends that the "comandante's" brush with the DEA didn't seem to deter him one bit. He says that the day after the DEA agents were stopped in Juarez, Loya was responsible for "whacking another person and leaving another one near death."

"God knows how many more murders he and his men committed that we do not know about," the law enforcement source adds.

Unfortunately, we may never know. Within days of the traffic stop involving the federal agents, DEA officials tried to arrange a meeting between the informant and Loya, to create an opportunity for Mexican federal agents to swoop in and arrest Loya. According to law enforcement sources, someone at ICE or the U.S. Attorney's office in El Paso jammed them up and wouldn't let the informant arrange the meeting.

As a consequence, commander Loya and three of his associates, "vanished into thin air," one law enforcement source said.

The plan to snare Loya was undermined, law enforcement sources contend, because Loya could have fingered the informant as a co-conspirator in the murders at the House of Death. That, in turn, would have blown apart the legal cases against Santillan and the alleged cigarette smuggler Abraham. Politics also plays a role in keeping the comandante out of the picture. If Loya were to confirm to Mexican interrogators the informant's active role in the House of Death murders, those revelations would likely inflame international tensions between Mexico and the United States

One law enforcement official made it clear that the war on drugs is an ugly business on both sides of the border. The one thing that distinguishes the bad guys from the good guys in the so-called war, however, is that murder is a line the real good guys never cross.

"No matter what, you have a moral and legal obligation to prevent murder, even if it is one of the bad guys," stressed the law enforcement source. "We are taught from the beginning that murder is the crime of crimes, and we are supposed to do everything in our power to stop it, no matter who the target is."

In addition to the central role of the informant, the cases of Santillan and Abraham are linked by the following circumstances, according to law enforcement sources:

• Both cases were actively investigated by federal ICE agents in El Paso.

• Both cases fell under the jurisdiction of the U.S. Attorney's Office for the Western District of Texas — then headed by U.S. Attorney Johnny Sutton, a personal friend of this nation's 43rd president, George W. Bush. Prior to being named one of the nation's most powerful prosecutors, Sutton rode on Bush's coattails in Texas politics — serving for five years as the Criminal Justice Policy Director for then-Governor Bush and, after Bush was elected president in 2000, as a policy coordinator for the Bush-Cheney Transition Team.

• The same attorney, Joseph Sib Abraham Jr. of El Paso, represents both Santillan and Abraham. The same informant, known as Jesus Contreras, or Lalo, an alleged Juarez Cartel operative, was central to both the Santillan and Abraham criminal cases.

• Chihuahua state police commander Loya is named in a federal indictment as one of a group of individuals who belongs to Santillan's criminal organization, which from late February 2003 to mid-January 2004 was allegedly responsible for the distribution of about four tons of marijuana and more than 29 kilograms of cocaine. The indictment also alleges that Santillan's organization employed "enforcers ... and assassins who killed rival drug traffickers, persons suspected of being police informants and members of the organization who Santillan believed had failed to carry out their duties for the organization."

• The same El Paso Assistant U.S. Attorney, Juanita Fielden, who is the lead prosecutor on the Santillan case also worked closely with the ICE supervisors and agents who handled the informant at the center of both the Santillan and Abraham cases.

• If all goes well for prosecutors, and convictions are obtained, both the Santillan and Abraham cases are potentially huge career-boosters for the law-enforcement officials involved, particularly prosecutors. Santillan is allegedly a top dog in the Juarez Cartel, a notorious drug-smuggling organization based in Juarez in the state of Chihuahua, Mexico — a stone's throw across the Rio Grande from El Paso. Abraham is allegedly the big fish in a nationwide smuggling ring that was taken down by what the U.S. Department of Homeland Security (DHS) describes in a press release as "the largest investigation to date involving the smuggling of cigarettes into the United States."

* * *

These connections are vital to understanding some serious accusations that have been leveled against the informant Contreras, his ICE handlers and the U.S. Attorney's Office by multiple sources within law enforcement. These whistleblowers, who asked that their identities remain secret because they fear retaliation, allege that officials with the U.S. Attorney's Office and ICE, in their overzealous quest to make the big cases against Santillan and Abraham, allowed their informant to literally get away with murder. And, they say, after U.S. officials became aware that it happened once, they still kept the informant in the field where he participated in or abetted at least eleven more homicides.

To make matters worse, if that's possible, these same sources contend that a coverup strategy was pursued at DHS, which oversees ICE; and at the Department of Justice (DOJ), which oversees U.S. attorneys and the DEA — all to prevent the facts of what happened from surfacing in the media and courts.

Daryl Fields, spokesman for the U.S. Attorney's Office in San Antonio, which also oversees the El Paso U.S. Attorney's office, declined to comment on the allegations.

The extent of the alleged coverup is not clear, according to the law enforcement sources. But they contend it goes at least as high as the field supervisory level at ICE and the prosecutorial level within the U.S. Attorney's Office.

Carl Rusnok, spokesman for ICE, says, "it is our longstanding policy not to comment on pending criminal cases." He adds, "In general, ICE takes any and all allegations of misconduct seriously and resolves them with expediency."

In this case, though, expediency proved to be a tall order. The law enforcement sources who came forward in 2004, when the Santillan case was still pending, and since then, said the details of the alleged coverup and corruption, once laid bare, threatened to unravel the career aspirations of a number of high-level government officials, including U.S. Attorney Sutton himself. Such a scandal also threatened, at the time, to give a black eye to the Bush administration, then in the heat of a re-election campaign.

Also, at stake were both the Santillan and Abraham criminal cases. One law enforcement source stressed that both cases were destined to "fall" if the full extent of the informant's role in the House of Death murders were made public prior to or during a trial.

If the U.S. Attorney's office in El Paso was aware of the informant's participation in multiple murders, as law enforcement sources allege is the case, then it appears the informant's ICE handlers are not the only ones operating out of bounds. According to guidelines issued in May 2002 by U.S. Attorney John Ashcroft, a Department of Justice agency, such as a U.S. Attorney's Office, "is never permitted to authorize a CI (confidential informant) to participate in an act of violence."

Even before the murders came to light, the informant allegedly influenced the U.S. Attorney's Office in El Paso to delay the indictment of Abraham in the cigarette smuggling case. The investigation in that case was launched in 2000 and was wrapped up by the winter of 2003 — as the House of Death murders were in full motion. The decision was made to delay the indictment, however, law enforcement sources claim, because it was feared the identity of the informant would surface in a trial, thereby jeopardizing the informant's infiltration of the Santillan organization.

When contacted by *Narco News*, Joseph Abraham Jr., the attorney for both Santillan and Abraham, declined to comment on his clients' cases. "All I can say is this is a very serious matter," he added, referring to the activities of the ICE informant Lalo.

* * *

The *Dallas Morning News,* the Associated Press and *Washington Post,* among other media outlets, reported pieces of this story. Loyal to the script, to the formula of drug-war reporting along the border, the U.S. media reports have focused on corruption by Mexican law enforcement officials, largely looking the other way at the pivotal role of U.S. agencies in allowing the House of Death and its serial murders to continue with the active participation of their own informant.

The sources that have come forward to me and the publication I wrote for at the time, *Narco News*, however, take us behind the door of the seedy underworld of prohibition-era narco-trafficking to reveal the sordid details of the "war on drugs." As it is practiced along the U.S.-Mexico border, it would be better described as the "war for drugs." These sources, their claims verified independently, describe two big cases made by overzealous U.S. prosecutors and agencies that drove the entire chain of regrettable, and probably preventable, events.

The "why" in this story is all about drugs and money. In order for federal agents and supervisors in the field to get the big salaries and power to run career-making cases, they have to impress the brass in Washington, D.C. And the brass want to impress their political bosses who, in turn, are impressed by big headline-generating drug busts that impress voters. And arrests and indictments connected to international narco-syndicates located in predominately brown nations, like Mexico, offer the political advantage of putting xenophobia and racism in play — to be exploited to further stoke voter engagement.

Building a case against the infamous Juarez Cartel, then, can be as addictive to blindly ambitious law enforcers and prosecutors as uncut cocaine.

In that quest, Lalo became indispensable, because he was the ticket to getting inside both the Santillan and Abraham organizations.

In the Santillan case, it was primarily Mexican drug dealers who were being murdered. Law enforcement sources contend that made it easier for some at DOJ and DHS — and within agencies under their umbrella, specifically DEA and ICE, respectively — to rationalize the torture and homicides at the House of Death as simply being an inevitable outcome for those victims anyway, regardless of their informant's involvement.

Honest law enforcers worry, however, that an "institutionalized racism" in U.S. law enforcement agencies, a problem that law enforcers have tried to blow the whistle on for years, has now led to officially sanctioned murders along the U.S.-Mexico border. The payoff for those willing to turn a blind eye to bloodshed was more money for their cases and more juice for their law enforcement careers.

"This is all about power," one law enforcer explained.

Another federal agent, who fears retaliation like other unnamed sources quoted in these dispatches, added: "One thing is for sure, the Santillan case goes to shit as does the cigarette case once the true story comes out. The kicker is that the U.S. Attorney's Office is in the middle of all this, and so who's going to investigate them? That's never going to happen unless there is enough public pressure brought to bear."

Dispatch 3
December 30, 2004

ICE announced in late 2004 that a plea agreement had been reached with accused cigarette smuggler Jorge Abraham. What the press release fails to mention is that the Abraham case also is linked to a major smuggling case involving Heriberto Santillan Tabares, a boss in the Juarez Cartel.

In addition to his mole role in the Santillan investigation, the ICE informant Contreras was employed as an informant in the Abraham case. Consequently, Contreras faced the prospect of being called as a witness in the Abraham case, if it went to trial. That put the U.S. Attorney's Office in San Antonio, which oversees the El Paso office, as well as officials at ICE in an awkward spot. Contreras could expose a lot of dirty laundry that would likely jeopardize the Santillan and Abraham cases. As damaging, or more, he also could shine a spotlight on the attitudes and actions of the agents supervising him while he was on the payroll of ICE.

As a result, Abraham's attorneys had a great deal of "leverage," DHS sources said at the time. So, here's how the Abraham case played out. In January 2004, ICE announced the following about the December 10, 2003, indictment of Abraham:

> The probe (of the Abraham organization) has resulted in a 92-count federal indictment against defendants accused of participating in a scheme to smuggle more than 107 million cigarettes with a potential street value of $37.5 million into the nation.
>
> The organization targeted today is believed to have cost the federal government, as well as three state governments, at least $8 million in lost tax revenue, while allegedly reaping enormous illicit profits.

If found guilty of the cigarette smuggling and related charges against him, Abraham faces a potential maximum 538 years imprisonment, as well as $30.5 million in fines, seizures and restitution.

In a press release issued on December 16, 2004, roughly one year after the indictment, ICE announced a plea bargain had been reached with Abraham, a U.S. citizen accused of heading an international cigarette-smuggling organization. The deal allowed Abraham to plead guilty to one felony count of the original 92 criminal counts he faced related to cigarette smuggling and trafficking. From the press release:

> Abraham, 34, faces a maximum sentence of five years. ... The total loss of revenue to the federal government and various state governments (New, California and Texas) was about $9.2 million.
>
> "This organization made large profits from circumventing the system and not paying the required taxes, cheating the American taxpayers from millions of dollars," said [Ronald] Wood, who leads ICE's El Paso Office of Investigations. "The agency appreciates the efforts of U.S. Attorney [Johnny] Sutton, his office, and the men and women of the various law enforcement agencies who worked with us to successfully bring this complex case to conclusion."
>
> As part of his guilty plea, Abraham agreed to pay restitution to the state and federal entities to which taxes and duties should have been paid. The court will sentence him and determine restitution and fines at a later date.

That's some kind of leverage, to go from a 92-count indictment and facing more than 500 years in jail to a plea deal that nets one count and a possible jail sentence of five years or less. The U.S. Attorney's Office and ICE also were facing heat from the civil lawsuit filed by the wife of one of the House of Death victims, Luis Padilla — the "kid from Socorro, Texas."

Padilla is now silent, but his family has fought to get his voice heard. They filed a lawsuit in federal court in El Paso in the fall of 2004 alleging that five ICE officials and an assistant U.S. attorney in El Paso bore some measure of responsibility in the murder of their loved one at the House of Death.

"Apathy, marred by incompetence characterized the operations run by ICE and the United States Attorney's office in El Paso. Yet the facts would reveal that both agencies were consciously aware of the ongoing killings," the lawsuit alleged.

The litigation sought unspecified economic penalties against the following defendants: ICE supervisors Giovanni Gaudioso, Patricia Kramer, Curtis Compton and ICE field agent Raul Bencomo. All of them worked in El Paso at the time of the House of Death murders. The other defendants are El Paso-based Assistant U.S. Attorney Juanita Fielden and Michael Garcia, the DHS assistant secretary who oversaw ICE.

The ironic twist in the Abraham case, law enforcement sources said at the time, was that some ICE agents were ready to move on his indictment in early 2003 but were forced to hold off for fear that a speedy trial for Abraham might expose Contreras as an informant, thereby compromising his work on the Santillan/Juarez Cartel case.

As it turned out, if Contreras had been exposed in early 2003 due to the Abraham case, it might have helped prevent some or all of the dozen or so murders that took place at the House of Death between August 2003 and January 2004.

The Santillan Case

U.S. Department of Justice officials took the predictable path in the House of Death mass-murder case by allowing the snake to swallow its tail.

U.S. Attorney Johnny Sutton in San Antonio, Texas, announced in late April 2005 that his office cut a plea bargain with Santillan. He had been charged with cocaine and marijuana smuggling along with five counts of murder. His case was slated to go to trial the following month in federal district court in San Antonio.

The plea deal capped more than a year-long effort by federal prosecutors and ICE officials to keep a lid on the U.S. government's role in an ICE informant's participation in murder in the Mexican border town of Ciudad Juarez. Under the plea deal, Santillan was sentenced to 25 years in prison for overseeing a criminal organization. All of the murder charges against him, however, were dropped.

The U.S. Attorney's Office in San Antonio, in a press release it issued outlining the plea bargain, offers a diplomatic rational for dropping the murder counts against Santillan:

> U.S. Attorney Sutton explained that the 25-year sentence imposed on Santillan Tabares effectively takes him off the street and removes him from the drug organization and the drug trade for the rest of his life. ... All of the murders were committed in Ciudad Juarez, by Mexican citizens, including law enforcement officials, and all of the victims were citizens of Mexico. While much of the evidence relating to the murders is from Mexico, Sutton said his office would share with Mexican authorities any evidence developed in the United States.

Santillan's attorney, Sid Abraham [no known relation to Jorge Abraham], in comments he made to the media, put the blame for the botched case against Santillan squarely on the shoulders of the U.S. government. From an article in the Associated Press: "Their star witness [the informant Lalo] is a renegade, untrustworthy and a scam," said Santillan's lawyer, Sid Abraham. "I think the government didn't want him to take the stand."

Despite all the posturing by the U.S. Attorney and Santillan's lawyer, it is clear that both sides in this case had a vested interest in cutting a deal. By avoiding a trial, U.S. law enforcers who might be seen by a jury as culpable in some way for the House of Death murders or the subsequent coverup efforts, avoid potentially career-ending public exposure.

Santillan, for his part, must know he has sinned against the Juarez Cartel. He could well be a dead man walking the minute he crosses the bridge into Mexico. His transgressions: 1) getting caught and 2) allowing an informant to get deep inside the narco-trafficking operation. As a result, Santillan may actually stand better odds of surviving if he is sent to a prison in the United States. He might even find himself relatively safe while there, as his continuing prison sentence is some proof that he hasn't squealed. Calculating those odds, though, is better left to Las Vegas.

Still, the whole case seems a blatant miscarriage of justice because it essentially allows people to get away with murder. We have to keep in mind what happened here. We must not forget that the focus of all of this backroom maneuvering is protecting the money interests of ruthless narco-traffickers as well as the career interests of well-heeled federal prosecutors and upwardly bound ICE supervisors and agents.

Not well-represented at the table of justice in this case are the victims, whose lives were spent like poker chips to advance these interests. Our government wants this case to be forgotten — covered up like a pauper's coffin in the ground. But for those who care to look, this case is a portal into the horrors of a pernicious, racist war for drugs. Ignoring those horrors, that reality, isn't the solution — because the next House of Death is still out there, waiting, maybe for me or you.

The Miguel Loya Case

The U.S. Attorney's Office in San Antonio did it yet again. Sutton announced in May 2005 that DOJ was not going to pursue charges against Mexican state police commander Miguel Loya Gallegos.

Juarez Cartel operative Santillan and Mexican state police commander Loya, who also is Santillan's nephew, each had been facing murder and drug-trafficking charges stemming from their roles in the torture and slayings of a dozen people later found buried at the House of Death in Juarez. Now both have scored very favorable outcomes through Sutton's office.

The *San Antonio Express-News* on May 4, 2005, reported the following in relation to House of Death killer Loya and his accomplices: "In a prepared statement, San Antonio-based U.S. Attorney Johnny Sutton said Mexico has a superior interest in prosecuting those responsible for the slayings."

That exact same reasoning, that Mexico has a superior interest in the case, is what Sutton advanced in dropping the murder charges against Santillan a month earlier.

So, the U.S. Attorney in San Antonio, in effect, turned a blind eye to murder, with the justification that it was Mexicans who were slaughtered, not U.S. citizens — even though a paid ICE informant was part of the execution team.

A message is being sent here, one that tells us that maintaining the pretense of the war on drugs is more important than pursuing murderers.

The Whistleblower

Sandalio Gonzalez is a man of average height and build, dark eyes and a neatly trimmed pepper-gray beard. He emigrated to the United States when he was a child, as part of the wave of so-called "Pedro Pan" refugees. They were all children, some 14,000 kids who exited Fidel Castro's Cuba in the early 1960s with the help of their Cuban parents, the Catholic Church and the U.S. government — with the goal of later being reunited with their parents.

In Gonzalez' case, it took some four years for his parents to join him in the U.S. after he first arrived in Miami on a Pan American flight via Havana at the age of 11. In the meantime, he lived for a short time in a camp run by Catholic nuns in Miami, then with family friends in New York City and finally with an uncle in California who had emigrated from Cuba.

While he was teenager living in the Big Apple, Gonzalez recalls that an individual broke into their apartment. Frightened for his life, he ran into the street yelling for help in an effort to get away from the invader. A New York policeman came to his rescue, chasing down the man and arresting him. Gonzalez, now a U.S. citizen, says that experience made him think he might want to become a police officer.

And, at the age of 21, Gonzalez did just that, joining the Los Angeles County Sheriff's Department and later the Huntington Park Police Department, before getting called up in 1978 to the big leagues: the U.S. Drug Enforcement Administration.

Over the next 26 years, Gonzalez rose through the ranks at DEA. He ended his career in the Lone Star State, working for DEA's El Paso field division, where he was the boss, or special agent in charge. Prior to that, he served as associate special agent in charge of DEA's Miami field division. And before the Miami post, he oversaw a good share of

DEA's Latin American operations as chief of the South American Section in the Office of International Operations.

I first met Sandalio, or Sandy as he is called by friends and acquaintances, decades ago in San Antonio — located in the heart of South Texas about an hour's drive south of Austin, the state capital. I recall at that meeting, held at a warehouse building on San Antonio's hardscrabble West Side, that he was working a case he couldn't talk about. But then he wasn't in San Antonio that day to talk about the drug war. Rather, he and a number of other federal agents who had reached out to me at the time, were focused on the war being waged against Latino and Latina special agents by their own government.

It was a war fought on the battle lines of their careers. They were being held back because of the color of their skin and their bilingualism, a skill that meant they would be regularly recruited for dangerous undercover work on the front lines of the drug war. It was a role that offered them little opportunity for acquiring management experience to advance on the job, so many never made it to the top ranks of the law enforcement bureaucracy. And the few who did advance either conformed to the sycophantic ways of the entrenched, largely white good 'ol boy networks that exerted great control within U.S. federal law enforcement agencies, or they found themselves isolated, ostracized and their careers stalled or ruined.

All this and more was fodder for another book I wrote called *Borderline Security: A chronical of reprisal, cronyism and corruption in the U.S. Customs Service.* It was published by the nonprofit, reader-supported newspaper *Narco News* in 2004 during the "coming of age" of the internet — as New York magazine dubbed the period at the time.

So, racism-fueled discrimination against brown-skinned people in law enforcement was the subject of the meeting that evening in the early 2000s in a small office inside a warehouse building on the Alamo City's West Side. That was the story I was pursuing as a journalist at the time. But my next encounter with Sandy, a few years later, was laser focused on murder, multiple murders, and the drug war. Yet, still undergirding it all, was the intolerance and cold-heartedness that racism breeds in our bureaucracies, law enforcement and the larger society. Injustice in America, however, always seems to leave behind a paper trail, one that can be followed. In this case, that trail leads to a House of Death.

Dispatch 4
February 18, 2005

Former DEA agent Sandalio Gonzalez throws down the gauntlet on the U.S. Attorney's Office in San Antonio in the form of one short paragraph tucked into the pleadings of a pending employment discrimination lawsuit he filed against the Department of Justice in the spring of 2002.

Gonzalez, until his retirement from DEA in early 2005, oversaw DEA's El Paso, Texas, field office. He makes the following claim in a legal motion he filed in early February 2005, a month after retiring, that updates his original racial discrimination lawsuit then still pending in federal district court in Miami:

> On August 20, 2004, defendant [the Department of Justice] continued to retaliate against plaintiff [Gonzalez] for exercising his protected rights by issuing him a performance appraisal record that was a downgrade from his previous outstanding appraisal, due to [DOJ's] unfounded allegations that [Gonzalez] exercised "extremely poor judgment" when [he] issued a letter to the special agent in charge of the ICE, El Paso, Texas field office, and the Office of the United States Attorney, Western District of Texas, [headed by U.S. Attorney Johnny Sutton] expressing his "frustration and outrage" at the mishandling of an informant in a drug investigation that resulted in several preventable murders in Ciudad Juarez, Mexico, and endangered the lives of DEA special agents and their families assigned to duty in Mexico. ...

In plain English, Gonzalez claims the DEA brass retaliated against him because he ruffled the feathers of a big-shot U.S. Attorney in San Antonio. The reason Gonzalez was slapped for writing the letter, according to law enforcement sources familiar with the case, who asked not to be named, is that the U.S. Attorney's Office in San Antonio was concerned that it "created discoverable material" in the Santillan murder case. "The U.S. Attorney's Office cannot prosecute someone for murders that could have been prevented by the government," explains one law enforcement source.

In other words, Gonzalez' letter, which was penned in February 2004, represents evidence that the government screwed up, and the U.S. Attorney's Office didn't want that letter being thrown in their prosecutors' faces during a possible future trial. As a result, Gonzalez was told to shut up, his work record tarnished in retaliation, and the letter buried — that is, until it can be unburied with the tools journalism offers us.

The House of Death wasn't Sandalio Gonzalez' first rodeo in the narco wars. He has a track record of standing up for what he believes in, even at the expense of his career. The original discrimination complaint he lodged in federal court in Miami stems from another drug-related case where Gonzalez refused to turn a blind eye to injustice.

Gonzalez is a 30-year-plus veteran of law enforcement. With his appointment in September 1998 to associate special agent in charge in Miami, Florida, he became the highest-ranking Cuban-American in DEA and the second in command of the Miami Field Division.

Over the course of his career with DEA, Gonzalez took on a number of domestic and foreign assignments, including his stint in Washington, D.C., as chief of South American Operations, just prior to coming to Miami.

But Gonzalez' move to Miami would prove to be career-altering. It was there that he ran headfirst into a suspected coverup that thrust him into a major legal battle with the DEA.

Following a November 1998 search of a suburban Miami house, a joint DEA/Miami-Dade Police team came up short on a stash of cocaine. Prior surveillance of the house indicated there should have been about 32 kilograms of cocaine on the premises, but the total amount accounted for after the search fell 10 kilos short of that mark. A kilo is equivalent to about 2.2 pounds.

Enrique Bover and his wife, Gisel, who each had prior drug convictions, were the targets of the raid. After their arrest, the Bovers agreed to become confidential informants in a play for leniency in their case. Their cooperation did lead to several arrests.

The Bovers assert that they informed DEA agents about the missing cocaine immediately after their arrest and that the information was ignored. Months later, the Bovers found themselves being accused of taking the 10 kilos of coke.

Gonzalez, however, suspected a set-up. He says the same Miami-Dade Police team involved in the Bover raid was responsible for "compromising three prior drug cases."

Gonzalez was clued into the potential corruption after receiving a memo from one of his agents outlining "apparent official misconduct ... and violations of federal law," he reveals in his discrimination lawsuit filed in federal court in Miami.

"It was alleged that police officers may have taken the cocaine," Gonzalez asserts in the lawsuit.

However, the fix was in, according to Gonzalez, who claims in his lawsuit that the "good ol' boys" within DEA and the U.S. Attorney's Office closed ranks to protect the "non-Hispanic/non-minority" DEA agents involved in the Bover raid.

The goal of the alleged coverup, Gonzalez claims in his litigation, was to prevent "any type of scrutiny regarding the Bover allegations" of police misconduct. Specifically, the lawsuit asserts that DEA brass wanted to ward off scrutiny of the DEA agents' "association with the Miami-Dade Police Department squad" that was involved in the Bover raid.

"The Bovers were deactivated as ... informants in January 1999, following the arrest of Enrique Bover," Gonzalez' lawsuit states. "This arrest was based on what was clearly questionable information and evidence produced by a Miami-Dade detective who worked closely with [DEA agents and] who Gonzalez subsequently learned was under investigation by his own police department's Internal Affairs office, as well as by the Miami-Dade County State Attorney's Office. The January 1999 case against Enrique Bover was consequently dismissed for lack of evidence."

Gonzalez' problems, however, were only beginning.

"I took a stand on the missing 10 kilos of cocaine and insisted that that they (DEA) do an investigation," Gonzalez says. "And that was it."

In the wake of pushing for that investigation into the missing cocaine, Gonzalez found himself the target of a series of actions by his superiors that he claims were designed to intimidate, embarrass and ultimately silence him. Gonzalez subsequently filed Equal Employment Opportunity (EEO) claims against his superiors for their actions and ultimately took his EEO case into federal district court in Miami – a last-resort option under the law.

In addition to suffering retaliation and discrimination designed to "harass and humiliate (him) and slander his character and damage his reputation," Gonzalez asserts in his lawsuit that in January 2001 he was transferred involuntarily to the less-prestigious post of special agent in charge of the El Paso, Texas Field Division.

"The prohibited actions cited ... were undertaken by the Department of Justice-Drug Enforcement Administration and the U.S. Attorney's Office for the Southern District of Florida personnel, all sanctioned and encouraged by management officials of the DEA, who also participated in the prohibited actions, and furthered an entrenched DEA policy or philosophy of racial profiling and retaliatory actions against minorities, specifically Hispanics," Gonzalez alleges in his lawsuit.

Gonzalez' legal case was dismissed on a technicality by a federal judge in the spring of 2003. A federal appeals court later reversed the decision, and Gonzalez' case was sent back to the federal district court for further review.

In addition to the revelation about the House of Death letter he penned, pleadings Gonzalez filed in the Miami case also detail additional retaliation he suffered after winning his court appeal.

That alleged retaliation included more than a dozen instances in which Gonzalez was passed over for a promotion or a transfer — and other less-qualified DEA officials were promoted or transferred in his place, according to the court filing.

The Department of Justice, the defendant in Gonzalez' lawsuit, contends the charges made in the case are without merit. Gonzalez, though, says his career did not merit being turned upside-down for reporting suspected law enforcement corruption.

"The missing cocaine is definitely the catalyst of my problems," he says. "The coverup [since then] has been amazing. They [his superiors] look at you blank-face and then look the other way."

This time, it's more than cocaine they have to turn away from. With the House of Death, we are being asked to disappear mass murder.

* * *

Gonzalez' court litigation in Miami related to the missing cocaine was not the only path he pursued in seeking justice. He also filed a case with the federal Merit Systems Protection Board (MSPB), which handles appeals by federal employees who claim they have faced retaliation due to whistleblowing activity.

Gonzalez took this step after both the Office of Special Counsel and the Justice Department's Office of Inspector General declined to investigate his whistleblower claims related to the House of Death mass murder case in Juarez. I filed a **Freedom of Information Act (FOIA) request** with the MSPB as a correspondent for *Narco News* to obtain whatever records I could from Gonzalez' case.

There was a wealth of information in the FOIA records released by the **MSPB**. This look behind the veil of government secrecy exposes the bombshell letter penned by Gonzalez. Although certain words in the letter were redacted in the original FOIA records, months later I obtained an unredacted version of the letter. (Information in the letter below in [brackets] has been inserted for clarification purposes.)

February 24, 2004

Mr. John Gaudioso

Special Agent in Charge

Department of Homeland Security

Bureau of Immigration and Customs Enforcement

4191 North Mesa

El Paso Texas 79902

Dear Mr. Gaudioso:

Since our meeting on January 25, 2004, and our telephone conversation on February 14, 2004, I've had an opportunity to digest what you've said as well as to conduct a careful review of the material in this case. I am now writing to express to you my frustration and outrage at the mishandling of the Heriberto Santillan Tabares investigation that has resulted in unnecessary loss of human life in the Republic of Mexico and endangered the lives of special agents of the Drug Enforcement Administration (DEA) and their immediate families assigned to the DEA office in Ciudad Juarez, Chihuahua, Mexico.

There is no excuse for the events that culminated during the evening of January 14, 2004, and absent a complete and logical explanation of these events, which led to the emergency evacuation of our personnel and their families in Ciudad Juarez, I have no choice but to hold you responsible for this unfortunate situation.

Rather than join with others in petty finger pointing, I will limit this letter to the following irrefutable facts:

This chain of events began when hired killers working for Santillan went to the residence of a DEA agent in Ciudad Juarez, and later caused local police to make a traffic stop of the agent's vehicle, which at the time was occupied by the agent and his wife and two daughters. We must not forget this.

During the early part of 2002, my office initiated Operation Sky High, a U.S. multi-agency bilateral investigation with Mexican federal authorities, targeting the Vicente Carrillo Fuentes organization. Coordination meetings in El Paso were convened among the participants, which included DEA, FBI, ICE, the U.S. Attorney's Office (USAO), and Mexican federal officials representing the Office of the Attorney General (PGR). Everyone agreed to work together and do everything possible to disrupt and/or dismantle the Vicente Carrillo Fuentes organization on both sides of the border. To this date, the only U.S. agency that has honored that gentleman's agreement is the DEA.

From the very beginning, ICE personnel and the prosecutor from the USAO [U.S. Attorney's Office] have exhibited an unfounded and indeed inexcusable lack of trust of DEA personnel, in particular agents stationed in Mexico. Allegedly, our agents in Mexico share too much information with their Mexican counterparts. This mistrust is insulting and runs contrary to the agreement made at the start of Operation Sky High.

DEA agents in both El Paso and Ciudad Juarez have honored every request made by your agents, as well as by the prosecutor, to not share information with Mexican authorities even though those requests, and the attitude in general of your agents and the prosecutor, go against the spirit of cooperation agreed upon by everyone present at the Operation Sky High meetings in El Paso.

On/about August 5, 2003, while working for your agency, the ICE confidential source [CS] identified as SA-913-EP [Jesus Contreras or Lalo] participated in a murder in Ciudad Juarez. Shortly thereafter the actions of [Contreras] were misrepresented to Mexican authorities that were told via official ICE correspondence that [he] had merely "witnessed" a murder and would soon be available to provide testimony to the PGR [Mexican Attorney General's Office]. [Contreras] was in fact a participant in the torture/murder of Fernando [Reyes Aguado, an attorney and alleged drug trafficker from Durango, Mexico], as reflected in [the informant Contreras'] debriefing report [with ICE] dated August 25, 2003, which clearly states that [he] supervised his murder.

When considering this situation, it is not surprising to me that people in your agency and the USAO would be concerned about DEA agents sharing "too much information" with their Mexican counterparts. While DEA personnel have done everything possible to assist Mexican officials without compromising ICE information, ICE personnel have thrown obstacles in our way and concealed vital information that could have saved lives.

Following the murder of Fernando [Reyes] in August 2003, your agents requested several country clearances for the [informant] to travel to Ciudad Juarez, and they continued sending the [informant Contreras] to Juarez while failing to report his activities to DEA as required by our own internal agreements. I have been told that over 200 reports of investigation were written regarding this case by ICE/El Paso and that none of these were distributed to your own personnel assigned in Mexico.

ICE agents failed to provide DEA agents in Juarez with the exact location where the body of Fernando [Reyes] was buried, stating that the information given by the [informant Contreras] was vague, thereby obstructing a murder investigation in Mexico, and eventually placing the lives of DEA agents and their families in Ciudad Juarez in grave danger. During his debriefing by ICE agents, the [informant] admitted to killing Fernando [Reyes] as well as to knowing the exact location of the burial site because following the debriefing he went back to the house in Juarez to give money to Alex Garcia [one of Santillan's crew]. This information is in the ICE debriefing report dated August 25, 2003.

On August 11, 2003, DEA Group Supervisor David Jenkins was asked by [ICE] Associate Special Agent in Charge [Patricia] Kramer to convene a meeting with FBI, DEA and ICE personnel to discuss the informant/murder issue as well as the issue of Mexican police corruption. The meeting was scheduled to take place in the DEA office on August 15, 2003, at 2 pm; however, ICE personnel did not show up as scheduled, and Group Supervisor Jenkin's ICE counterpart notified him that the meeting had been cancelled. That was the last time we heard about the issue until recently.

Following the August 2003 murder of Fernando [Reyes], ICE personnel and the prosecutor ignored well-founded recommendations made by DEA agents to arrest Santillan and "take down" the case, thereby allowing at least thirteen other murders to take place in Ciudad Juarez, in what can only be described as a display of total disregard for human life, and disrespect for the rule of law in Mexico. Much of this, I'm told, to protect the drug case against Santillan and a cigarette-smuggling case in which [the informant Contreras] is a witness.

On/about December 19, 2003, your office submitted a request to lure Santillan into the U.S. without the requisite ASAC [associate special agent in charge] level of coordination with my office or with DEA in Mexico City. This was after DEA agents assisted and participated in the drug case against Santillan, since it fell under the umbrella of Operation Sky High. During our telephone conversation, you referred to the matter of the lure as a "minor issue."

Santillan and [Contreras] were allowed to continue their activities in Mexico following the August 2003 murder of Fernando, and on January 14, 2004, DEA agents and their families stationed in Ciudad Juarez were and remain evacuated from their residences because hired killers working for Santillan tried to identify two of our [DEA] agents through [Contreras] under the ruse of a traffic stop.

Santillan and others, with the assistance and participation of [Contreras], committed a series of murders in Ciudad Juarez that have shocked the conscience of decent, law-abiding citizens on both sides of the border.

Following the evacuation of our [DEA] personnel from Ciudad Juarez, ICE agents, with your concurrence, refused to immediately present the [Contreras] to Mexican federal authorities so that his testimony could be used as the probable cause necessary to arrest the corrupt police officials in Juarez. Your failure to present [Contreras] to Mexican federal officials resulted in a one-week delay before probable cause could be established to search for the dead bodies [at the House of Death].

These officials told our [agency] attaches in Mexico that they would have to wait to discover the bodies prior to arresting the corrupt officers. Now these dangerous killers [including Mexican state police commander Miguel Loya Gallegos] are at large. To make matters worse, you would not allow [Contreras] to call Comandante Loya so that Mexican federal authorities could arrest him for his participation in the [House of Death] murders. You and the prosecutor [in El Paso, Juanita Fielden, who works under U.S. Attorney Johnny Sutton in San Antonio] until last week refused our repeated requests for direct access to [Contreras] so that we could at least attempt to resolve the threat. In fact, the prosecutor stated that she had ordered ICE personnel to refuse DEA access to tapes of [Contreras], while expressing concern regarding our [DEA] sharing of information with Mexican federal authorities. You allowed a prosecutor to make an operational decision that interfered with the investigation of a threat against the lives of fellow U.S. federal agents and their families.

It was not until the [DEA] Chief of Operations met with his counterpart in your agency [ICE] that you agreed to allow our agents direct access to [Contreras]; however, you then placed restrictions on that access that are inconsistent with both the spirit of cooperation that should exist between our two agencies, and with good law enforcement practices and procedures. Your reasoning for doing this was that, in your view, DEA agents were targeting [Contreras], and you could not allow that to happen.

In light of that, we cannot help but wonder why you would go to such extreme lengths to protect this "homicidal maniac" informant. In fact, the procedures employed in the handling of this informant, the fact your agents continued working with him after he tried to run a 100-pound load of marijuana behind our back last June [2003], and his incredible story after he tape-recorded the murder of Fernando, leads me to conclude that the informant may have been controlling the agents. ICE agents allowed [Contreras] to continue on an unabated crime spree while under their so-called control.

The restrictions you [ICE] placed on our interview of [Contreras] had the effect of obstructing the investigation of the threat against our [DEA] agents, a threat that should have never taken place, and that came about as a result of cold killers who went to an agent's residence, and later caused local police to make a traffic stop of the agent and his family for purposes of identification and possibly their abduction and murder.

This situation is so bizarre that even as I'm writing to you it is difficult for me to believe it. I have never before come across such callous behavior by fellow law enforcement officers. The bottom line is that as a result of these actions, Comandante Loya and other murder suspects are now fugitives. There was no logical reason to prevent [Contreras] from calling Loya so Mexican authorities could arrest him. What is more important here, the safety of agent personnel and their families, or drug and cigarette smuggling cases? Santillan's subsequent indictment for murders that occurred after August 5, 2003, that could have been prevented, is disturbing.

You mentioned during our telephone conversation that one of our Juarez agents "lost his cool and made a fool of himself" while trying to obtain information regarding the threat. I strongly disagree with your assessment in that regard and propose to you that while there may be fools involved in this debacle, not one of them is employed by the DEA. I suggest that just for a moment you put yourself in that agent's shoes. What would you have done if you and your family had been threatened by [Juarez Cartel] killers, and I refused you access to a DEA informant who might be of help in the case?

[Contreras] knew on January 13, 2004, that Santillan was planning a "carne asada," for the Parsioneros house [the House of Death in Juarez] on the following day, and nothing was done about it until Santillan called [Contreras] on the night of the 14th to check the names of our [DEA] agents. By that time, three more human beings had been tortured and killed.

You told me that it was not until January 25, 2004, that you learned of [Contreras'] involvement in murders other than the one on August 5, 2003.

You also told me that your agents will no longer work with DEA personnel assigned to the Ciudad Juarez Resident Office. This is unacceptable and goes against the spirit of cooperation inherent in the reasons for creating the Department of Homeland Security.

It appears to me, after reading the statement given by [the informant Contreras] to the Mexican authorities, that [Contreras'] handlers may have known about the "carne asada" scheduled for January 14 [at the House of Death], and perhaps others prior to that. This of course begs the question, if the killers had not called [Contreras] to check on our agents on January 14, [2004] how many more dead bodies would we have by now?

Now, six months after the murder of Fernando [Reyes], the [Mexican Attorney General's Office] PGR has testimony from several members of Santillan's killing circle. The PGR knows that U.S. authorities could and should have taken steps to stop these assassins. Both of our agencies have spent countless hours building trust and sharing sensitive information without compromise with trusted counterparts in Mexico.

However, the developments in this case have, to say the least, strained that relationship and set us back years. Our regional director in Mexico and I have been discussing this at length on a daily basis. We both find this situation appalling, and he concurs with my comments.

Sandalio Gonzalez

Special Agent in Charge

cc Chief AUSA [Assistant U.S. Attorney], El Paso

Regional Director, Mexico City

Dispatch 5
March 26, 2005

The first sign that **DEA supervisor Sandalio Gonzalez** had hit a deep nerve with his letter of protest over ICE's handling of the House of Death murders materialized in May 2004, three months after the missive was delivered to El Paso ICE Special Agent in Charge John Gaudioso — with a copy also earmarked for the **U.S. Attorney's Office.**

It was then that Gonzalez claims he was threatened by the DEA's legal counsel during the course of settlement negotiations over his discrimination/whistleblower lawsuit filed in federal court in Miami. Essentially, Gonzalez was told that if he did not voluntarily retire from the agency by June 2004, he would receive a negative job-performance rating.

Gonzalez deemed the threat a reprisal for writing the House of Death letter to Gaudioso. In reaction, Gonzalez fired off a letter to the U.S. Department of Justice's Inspector General, then Glenn A. Fine, **asking that his office investigate** the retaliation he was experiencing due to his whistleblowing activities.

Fine's office declined to take up the case because the alleged retaliation occurred in the context of Gonzalez' still-pending federal litigation in Miami. "Because the matters you raise are related to your pending whistleblower litigation, we have decided not to initiate another investigation into the matter," Carol F. Ochoa, director of oversight and review at the Office of Inspector General, wrote in an August 12, 2004, reply to Gonzalez.

Despite the Inspector General's refusal to take action on his complaint, Gonzalez was not done fighting. He had no intention of being forced out of the DEA for telling the truth. In late August 2004, the agency followed through with its threat to slam his work record by giving him a negative job review. A few weeks later, on September 9, 2004, Gonzalez filed a complaint with the U.S. Office of Special Counsel — the OSC.

Gonzalez asked the watchdog agency to investigate his case, claiming that he was being retaliated against for disclosing "murder, gross mismanagement of a criminal case and (obstruction of) an investigation of a threat against the lives of a federal agent and his family."

Following is an excerpt from **Gonzalez' OSC complaint** as well as the **agency's response** — both of which were included with Freedom of Information Act records I obtained while working as a *Narco News* journalist. Content contained in [brackets] was added by me for clarity and, where necessary, confirmed with sources.

> This issue began on February 24, 2004, when I sent a letter to the Special Agent in Charge of the Bureau of Immigration and Customs Enforcement (ICE) in [El Paso, Texas] in essence holding him responsible for the actions of ICE personnel and one of their informants regarding the discovery of several bodies buried in the backyard of a residence located in the city of [Ciudad Juarez], Republic of Mexico, and the obstruction of an investigation about a threat against the life of a DEA agent and his family. Since a federal prosecutor was in the mix, I also sent the letter to the prosecutor's supervisor in the Office of the United States Attorney for the Western District of Texas, (in San Antonio).
>
> A few days later I received a telephone call from [name redacted], the Chief of Operations of the Drug Enforcement Administration (DEA), who informed me that the United States Attorney for the Western District of Texas [Johnny Sutton] had been given a copy of the aforementioned letter and that [Sutton] was very upset with it and had alleged that my letter had created discovery material in the federal case against [Heriberto Santillan Tabares]. [The Chief of Operations at DEA] also said that [Sutton] had gone directly to the Department of Justice (DOJ) to complain about me, and that DOJ officials had contacted [the] DEA Administrator [then Karen Tandy] to inform her about [Sutton's] complaint....

Several days later, I spoke with the Deputy Administrator of the DEA [Michele Leonhart] who told me that the Administrator [Karen Tandy] was very upset with me as a result of the letter, and that she had seriously considered calling me back to Washington to discipline me for sending the letter. [Leonhart] went on to tell me that she had convinced the administrator not to call me to headquarters because it would disrupt the Special Agent Promotion Program where I was serving as an assessor at the time; however, [Leonhart] went on to say that in her view, as well as in the opinion of the [DEA] administrator and the chief of operations, I had exercised "poor judgment" in sending the letter to the ICE SAC and the U.S. Attorney's Office. I respectfully disagreed with her, and we then went on to discuss other matters.

On May 4, 2004, regarding a whistleblower complaint and a Title VII lawsuit I previously filed in Miami against the DEA, the DEA attorney threatened me with a negative performance rating if I did not retire by June 30 of this year [2004] ....

NOTE: The Deputy Administrator [Leonhart], who is my first-line supervisor and the rating official in my performance appraisal, must approve all matters such as these. Since I did not retire on June 30, DEA carried out the threat in its May 4, 2004, letter when the issue in question was misrepresented in the [August 2004] appraisal under the job element of liaison/collaboration. [Leonhart, who later became DEA administrator, confirmed by the Senate in 2010,] wrote that my "extreme poor judgment" in writing the letter had caused DEA's relationship with ICE and the U.S. Attorney's Office in [El Paso and San Antonio] to worsen. [Leonhart] also lowered my overall rating from the previous year despite the fact that the list of accomplishments in this year's rating was far greater than last year's....

I believe that I'm being punished for speaking the truth about a serious matter of public concern that is not publicly known. When I made this known to the United States Attorney for the Western District of Texas [through the letter forwarded to Sutton in San Antonio], rather than take corrective action, he attacked my professionalism. And, [he] indirectly criticized my integrity, ironically for refusing to participate in a coverup, which may even constitute the criminal offense of obstruction of justice, misprision of a felony, or, to a lesser extent, a federal agency's negligence resulting in multiple homicides.

DEA officials that are fully familiar and upset with the issue of the murders, as well as the obstruction of the investigation of the threat against the life of a DEA agent and his family, and admitted this to me, are now following the political and personal agenda of the United States Attorney for the Western District of Texas [Sutton] by retaliating against me with a negative performance appraisal. In addition to all of the above, there is also a First Amendment violation here.

The Whistleblower Protection Act protects employees who (reasonably) disclose ... "a substantial and specific danger to public health or safety." I reported allegations of serious misconduct on the part of federal agents and an informant acting under the direction of the agents, arguably with the knowledge of a federal prosecutor....

In direct retaliation for the protected disclosures attributed to me, the agency lowered my performance appraisal and included negative information within the appraisal, specifically attacking the disclosures, an admission of its direct violation of the whistleblower statute. These notations irreparably tarnish my career and post government-service employment opportunities. My performance evaluation was lowered and contained negative information precisely [and only] because of my protected disclosure. A more transparent violation of the Whistleblower Protection Act is difficult to imagine.

The Office of Special Counsel replied to Gonzalez' complaint on November 19, 2004. Following are excerpts from that response:

Dear Mr. Gonzalez:

This letter is in response to your complaint to the U.S. Office of Special Counsel (OSC) against the Department of Justice (DOJ). You allege that the lowering of your performance rating from outstanding to excellent constitutes reprisal for whistleblowing.

The Office of Special Counsel is authorized to investigate allegations of activities prohibited by civil service law, rule, or regulation, and prohibited personnel practices. We have carefully considered the information you provided. .... However, for the reasons explained below, we have made a preliminary determination to close the investigation into this matter.

You state that on February 24, 2004, you sent a copy of the letter you wrote to Special Agent in Charge John Gaudioso to the United States Attorney for the Western District of Texas. In this letter, you reported your frustration and outrage at the mishandling of the [Juarez Cartel] investigation that resulted in the unnecessary loss of human life in the Republic of Mexico and endangered the lives of special agents of the Drug Enforcement Administration and their immediate families assigned to the DEA office in Mexico.

In order for a disclosure to be protected, the employee must have a "reasonable belief" that the information being disclosed evidences one of the improprieties mentioned in the statute — a violation of law, rule, or regulation; gross mismanagement; a gross waste of funds; an abuse of authority; or a substantial and specific danger to public health or safety....

We lack information that demonstrates how your report evidences one of the improprieties defined in the statue....

However, even if your report was determined to constitute a protected disclosure, we still would be unable to establish a connection between it and the personnel action....

Thus, while you may believe that agency officials took a reprisal action for your report, we cannot infer that this action was taken for reasons other than those given in your appraisal concerning your extremely poor judgment, and that your actions made already tense relationships worse....

Finally, with regard to your allegation that you engaged in protected speech which was in turn the motivating, substantial and exclusive factor for the agency official's retaliation, we analyzed this matter as a possible violation.

Speech involves a matter of public concern if it addresses items of political, social, or other concern to the community. However, federal employees enjoy a more limited right to free speech than other citizens when the federal government is acting as an employer.

We believe that your comments did not amount to public speech protected by the First Amendment. Rather, as stated above, simply expressed your observations of, and dissatisfaction with, the Bureau of Immigration and Customs Enforcement management officials and their handling of a federal case.

Further, even if we assumed that the letter touched upon a matter of public concern, it appears management's right to restrict an employee's on-duty speech that has the potential to disrupt the work environment would outweigh your rights in this situation.

As indicated above, we have made a preliminary determination to close our inquiry into your complaint based on the reasons we cited for each allegation you made....

Sincerely,

Colette A. Key

Complaints Examiner

Complaints Examining Unit

So, some nine months after his House of Death protest letter was sent to ICE supervisor Gaudioso and U.S. Attorney Sutton, Gonzalez found himself running out of options in dealing with the resulting reprisal he was convinced had come his way. Two major government watchdog agencies had now chosen to hide behind legal loopholes to look away from the House of Death mass murder and its tomb of lies.

Gonzalez' federal whistleblower/discrimination lawsuit in Miami was still pending, but with no end in sight. And, Gonzalez claims, there was no end in sight to the retaliation he was facing from the DEA. As a result, Gonzalez decided to turn in his gun and badge for good.

"On January 8, 2005, [Gonzalez] had no choice but to retire after 26 years of service with the agency when it became obvious that his career was all but over due to the numerous acts of retaliatory conduct on the part of [the DEA], essentially making it the same as a constructive discharge," Gonzalez' attorney asserts in pleadings in his **federal lawsuit in Miami**.

Gonzalez' letter exposed the role played by an ICE informant in the multiple murders in Juarez while under the supervision of U.S. federal agents. The same ICE informant assisted with and even participated in some of those murders carried out by the Juarez Cartel. He then later helped ICE snare the chief author of the homicides, Heriberto Santillan Tabares, who U.S. prosecutors portray as a rising figure in the Juarez Cartel.

Despite all this, it is Gonzalez that is deemed to be the one out of line for speaking the truth to power. So, why should it be any surprise that the ICE informant is allowed to play outside the rules on that bridge between worlds in the war for drugs, enabled by U.S. law enforcers with a pass to commit murder?

A May 2005 report in a leading Mexican news magazine, *Proceso,* (which was reprinted in the daily Mexican newspaper *Por Esto!)* claims that the informant Lalo — also known as Jesus Contreras — is a former officer with the now-defunct Mexican Federal Highway Police. The *Proceso* report also indicates that Lalo's real name is likely Eduardo Martinez Peyro. U.S. government documents will surface later showing that name is close, but still off the mark.

So, who is this informant, really? Clearly, his identity is shrouded in layers of deception for his own protection, so his true name is hidden beneath a mask of aliases. He is essentially a man with many names. Johnny Sutton, however, we do know. Veteran DEA agent Gonzalez has accused Sutton of retaliating against him for blowing the whistle on a paid ICE informant's "homicidal" role in the narco-related murders of a dozen people in Ciudad Juarez, Mexico.

Sutton at the time of the House of Death murders had close ties to President George W. Bush. He also had worked previously with Bush's second Attorney General, Alberto Gonzales.

Sutton, a former assistant district attorney in Harris County, Texas, hitched his star to the Bush political machine early on in his career, while George W. was governor of Texas. After Bush was elected president, Sutton's devotion paid off, and he was named associated deputy attorney general at DOJ in Washington, D.C., and also served as a policy coordinator for the Bush-Cheney presidential transition team. In late October of 2001, Sutton was appointed by Bush to serve as U.S. Attorney for the Western District of Texas in San Antonio. The U.S. Senate confirmed the appointment a month later. So, Sutton does indeed have friends in high places, including his most recent boss at the Department of Justice (DOJ).

San Antonio native Alberto Gonzales also skyrocketed into the big time on the coattails of the Bush machine. Like Sutton, Gonzales also practiced law in Harris County (Houston) prior to joining then-Gov. Bush's staff. Gonzales served as general counsel and a senior advisor to Gov. Bush while Sutton also was on the governor's staff as a legal advisor. After Bush was elected president in 2000, Gonzales was upgraded to White House Counsel, a position he held until February 2005, when he became the boss at DOJ, replacing John Ashcroft.

Despite the allegations about a coverup in the House of Death case, Attorney General Gonzales still appointed Sutton to the post of vice chairman of his Advisory Committee of U.S. Attorneys, which plays a key role in determining DOJ policies and programs.

Sandalio Gonzalez, a 26-year veteran of DEA, has a demonstrably stellar track record with the agency. As mentioned, previous to his post as head of DEA's field office in El Paso, Gonzalez served as associate special agent in charge of DEA's Miami Field Division. Prior to that, he oversaw DEA's operations in much of Latin America as chief of the South American Section in the Office of International Operations.

Sutton, however, was seemingly not impressed with Gonzalez' background, or at least did not feel compelled to meet with him after receiving his letter denouncing ICE's informant and his role in the House of Death murders. Instead, Sutton's reaction was to reach out to his high-level contacts within the DOJ in Washington, D.C., to bring pressure to bear on Gonzalez, to shut him up and to ensure the letter he penned was buried.

"When a U.S. Attorney gets a letter from another senior government official in DOJ, and his first reaction is to go after that official behind his back instead of looking at the issues, that is suspect," Gonzalez said in an interview with me for *Narco News*. "If he was on the up and up, he should have at least called me to set up a meeting with me.

"Instead, he goes behind my back to DOJ to complain. This is indicative of the way the government works against all whistleblowers. When they go against the grain, no matter how right they are, the government goes after them. The record is rather clear on this."

And in this case, Gonzalez' whistleblowing about a "homicidal" ICE informant — with the cover name of Jesus Contreras, or Lalo — threatened to expose a corruption that U.S. prosecutors likely could not overcome.

"No way they could afford to put Lalo on the stand and have him testify to all of this," Gonzalez said in a 2008 interview with *Reason* magazine "...The murders had to be dismissed because the government's star witness and informant, Lalo, would have had to testify that he took part in them. At that point, any defense attorney worth his salt would've gotten out of Lalo that he was reporting these murders to federal agents before they happened."

Dispatch 6

September 12, 2005

The one consistent thread in following the House of Death story that became clear with time is that coverups rarely succeed in concealing the evidence, and so eventually, to succeed, they must concentrate on silencing the messengers. Still, the evidence exists. Additional documents that I obtained through Freedom of Information Act (FOIA) requests filed as a *Narco News* correspondent pull back further the dark shroud hung over the House of Death. The documents, released by the U.S. Merit Systems Protection Board (MSPB), include internal Department of Justice e-mails focused on the House of Death case.

Recall that in addition to his federal court case in Miami stemming from alleged law enforcement corruption related to missing cocaine, Gonzalez also lodged a complaint with the federal Merit Systems Protection Board (MSPB), which hears cases involving federal employees who claim they are facing retaliation due to whistleblowing activity. Gonzalez took this step after both the Office of Special Counsel and the Justice Department's Office of Inspector General declined to investigate his claims related to ICE's handling of its informant in the Santillan/House of Death mass murder case in Juarez.

In general, the FOIA documents obtained from the MSPB are heavily redacted — based, in part, on alleged privacy-protection exemptions. As it turns out, among the items redacted in the e-mails are the names of the high-ranking Department of Justice officials who drafted or received the e-mails as part of performing their public duties. *Narco News* filed a FOIA appeal seeking the release of all the documents in former DEA supervisor's Sandalio Gonzalez' MSPB case and asked that all the names of public officials in those documents be "un-redacted." That appeal was not successful, but un-redacted versions of some of the documents appeared later as exhibits in court cases, and law enforcement sources familiar with the House of Death case also assisted in filling in some of the missing information.

Other important documents surfaced through the FOIA request include two emails drafted in early March 2004, shortly after Gonzalez sent his House of Death letter to U.S. Attorney Johnny Sutton exposing the murderous activity of the informant Contreras while he was under the supervision of ICE agents and a U.S. prosecutor.

Well-placed law enforcement sources familiar with the House of Death case told me at the time, in the fall of 2005, that the individuals who either wrote the e-mails or received copies of the e-mails included the following: Karen Tandy, administrator of the DEA; Catherine M. O'Neil, associate deputy attorney general at DOJ; and the number two person at DOJ, then-Deputy Attorney General James B. Comey – who would later become director of the FBI.

In the following email correspondence, text that is inside [brackets] was added for clarity or represents reconstructed or later-revealed information previously hidden behind redactions – with all of the revelations based on court records and/or assistance from law enforcement sources.

Drafted March 4, 2004

From: Catherine M. O'Neil, Associate Deputy Attorney General and Director of the Organized Crime Drug Enforcement Task Force (OCDETF)

To: Jeff Taylor, Counsel to the Attorney General for Criminal and National Security Matters; David Ayers, Chief of Staff to the Attorney General; and James B. Comey, Deputy Attorney General

CC: Karen Tandy, Administrator of DEA

Subject: Possible press involving the DEA [Juarez]-ICE informant issue

We just heard from Johnny Sutton that the DEA SAC in El Paso [Special Agent in Charge Gonzalez] wrote a rather lengthy and inflammatory letter to the ICE SAC regarding the "mishandling of the [Santillan/House of Death] investigation that has resulted in unnecessary loss of human life in the Republic of Mexico and endangered the lives of DEA agents." [REDACTED] and I are getting a copy of the letter, as well as an ICE response. I am also speaking with [U.S. Attorney Sutton] at 8 pm (CST) tonight on this matter. He was driving and could not talk at length.

Please be aware that, according to [Sutton], [REDACTED] has reached out to get a copy of certain reports of interview of the CI [the confidential informant Jesus Contreras, or Lalo] in the investigation. The [REDACTED] Times apparently had enough information to ask for the report which states that the CI [Lalo] "supervised the murders" of certain individuals. [Sutton] was not sure who was talking, but we are certainly concerned that there may be press and there may be inquiries here in DC as well.

I have been unable to reach [Mike Furgason, chief of operations at DEA] to find out whether DEA HQ knew anything about the SAC's [Gonzalez'] letter. I'd be surprised if HQ saw it, since, in our meeting on [Tuesday, Furgason] did not mention any letter and, in fact, said they were finalizing the reports of interview from the team that was looking into the matter. I will keep following up.

[REDACTED]: Once I talk with [Sutton] and get a better handle on what's going on in [El Paso/Juarez], I'd be happy to try to get you up to speed on whatever you may need, in case you need to have a statement prepared to respond to any inquiries. My sense is, we don't want to be saying much, since we don't have all the facts yet. However, these are serious allegations between the agencies, including a Justice agency, so we may need to be ready to say something.

Catherine O'Neil
Associate Deputy Attorney General
and Director OCDETF
950 Pennsylvania Avenue, Washington, DC 20530

On March 5, 2004, DEA Administrator Karen Tandy sent an email to the following officials. Their titles are current as of 2004, unless otherwise noted:
• Catherine M. O'Neil, associate deputy attorney general and director of the Organized Crime Drug Enforcement Task Force.
• Jeff Taylor, counsel to the attorney general for criminal and national security matters.
• David Ayers, chief of staff to the attorney general, then John Ashcroft.
• And the number two person at DOJ, Deputy Attorney General James B. Comey — who later took a job as general counsel for defense contractor Lockheed Martin Corp. and eventually, under the Obama administration, was named head of the FBI.

Others within DOJ who received a copy of Tandy's e-mail included:
• Michele Leonhart, deputy administrator of DEA — who later became DEA administrator, resigning in 2015 in the wake of a Congressional hearings focused on a sex-party scandal in Colombia involving DEA agents and prostitutes paid for by narco-traffickers.
• Stuart Levey, former principal associate deputy attorney general, who later became under-secretary of the treasury for terrorism and financial and intelligence.
• Chuck Rosenberg, former chief of staff for Deputy Attorney General James Comey, who later served as Comey's chief of staff at the FBI and, for a time, as the acting administrator of DEA after Leonhart resigned from the post in May 2015.
• And Mark Corallo, director of public affairs for the Justice Department — who later served for a time as spokesman for President Donald Trump's legal team.

Strangely, as mentioned, the version of the email provided to me through the FOIA request was heavily redacted, including all of the names of both the senders and the receivers. I later obtained an unredacted copy of Tandy's e-mail, however. It was filed by a U.S.

prosecutor as an exhibit in former DEA Special Agent in Charge (SAC) Gonzalez' lawsuit lodged in federal court in Miami. Why government censors decided to redact the FOIA version of the e-mail but failed to do the same for the court-exhibit version is not clear. You can be the judge of this bit of bureaucratic bumbling. The unredacted text of the Tandy email follows; the "el paso SAC" is Sandalio Gonzalez:

Drafted March 5, 2004

Subject: Re: Possible press involving the DEA Juarez /ICE informant issue

DEA HQ officials were not aware of our el paso SAC's inexcusable letter until last evening — although a copy of the letter first landed in the foreign operations section sometime the day before. The SAC did not tell anyone at HQ that he was contemplating such a letter and did not discuss it or share it with HQ until we received the copy as noted above, well after it was sent.

I apologized to Johnny Sutton last night, and he and I agreed on a no comment to the press. Mike Furgason, Chief of Operations, notified the El Paso SAC last night that he is not to speak to the press other than a no comment, that he is to desist writing anything regarding the Juarez matter and related case and defer to the joint management and threat assessment teams out of HQ — and he is to relay these directions to the rest of his El Paso Division. The SAC, who reports to Michele [Leonhart], will be brought in next week for performance discussions to further address this officially.

It is important to note that at this point nobody in the Tandy e-mail chain, nor then-U.S. Attorney Sutton, had announced any criminal investigation into the specific claims raised by Gonzalez in his February 24, 2004, letter calling out ICE agents, their informant and an assistant U.S. attorney in El Paso for their roles in the House of Death homicides. Specifically, Gonzalez' U.S. Office of Special Counsel complaint alleges that parties involved in the House of Death case orchestrated a "coverup" that may "constitute the criminal offense of obstruction of justice, misprision of a felony, or, to a lesser extent, a federal agency's negligence resulting in multiple homicides." Instead of addressing Gonzalez' serious allegations, DOJ's energies appear to have been focused on concealing his allegations from the public and retaliating against the whistleblower.

Also keep in mind that even though the e-mail correspondence and resulting scurry to deep-six Gonzalez' House of Death letter occurred under the reign of then-Attorney General John Ashcroft, his successor, Attorney General Alberto Gonzales, post-House of Death actually promoted Sutton to a policy-making post within DOJ — as vice chair of the Advisory Committee of U.S. Attorneys.

So, what exactly are these government officials trying to keep under wraps? The raw statistic — a dozen people murdered — doesn't get beneath the skin like the truth. So, we need to meet the devil in the details. For that, we turn to an account provided by the informant known as "Lalo" or Jesus Contreras. Immediately after the murder of Mexican attorney Fernando Reyes Aguado at the House of Death in early August 2003, the informant Lalo returned to El Paso to be debriefed by ICE agents. An ICE report based on that debriefing was generated on August 25, 2003.

Following, from that report — obtained through a FOIA request and later found in court pleadings — is the informant version of the first murder he "supervised" — and tape-recorded clandestinely. Lalo, along with Jesus Contreras and cooperating source SA-913-EP, are the same individual, the House of Death informant — whose real name is concealed to protect his identity and the cases he is working for the U.S. agents and prosecutors.

Date: [August 25, 2003]

File [ENF-1:OI:EP:LG]

From: Special Agent [Luis Garcia, El Paso]

Subject: [<u>August 6, 2003 Debrief of SA-913-EP</u>]

The purpose of this memorandum is to document information obtained during a debrief of SA-913-EP, which took place on

Wednesday, August 6, 2003. ... The murder of Fernando LNU [last name unknown, though later revealed in public records as Reyes] was ordered by Heriberto Santillan Tabares, who is a gatekeeper for the Vicente Carrillo Fuentes organization. According to Santillan, Fernando was a childhood friend who had entrusted him with the delivery and transportation of 1,000 pounds of marijuana.

An agreement between Santillan and Fernando had been reached, at which time Santillan lured Fernando to an undisclosed location in Juarez, Mexico [the House of Death] for the purpose of meeting SA-913-EP [the informant Lalo]. The purpose of the meeting was to hand over the phone numbers for the people that were responsible for accepting the marijuana in El Paso, Texas. As Santillan entered the location [the House of Death], Ferando was told to give the phone numbers to SA-913-EP. As the information was relayed, Santillan exited the residence, at which time Fernando was subdued and murdered.

The participants in the murder were Alex Garcia and two Juarez judicial police officers. SA-913-EP [the informant, Lalo,] supervised the murder and had minimal participation in the act.

[Lalo] told [Santillan] that he would take his own vehicle because he was going to buy some lime and duct tape, and that he would meet the two Police officers at the residence [the House of Death in Juarez].... At approximately 11:15 a.m. [on August 5, 2003, Lalo] arrived at the house.... [Lalo] entered the residence and at this time thought, "If they were going to kill me, this would be the time." [The informant] sent one of the police officers outside so that if a confrontation ensued inside the house, it would be with only the other police officer, which would give [the informant] better odds of surviving.

[Lalo] entered the residence and began to visually scan the residence looking for anything unusual. [He] dropped the sack of lime on the floor, while still holding [a] handgun, and looked at the other police officer. [Lalo] began fidgeting with the gun and asked the [Juarez] police officer what the plan was. [It's worth noting that Lalo's informant contract specifically forbids him from "carrying a weapon" while working as an ICE informant.]

[Lalo, still inside the house] walked towards the front door, at which time he observed [Santillan's] vehicle parked in front of the residence. [Lalo] observed [Santllan, Garcia and Mexican attorney Fernando Reyes] walking toward the residence. [Lalo] stated that at that time he felt a big wave of tranquility and calmness. [Lalo] stated he now knew that he was not going to be killed, and that it was [Fernando Reyes] they were going to kill. Fernando went to sit down on the only chair in the living room, which was a folding chair located in the middle of the room. Santillan then exited the residence.

As [Fernando Reyes] is sitting on the chair [in the living room], [Garcia] pulls out his weapon and places it up against the right side of [Reyes'] face. [Reyes] sees the weapon and begins to scream, "Why, please don't kill me, don't kill me!" The first police officer came out from behind [the informant Lalo] and ran to [Reyes]. The police officer, already with the tape in his hand began to unwind it and forced a portion of the tape into [Reyes'] mouth. The police officer began to wrap the tape around [Reyes'] head, and [Reyes] responded by trying to fight his way out.

The second police officer appeared and began to assist [Garcia] and the other police officer. The first police officer continued to wrap the tape around [Reyes'] head in an attempt to smother him with it. [Reyes] continued to fight, at which time the two police officers and [Garcia] push [Reyes] to the ground and began to tape his hands. [Reyes] begins to kick his legs at which time [Garcia] looked at [Lalo]. The look made [Lalo] feel uncomfortable. Based on the look, [Lalo, the informant] felt forced to assist in the restraining of [Reyes] by the legs.

The police officers began to tape [Reyes'] feet together. One of the Police officers then grabbed an extension cord and wrapped it around [Reyes'] neck. The Police officer then began to violently pull on the cord in an attempt to choke out [Reyes]. During this time, the cord broke and part of the cord remained around [Reyes'] neck at which time one of the Police officer asked, "Now what?" [The informant, Lalo,] then pointed to a plastic bag. One of the police officers grabbed the plastic bag and placed it over [Reyes'] head. [Garcia] then began to wrap the duct tape around the bag, therefore, suffocating "Fernando" [Reyes].

They all stood around and watched [Reyes'] body as his movement became less and less. One of the police officers then went and grabbed a shovel and began to strike [Reyes] in the back of the neck area. [Lalo] stated that he believed the violent striking of the neck caused it to break. [He] walked out of the residence in an attempt to find Santillan and inform him of Ferando [Reyes'] death. [Lalo] found Santillan at the corner store [and he] told Santillan of the death.

[Santillan] praised [Lalo] for his participation in the murder and that his participation could lead to his meeting with Vicente Carrillo Fuentes. Santillan also told [Lalo] that he was now number four in running the narcotics business for the VCF organization. They proceeded to a residence in the area.

The residence is considered to be a "safe-house." The residence is for high-ranking [Juarez Cartel] organizational members only. [Santillan] introduced [Lalo] to certain people in the residence and told them that (Lalo) has permission to come to the residence, and for the people to be hospitable towards him. [Lalo] stated that the house is where all the high-ranking organization [Juarez Cartel] members stay when in [Juarez] Mexico. They have everything they could need, stemming from groceries to women.

After Lalo was debriefed about his participation in the murder of Reyes, ICE officials notified DEA's assistant regional director in Mexico City that the informant had only "witnessed" a murder, failing to note that Lalo had actually supervised and assisted with a brutal, premeditated homicide. DEA's Mexico operations, including Juarez, were not under DEA supervisor Sandalio Gonzalez' chain of command. He oversaw only U.S. operations as head of DEA's El Paso field office, so Gonzalez was not privy to all the information at that time.

Officials with the Department of Homeland Security, which oversees ICE, did tell Mexican officials about the murder, but also misled them about the true facts by failing to reflect in that communication that Lalo actually "participated" in the murder. Consequently, the Mexican authorities also were led to believe that the informant did not know where Reyes was buried — even though Lalo supervised the murder and the House of Death burials.

Following, obtained through FOIA records as well as court pleadings and translated into English, is the text of the letter sent to Mexican officials:

August 15, 2003

Lic. Jorge Rosa Garcia

Acting Chief of the Office of Special Investigations on Organized 7

Dear Lic. Rosas:

We wish to inform you that a source of information from the Department of Homeland Security traveled to the state of Chihuahua, Mexico, [on August 3, 2003], to meet with members of the contraband organization of Vicente Carrillo Fuentes to discuss the transport of a cargo of marijuana. On August 5 of this year, the informant [Contreras] was a witness to the assassination of the owner of the drugs [Fernando Reyes].

According to the conversation we had with you on August 6, 2003, we agreed that the informant would continue with the work he/she was undertaking in Chihuahua, Mexico, in order to obtain more information about the drug-trafficking organization of Carrillo Fuentes, as well as to try to obtain information on the whereabouts of the body of the person [Fernando Reyes] who supposedly had been assassinated. As soon as the U.S. Department of Homeland Security decides to discontinue this investigative work for security reasons or any other motive, we'll make the informant [Lalo] available to you to take his/her statements, and we will provide you with intelligence, including telephone numbers, names of people involved, etc., that might help you to continue this investigation together with the Mexican authorities. With nothing further, I take this opportunity to send you my kindest regards and remain available for any further information you might need in this regard.

Sincerely,

Luis Alvarez
Customs Attaché
U.S. Department of Homeland Security

So, in effect, ICE officials and the U.S. prosecutor in El Paso sat on their hands after the first murder, hoping to continue running their informant to make that career-boosting case against Santillan and the Juarez Cartel leadership. As a result, over the next six months, at least another 11 victims were murdered and buried at the House of Death in Juarez, with the informant overseeing the torture/murder house and its "carne asadas" as well as the burial of the corpses in the backyard of that grim abode, according to FOIA records.

In U.S. government's pleadings filed in the fall of 2006 as part of a civil lawsuit brought by Janet Padilla, wife of one of the House of Death victims, the ICE agents and U.S. prosecutor who were part of the House of Death investigation deny any wrongdoing in their handling of the case or of the informant Lalo, however. They claim they were not aware of any House of Death murders while they were occurring or in advance of a murder taking place:

> Defendants [several ICE agents in El Paso and the head of ICE itself, as well as a U.S. prosecutor and leadership of the agencies involved, ICE, DEA, DOJ and the U.S. Attorney's Office] all acted within the course and scope of their employment at all times and related to all incidents alleged in the complaint [focused on the House of Death murders] and, as such are protected by immunity ....

Translated, that means qualified immunity, which extends to federal law enforcers while acting under the color of law. The legal publication Lawfare explains: "Qualified immunity is a judicially created doctrine that shields government officials from being held personally liable for constitutional violations — like the right to be free from excessive police force — for money damages under federal law so long as the officials did not violate 'clearly established' law."

As part of ICE supervisor Curtis Compton's affidavit filed in the Padilla case, he explains that in July or early August 2003, "My group was designated to play a supporting role in the Santillan investigation." Compton adds that his group's role was "to assist Group supervisor [Todd] Johnson's team in the operation, and in particular, the court-authorized wiretap interceptions and administrative tasks."

Both Compton and Johnson, who was ICE agent Raul Bencomo's direct supervisor, were under the management arm of Giovanni Gaudioso, who was promoted to Special Agent in Charge of the ICE El Paso field office in July 2003, after having served just prior to that as the associate special agent in charge of what was then the U.S. Customs Service's Tampa office, according to the affidavit he filed in the Padilla case.

It's important to note the date of all these changes. The informant Lalo helped to murder Mexican attorney Reyes on August 5, 2003, around the time Compton claims his group was first assigned to the case and only about a month after Gaudioso took over as head of the ICE El Paso office, which was spearheading the Santillan House of Death case using the informant Lalo. In addition, 2003 was the transition year when the U.S. Custom Service was dissolved, and its investigative arm was merged into the Department of Homeland Security to create ICE. And finally, ICE agent Bencomo, who recruited Lalo as an informant in 2000 and was his direct handler for years, claims he was removed from that role for a short time during a critical period.

"The Santillan investigation began in February 2003," Bencomo states in an affidavit filed in the Padilla case. "I was [Lalo's] handler at that time. As his handler, I was the primary person responsible for communications with him. I was removed as [Lalo's] handler in late June 2003 and reinstated as his handler in mid-August 2003."

That means, if accurate, that Bencomo may have been in the dark about the murder of Mexican attorney Reyes because he was not overseeing the informant Lalo when he assisted with Reyes' murder — which was the first homicide at the House of Death in Juarez. All of these factors — Gaudioso and Compton's late arrival to the case, the transition of U.S. Customs to ICE in 2003, and Lalo's longtime handler Bencomo being yanked from that role at a critical juncture — seem to have contributed to a perfect storm of dysfunction and confusion, and bloodshed.

The stench of this whole drug-war nightmare hit the open air on January 14, 2004, after Santillan's henchmen mistakenly pulled over the car of a DEA agent and his family, seemingly thinking maybe the agent was a dope smuggler or corrupt law enforcer who had crossed Santillan's turf.

After the dirty little secret of the murders at the House of Death had surfaced within law enforcement circles, FOIA records show, ICE officials and Fielden allegedly continued to advance the coverup by obstructing the DEA's efforts to capture Mexican state police commander Loya — the chief enforcer of the House of Death hit squad. As a result, Loya and several of his assistant assassins disappeared into the ether and remain at large. From former DEA commander Gonzalez' MSPB pleadings:

> To make matters worse, ICE officials would not allow the informant to call one of the suspects [Loya] and arrange a meeting so that Mexican federal authorities could arrest him for his participation in the murders. Furthermore, the U.S. prosecutor refused the repeated requests by DEA for direct access to the informant [Lalo] so that at least attempts could be made to resolve the alleged threat against the DEA personnel and their families stationed in [Juarez].

> In fact, the U.S. prosecutor stated that she had ordered ICE personnel to refuse DEA access to tape-recorded conversations of the informant, while expressing concern that DEA personnel would share information with Mexican federal authorities.

Before Mexican state police commander Loya vanished, however, he took care of one other loose end on behalf of the Juarez Cartel, FOIA records show. On January 16, 2004, two days after the last of a dozen bodies were buried at the House of Death in Juarez, Loya carried out yet another act of brazen brutality. From a DEA Timeline document that chronicles the House of Death murders:

> [Two males] in a white pickup truck were shot after being stopped by two subjects reportedly acting as police officers. The targets were stopped upon departing the gated residential subdivision identified as Fraccionamiento Maese located at Calle Calzada Del Rio No. 8010, Ciudad Juarez. The subjects were asked for identification by one of two alleged officers who approached them. Immediately upon identifying the driver, one of the suspects fatally shot the driver in the face and head with a 9-mm handgun.
>
> The CJRO [Juarez DEA field office's] Chihuahua State Police SOI [source of information] indicated that the subject was identified by their reporting as Rodolfo Renteria Cervantes. Further, the SOI reported that [Mexican State police commander] Miguel Loya Gallegos directed the killing of Renteria due to the loss of a 4,000-pound load of unspecified drugs. The other occupant of the vehicle was shot in the mouth and neck. He remains in critical condition in a local hospital and has not been able or willing to give a statement

Given this whole misguided affair has been documented, and by the government's own records, we are left to wonder why the cloak of immunity shielding U.S. law enforcers in this case simply doesn't unravel. Unfortunately, the cobwebs of the House of Death horror story by now have been spun intricately through the U.S. Justice System.

Still, of all the questions that yet remain unanswered to this day, among the biggest, for me, is where is the outrage from our political leaders? Have we really become a nation that tolerates, maybe even condones, murder in the pursuit of career, politics, power and money? That is an ugly thought, but then there is really nothing pretty about homicides.

As for former DEA agent Gonzalez, he is only asking for the truth to be told. Maybe that's a starting point; maybe it's time someone starts listening to him.

"This is not about me," Gonzalez says. "What happened to me is minor compared to the enormity of what took place here, and the fact that nobody is focused on it.

"We need an independent investigation of this by someone outside the executive branch. And then we can let the chips fall where they may."

Dispatch 7

September 30, 2006

High-level officials within the departments of Justice and Homeland Security did know about the activities of a U.S. government informant who supervised and participated in murder in Juarez, Mexico, and yet they allowed that informant to continue his bloody assignment at the House of Death.

A sworn legal affidavit prepared by the U.S. prosecutor (Juanita Fielden) who oversaw the House of Death case confirms that fact. Fielden's affidavit is included as an exhibit in a civil rights case filed against U.S. law enforcement officials by the families of the victims in the House of Death mass murder. That case was filed in U.S. District Court in El Paso, Texas.

Fielden's affidavit starts out by providing details about how DOJ and ICE officials responded to the news that the House of Death informant had been caught smuggling drugs in New Mexico about a month prior to the August 5, 2003, murder of Fernando Reyes at the House of Death.

At this time (in June 2003), DEA also was using Lalo as an informant. In the wake of his New Mexico drug bust, however, DEA decided to end its relationship with the informant. It seems ICE officials, and Fielden, felt a greater sense of loyalty to the informant, despite his act of betrayal. That loyalty stemmed from their desire to protect career-enhancing cases that were making use of the informant Lalo. Fielden's affidavit, excerpted below, reveals the extent of that loyalty:

> On the evening of June 28, 2003, I was contacted by ICE group supervisor (GS) Todd Johnson who advised me that a confidential informant [SA913-EP, or Lalo] had been stopped at a U.S. Border Patrol checkpoint in Las Cruces, New Mexico, in possession of

approximately 100 pounds of marijuana which was concealed in his vehicle. This was unauthorized criminal activity on the part of [Lalo]. [He] was arrested by Las Cruces, New Mexico, DEA Special Agent Mike Garcia and the case was referred to the state prosecutor.

The next week a meeting was held at the United States Attorney's Office regarding the ramification of [Lalo's] arrest. Attending this meeting were members of ICE management (Assistant Special Agent in Charge Fred Schroeder, Group Supervisor Todd Johnson and Group Supervisor Curtis Compton) and AUSAs [Assistant U.S. Attorneys] Margaret Leachman, Jose Luis Gonzales and me [Juanita Fielden]. After a lengthy discussion, the consensus was that if [Lalo] was closely monitored he could continue to be effective and provide significant information on both the El Paso investigations [which includes the Santillan investigation in Juarez], as well as a Chicago investigation.

The ICE agents indicated that, pursuant to ICE policy, they would attempt to get the approval of the Special Agent in Charge (at the time it was an Acting SAC) to continue to use [Lalo]. If the agents obtained approval to continue to utilize [him], I would call the state prosecutor in New Mexico and ask that they suspend prosecution based upon [Lalo's] continued cooperation. Group Supervisor Todd Johnson called me later and said the state prosecutor who agreed to defer prosecution of [Lalo] as long as [he] cooperated. The state charge was eventually dropped in December 2003, at my request.

So, Fielden admits that Lalo not only broke the law but deceived his ICE handlers more than a month prior to the first murder at the House of Death, yet the decision was still made, through the ICE and DOJ chain of command, to continue using Lalo in order to make a drug case against the Vicente Carrillo Fuentes organization. Had Lalo been deactivated by ICE in June and prosecuted for his marijuana-smuggling crime, a dozen people might still be alive today.

And even though DOJ and ICE officials had knowledge of the Lalo's active role in at least the first murder in early August 2003, Fielden still chose to drop the drug-smuggling charges against the House of Death informant some four months later, in December 2003. It is not clear if Fielden ever informed the state prosecutor in New

Mexico that Lalo had been involved in a murder prior to requesting that the charges be dismissed.

Another puzzling revelation is the notion that ICE officials continued to use Lalo as an informant in the House of Death investigation in Mexico after his drug bust. How could ICE possibly "closely" monitor his activities while he was operating inside a Juarez Cartel-affiliated criminal cell in Mexico — where he admits to carrying a gun, despite a prohibition against that act in his **informant contract** with ICE? In any event, as evidenced by the fact that the first murder at the House of Death occurred about a month after Lalo was busted for smuggling cannabis, it is clear that ICE, in fact, did not have control of the situation.

More from **Fielden's affidavit:**

On July 25, 2003, United States District Judge Phillip Martinez for the Western District of Texas signed an order authorizing an anticipatory interception of a cellular telephone (915-892-8888) which was to be given to Santillan Tabares by [Lalo, aka, Jesus Contreras]. The court was notified of [Lalo's] arrest [on the drug charges] at that time.

On or about August 5, 2003, I was contacted at home by ICE GS [Group Supervisor] Curtis Compton and advised of a murder that had taken place in Juarez, Chihuahua, Mexico, in which Santillan Tabares was involved. The incident had been recorded by the CI [Lalo].

I, in turn, contacted my supervisor, Assistant United States Attorney Margaret Leachman. She later told me that she had advised Richard Durbin, chief of the criminal division for the Western District of Texas, of the incident. The next morning I spoke with my OCDETF [Organized Crime Drug Enforcement Task Force Office] advisor, Greg Surovic, and told him of the incident. It was sometime later that I learned that the individual murdered was identified as Ferando Reyes.

Interestingly, Fielden's boss in San Antonio, U.S. Attorney Sutton, is never mentioned in her affidavit. However, Gonzalez, a long-time DEA commander and head of the agency's El Paso field office when the House of Death murders played out, has dealt with many U.S.

prosecutors over the years. He insists that Sutton clearly would have been in the chain of communication on all these matters.

"Of course, Sutton was in the loop," Gonzalez says. "If the OCDETF attorney [Surovic] was in the loop, so was Sutton."

More from Fielden's affidavit:

> On or about August 25, 2003, I was provided an ICE memo prepared by SA Luis Garcia which detailed an August 6, 2003, interview of [Lalo] wherein he discussed the events surrounding the murder of Fernando Reyes on August 5, 2003. [Lalo] stated he feared for his life during this event.
>
> It was my understanding that from August 6, 2003, until August 21, 2003, Santillan Tabares was in the interior of Mexico. I am aware that the El Paso ICE agents notified ICE management in Washington, D.C., and Mexico City, Mexico, of the murder, which occurred on August 5, 2003, and that ICE management in El Paso and in Washington, D.C., approved the continued use of [Lalo] and the continued investigation of Santillan Tabares.
>
> On September 4, 2003, United States District Judge Phillip Martinez, Western District of Texas, signed an order authorizing the continued interception of a cellular telephone (915-892-8888). The affidavit for the continued wire interception discussed the murder of Fernando Reyes on August 5, 2003. This affidavit was prepared by ICE Special Agent David Ortiz, reviewed and approved by his chain-of-command, reviewed by me and the Office of Enforcement Operations Attorney Nancy Brinkac and her supervisor, and approved by Deputy Assistant Attorney General John G. Malcolm.

Fielden's affidavit omits an important fact. She claims officials in Mexico City were made aware of the first murder. What she fails to point out is that the Mexican government was only told that the informant was a "witness" to a murder in Juarez. There was no mention of the fact that he "supervised" and had "limited participation" in that murder, as an August 25, 2003, ICE memo clearly states. This selective use of the facts prompts former DEA agent Gonzalez to wonder what

ICE officials communicated to the federal judge in the affidavit when seeking authorization for the continuing wiretap for the phone number.

"What did they tell the judge?" Gonzalez asks. "Did they inform the judge [about the informant's role in the first murder] in the same way they told the Mexican government?"

Fielden's affidavit continues:

> In late September 2003, the investigation revealed that Santillan Tabares had again traveled to the interior of Mexico where he remained for several weeks, returning to Juarez, Mexico, sometime in mid-November 2003. During this time, I began preparing a grand jury indictment of Santillan Tabares and five other defendants for the March 2003 cocaine transaction [which occurred in the United States four months prior to the first House of Death murder].
>
> On December 10, 2003, a federal grand jury returned the indictment. Pursuant to Department of Justice policy, in order to lure an individual from Mexico into the United States to arrest him, authorization must be obtained from the Department of Justice – Office of International Affairs (OIA), after the agency has obtained approval from the ranking U.S. official in Mexico. I finally obtained DOJ OIA authorization on January 15, 2004.
>
> On January 14, 2004, I was called at home by ICE GS [Group Supervisor Curtis] Compton who requested that I come to the ICE office because of an incident that had occurred in Juarez, Mexico that day.

That incident involved a DEA agent and his family in Juarez being confronted by Santillan's men during a traffic stop. If it were not for the quick thinking of the DEA agent, he and his family, including two children, would have almost certainly been taken to the House of Death.

Fielden's affidavit continues:

> I notified AUSA [Assistant U.S. Attorney] Leachman and then went to the ICE office where I met with ICE agents; their associate special agent in charge, Patty Kramer; the Juarez DEA agents; and an El Paso

DEA crisis management team [assembled to deal with the DEA agent's encounter with Santillan's men]. I then sat in on a meeting with these individuals and [Lalo]. This is the first time I had met or spoken to the [the informant]. After this meeting I learned general details of some of the murders and burials [at the House of Death].

On January 15, 2004, after obtaining DOJ OIA approval, Heriberto Santillan Tabares was arrested in the United States on the December 2003 indictment. ...

Anyone who grew up watching the TV show *Hogan's Heroes* has to remember the line thrown out by the German soldier Sgt. Shultz whenever he was confronted with an uncomfortable fact: "I know nothing!" Well, it seems Fielden watched that show as well.

She also proves to be very adept at passing the buck. If you take her at her word, everyone above and below her in the chain of command was responsible for authorizing the actions that led to the House of Death mass murder, but she alone seemingly has no responsibility for the blood that was spilled.

From her affidavit:

On January 28 and 29, 2004, I interviewed [Lalo]. This was the first time I became aware of any further involvement in any murders by [Lalo] other than the August 5, 2003, murder.

With respect to the rules or policies concerning the use of confidential informants, I reviewed the Attorney General's 2002 Confidential Informant Guidelines, specifically, Section IV (B) - Notification of Unauthorized Illegal Activity. However, the final decision to continue to operate this particular informant, after his arrest in June 2003 [for marijuana smuggling], was made by ICE Acting Special Agent in Charge [SAC], pursuant to their department guidelines. As noted previously, the ICE El Paso SAC, as well as ICE management in Washington, D.C., also authorized agents to proceed with the investigation after the August 5, 2003 [initial House of Death] murder.

At no time prior to January 14, 2004, did I have access to the informant. At no time during this or any other investigation, did I directly or indirectly supervise the informant. In fact, I stated previously, [the] first time I met the informant was on January 14, 2004.

ICE managers supervised the investigation. I, as the OCDETF prosecutor, was consulted on various aspects of the investigation, supported the investigation by obtaining authorization for the wire interceptions, discussed options for prosecution, obtained the indictment and the DOJ portion of the lure approval.

At all times, I acted in my professional capacity and in accordance with Department of Justice guidelines. I consulted with my superiors and sought their advice whenever I was made aware of any problems with the investigation. ...

You, the readers, will have to weigh all these facts and assertions. But keep in mind that the ultimate truth of the House of Death was still very likely at this point in this story to remain shrouded in a coverup. It seemed that neither Fielden, nor any other U.S. government officials, would ever be subjected to cross examination under oath unless a then-pending civil case filed by the family members of the House of Death victims proceeded to trial. It was that case for which Fielden was compelled to prepare her affidavit.

On legal grounds, under the rules of civil court proceedings, Fielden's affidavit, and similar pleadings filed by other ICE officials, however, may well be all the judge needs to conclude that the case should be dismissed, given all of those ICE officials contend that they had no foreknowledge or responsibility for the House of Death murders. They were just doing their jobs — if you are to believe their pleadings in the case.

The Victims

Dispatch 8

November 6, 2006

Raul Loya, a Dallas civil rights attorney representing many of the family members of House of Death murder victims, filed litigation in federal court in El Paso in 2005 on behalf of the family of the first known murder victim at the House of Death, Mexican attorney Fernando Reyes. The litigation accuses the informant known as "Lalo," and his U.S. government handlers, of violating the constitutional right of Reyes and his family. Lalo, while working for ICE, allegedly supervised Reyes' murder in August 2003, according to the lawsuit.

"The right to be free from unwarranted bodily injury at the hands of law enforcement officers is supported by the Fourth Amendment guarantee of the right to be secure in one's person and the Fifth Amendment guarantee against the loss of liberty without due process of law," the Reyes litigation filed in federal court in El Paso asserts.

Several agents and supervisors with ICE who handled or oversaw the informant and were responsible for his activities, as well as an assistant U.S. prosecutor, are named as defendants in the lawsuit. They include El Paso ICE supervisors Giovanni Gaudioso, Patricia Kramer and Curtis Compton as well as Raul Bencomo, an ICE field agent and the informant's handler. None of the defendants, nor Sutton, who is not named in the lawsuit, ever agreed to speak on the record with me as a *Narco News* correspondent about the House of Death, although each of the individuals named in the litigation claim the charges of complicity and/or negligence leveled against them are without merit.

From the Reyes litigation filed in federal court by attorney Raul Loya:

> The actions and omissions of defendants [Guadioso, et al] ... in recruiting, encouraging and allowing [the informant Lalo] to torture and kill several victims, including Fernando Reyes, under the shield of law was characterized by ill will, spite, evil motive, and a purpose to injure constituting malice. Such malice gave rise to a reasonably foreseeable risk of harm to the decedent Fernando Reyes [the murder victim] and his survivors. As a result, the plaintiffs [the families of the House of Death victims] are entitled to recover all damages allowed by law on account of defendants ... actions and omissions constituting malice. ...

Loya's lawsuit seeks justice for the families of the known House of Death victims. The ICE informant Lalo, according to law enforcement sources and documents, assisted in some way with most of those murders — including prepping the house, luring individuals to it, and even helping to commit murder; and, also by supervising cleanup and burial after a murder was committed at the House of Death, or elsewhere.

He was physically present for at least five homicides linked to Santillan and the House of Death, according to a caretaker who assisted the informant. The informant's handlers — agents and supervisors with the El Paso office of ICE — were allegedly fully aware of the Lalo's complicity in the murders. They did nothing to stop the killing, however, allegedly out of fear of jeopardizing a multi-million-dollar cigarette-smuggling case against a quadriplegic named Jorge Abraham and a sprawling narco-trafficking investigation against the ruthless Juarez criminal-cell leader Santillan — an investigation that sought to target even bigger fish in the Juarez Cartel.

The informant had weeded his way deep into both cases and consequently was key to successfully prosecuting both cases. The cigarette and narco-trafficking cases were under the jurisdiction of U.S. Attorney Sutton in San Antonio in South Texas. The Alamo City (San Antonio's other moniker) is a 550-mile drive from the city of El Paso, which is located on Texas' far southwestern border, where Mexico, Texas and New Mexico meet. Assistant U.S. Attorney Juanita Fielden also worked closely with the ICE supervisors and agents in El Paso overseeing the informant Lalo — who also understood, and arguably exploited, his key role at the nexus of both criminal cases.

Among the other family members of the House of Death tragedy represented by Dallas attorney Loya was the wife of murder victim Luis Padilla, who filed a lawsuit in October 2004 against Fielden and the same ICE officials named in the litigation filed by the family of Fernando Reyes. Padilla in early January 2004 allegedly was picked up by some of Santillan's crew and brought to the House of Death in Juarez. He happened to be in the wrong place at the wrong time, or at least that's the theory. When he was kidnapped is not completely clear, but investigative reporting by *The Observer* in London, the *Houston Press* and the *Dallas Observer* on the Padilla case all report his disappearance and presumed kidnapping by Santillan's men occurred early in the day on January 14, 2004. That would mean Padilla, a truck mechanic, was one of the last three people killed at the House of Death — one of whom that day gave up the location of DEA agent Homer Glen McBrayer's home address in Juarez, leading to the near-fatal traffic stop targeting him and his family later that same day.

"Luis Padilla went missing since January 14, 2004," states litigation filed in federal court in El Paso by Padilla's family. "His body was later found in the backyard of a small house in Juarez, Mexico."

That "small house" was the House of Death at Calle Parsioneros 3633 in Juarez.

DEA documents also indicate that on January 26, 2004, one of the dozen corpses excavated at the House of Death was found wrapped in a newspaper dated January 14, 2004, the same day Padilla was kidnapped and killed. His corpse was found near another grave that contained only a pile of clothing — a clue that there may have been a 13th body buried at the House of Death that was subsequently moved for some reason.

The informant's statement provided to the Mexican government in February 2004 provides a name for only one of the three people murdered at the House of Death on January 14, 2004. That House of Death victim was Omar Cepeda Saenz.

"[Santillan] told me that the ones that had kidnapped Omar [Cepeda Saenz] and his [two] companions had been municipal policemen, and that they had handed them [the three victims] over [to Santillan's executioners] in an alley in Juarez," the informant Lalo says in his February 12, 2004, statement to the Mexican Attorney General's Office.

The DEA document, a timeline of events related to DEA's evacuation of its agents from Juarez, also does not indicate that Padilla was among the three victims murdered on January 14, 2004. The document mentions only one victim by name: again, Omar Cepeda Saenz. And it offers up only coincidence and miscues as the explanation for why DEA agent McBrayer's house in Juarez was targeted by Santillan's men.

From the DEA timeline document:

> [Juarez DEA] agents reviewed the recording of [a] conversation wherein Santillan identified Omar Cepeda as one of three individuals who were abducted, tortured and killed by [state police commander] Loya Gallegos and associates. Cepeda, during the torture, told Santillan about an alleged stash house in the vicinity of the McBrayer [home] which contained four thousand pounds of unspecified drugs. Santillan further related that Loya Gallegos, et. al., effected a surveillance and traffic stop wherein suspected DEA personnel were identified [by Santillan's execution crew] as associated with what they suspected to be the stash house. Santillan theorized to [Lalo] that Cepeda gave him the [bad] information in order to set Santillan up for retaliation from the DEA.

A question arises, naturally. How did Cepeda know about DEA agent McBrayer's house in Juarez in the first place, unless he or one of the other two victims that day knew McBrayer? Also, why did Santillan's enforcers stake out McBrayer's home instead of the actual supposed stash house, which was at a different address. Just a mistake and a huge coincidence? Another view is that it simply doesn't add up.

Attorney Loya confirmed that Padilla, who was a year shy of 30 at the time of his murder, was not a naturalized U.S. citizen. He was, however, a long-time legal resident of the United States — with three children. The son of migrant workers, Padilla graduated in 1995 from Socorro High School, where he excelled as an athlete. The community of Socorro is located on the Texas-side of the border just outside of El Paso. Padilla also had another side, revealed in an arrest record with the El Paso Police Department. Only a year prior to his murder at the House of Death, Padilla was busted for marijuana possession, police records show. Specifically, he was arrested on felony charges after the El Paso cops in January 2003 discovered a green duffel bag in his possession "containing 52 bundles of marijuana ... with a combined gross weight of 56.25 pounds," and a separate blue plastic bin "containing 59 bundles of marijuana ... with a combined gross weight of 63.65 pounds," the police report states. Padilla's bond was set at $3,000,

That arrest, no doubt, did not go unnoticed by the people who provided him with the marijuana. Nor did the fact that U.S. law enforcers, with that arrest, now had Padilla over a barrel and likely would try to squeeze him to give up the names of the "bigger fish" he worked with in the drug business, or otherwise coerce Padilla to do their bidding in the war for drugs. That creates a scenario where Padilla may well have been among the last three victims tortured and murdered at the House of Death, by design, and that he, not Cepeda, may have been the real source of information about DEA agent McBrayer's home in Juarez. Time may tell.

* * *

In late 2005, the Padilla and Reyes family members combined their civil claims with those of other family members of other House of Death victims and filed a joint legal action against the U.S. government in federal court in El Paso.

Loya's pleadings in the families' cases rely heavily on the contents of a letter written by Sandalio Gonzalez, the former special agent in charge of DEA's operations in El Paso. As you recall, that letter, drafted in February 2004, blew the whistle on the role federal prosecutors and ICE agents played in the House of Death homicides. Gonzalez' whistleblowing missive was surfaced initially through a Freedom of Information Act request.

Officials with ICE and DOJ, whose agents and prosecutors were building cases with the informant Contreras' help, when contacted for comment on Gonzalez' letter and the House of Death case generally, continued to either deny official complicity in the murders or simply refused to comment on the case.

Still, the truth of the House of Death murders continued to bubble up from the ground. As part of the litigation filed by the families of the House of Death victims, an affidavit was prepared and signed under oath by a former high-level DEA agent, who previously served as the head of the agency's Dallas field office and as head of DEA's El Paso Intelligence Center.

The former DEA agent, Phil Jordan, and his experiences, including the murder of his brother as a result of a suspected narco-trafficker payback, are the subject of a book called *Down by the River,* penned by the late, great journalist Charles Bowden. The book is considered a seminal work on the drug war and its pernicious and bloody reach across both sides of the border.

Jordan's affidavit is a crucial document because it brings sharply into focus what I had been reporting for years at *Narco News* about the House of Death mass murder. Information in the sworn affidavit to follow that is contained in [brackets] has been added for background and clarity-of-reading purposes. ICE officials mentioned in the affidavit are identified by the titles they held at the time the House of Death murders played out in 2003 and early 2004.

Plus, there is this big reveal. For the first time, the real identity of the House of Death informant is surfaced. So far, he has been known only by his aliases — Jesus Contreras, Lalo and SA-913-EP.

The ICE informant's legal name, the one he inherited from his parents (who are middle-class professionals living in Mexico) is Guillermo Eduardo Ramirez Peyro. The informant's **real name** appears in former DEA commander Jordan's affidavit but was initially made public through the informant's immigration-court document trail.

Affidavit of Phillip E. Jordan

My name is Phillip Jordan. I am over the age of 21 years and in all ways competent to make this affidavit. All of the facts stated herein are within my personal knowledge and are true and correct.

... I served with the Drug Enforcement Administration for over 30 years, from 1965 to 1996. I was the DEA Special Agent in Charge for the Dallas Division, and I was the former director of the El Paso Intelligence Center (EPIC). I was a senior inspector for the DEA in charge of inspections and overseeing the operations of confidential informants prior to my transfer to the Dallas Division. I supervised the compliance of numerous memorandums of understanding between DEA and the United States Customs [Service] and other agencies.

I have reviewed the affidavits submitted by [Assistant U.S. Attorney in El Paso] Ms. Juanita Fielden, [ICE agent] Raul Bencomo, [ICE supervisor] Curtis Compton and [ICE Special Agent in Charge of El Paso] Giovanni Gaudioso in this case.

With regard to Guillermo [Eduardo or "Lalo"] Ramirez Peyro, the informant .... Ms. Fielden's testimony is inconsistent and lacks credibility. Fielden admits that the first murder was recorded by the informant. Fielden does not reveal whether the Judge signed a T-III federal intercept order [referring to the Title III federal wiretap law]. And, if so, what did they tell the judge in the [required] 10-day report? The report would indicate whether they informed the judge that the informant supervised but did not participate in the murder. This would have been a mischaracterization and deceptive.

Fielden's statements indicate that she misrepresented the true nature of the informant's involvement. The Bureau of Immigration and Customs Enforcement [ICE] August 25, 2003, memorandum gives an incomplete account of the informant's involvement in the murder. Fielden and ICE's account of the murder of [Mexican attorney Fernando] Reyes [the first victim at the House of Death in Juarez] was not completely truthful, especially compared with [the informant [Guillermo Ramirez Peyro's] own statements.

Ramirez [Peyro] gave a sworn statement to the Mexican consulate in Dallas, Texas. He testified in immigration court. And, he has given a sworn deposition. In his deposition, Mr. Ramirez [Peyro] adopted the statement to the Mexican consulate as true and accurate. The statement gives a detailed account of the murder of Fernando Reyes that occurred in August 2003. By all indications, Ramirez [Peyro] was a key participant in the torture and murder of Reyes. Ramirez [Peyro] also admits his involvement in disposing of the bodies. It is my belief that [federal] Judge Phil Martinez would not have authorized the Title III [wiretap] intercept had he been informed of Ramirez [Peyro's] true involvement in murder.

Ms. Fielden and ICE agents deliberately excluded DEA personnel and concealed information regarding Ramirez [Peyro's] involvement in murders and other illegal activity. The cooperating individual referred to as the "CI" in the affidavit [confidential informant Ramirez Peyro], was arrested by New Mexico DEA Special Agent Mike Garcia. After the CI's arrest, Ms. Fielden held a meeting with ICE management, excluding DEA personnel. Under the established protocol, Ms. Fielden had no right to call this meeting without the arresting agency being present and did not have justification to request the dismissal of the charges [against Ramirez Peyro] that were pending in state court without DEA consultation. Under DEA policy, if an informant is arrested committing a crime, he is subject to being "blacklisted" and extraordinary precautions would have to be taken in order to continue utilizing this type of informant. Murder is not negotiable to continue the utilization of an informant.

Ms. Fielden makes no mention of any DEA consultation. Ms. Fielden claims to have obtained a "consensus" to continue using the informant. The reasons Ms. Fielden and ICE personnel concealed information from DEA is clear. Ms. Fielden and the ICE agents were aware of the CI's [Ramirez Peyro's] illicit activities, i.e., committing murder, which is totally against DEA and Department of Justice policy. It has always been DEA policy that an investigation is terminated when the CI is an accomplice, accessory, or is about to commit a murder. To allow a CI to continue cooperating with the government after having been involved in criminal wrongdoing, i.e., murder, is against all Department of Justice policies, and, most important, the United States Constitution.

Ramirez [Peyro] testified that his ICE handlers knew ahead of time that murders were planned. According to Ramirez [Peyro], the intercepts indicate the time, place and the person(s) targeted for torture and murder. I refer to the [immigration] court transcript of Ramirez [Peyro's] testimony as well as his media interview.

In his 18 years of law enforcement, [ICE Special Agent Raul] Bencomo has been trained to discontinue working with an informant that "supervised" and participated in a murder. It is simply not credible that Department of Justice officials would approve the continued use of an informant directly involved in murder.

Bencomo and [ICE Supervisor Curtis] Compton's claims that they were not aware of the killings prior to them taking place are contrary to the evidence. The DEA timeline of events shows that the ICE agents allowed Ramirez [Peyro] to return to Juarez armed with a firearm against both U.S. policy and Mexican law. The informant continued his involvement after each sequential murder and debriefing. Bencomo states they learned of the "murders" through "interviews" of Ramirez [Peyro] after the fact. He does not indicate how many interviews took place between August 3, 2003, and January 4, 2004. He does not indicate how many murders took place. There is no evidence to support [ICE supervisor Curtis] Compton's claim that the Mexican authorities authorized the operations to continue.

As a supervisor, Compton should have blacklisted the informant immediately upon learning of the first murder. Compton cannot explain why Ramirez [Peyro] signed the INSTRUCTION FOR CONFIDENTIAL SOURCES FORM under a fictitious name "Jesus Contreras." Furthermore, Ramirez [Peyro] was never required to sign another form after the first murder.

According to the Ramirez [Peyro's] media interview [with producer Mark Smith of WFAA-TV in Dallas as well as a *Narco News*' interview with the informant], ICE took no action to prevent the murders from occurring and stop the operation. Ramirez [Peyro] was specifically instructed not to record any more murders, thus giving the informant a false impression that he had license to kill.

Bencomo and Compton admit Ramirez [Peyro] told them where the murder took place, giving the exact address. This means El Paso ICE lied to the DEA in Juarez, and to the Mexican authorities in the letter dated August 15, 2003. The letter to the PGR [Mexican Attorney General's Office] stated that the informant "witnessed" a murder and suggested they didn't know where the murder took place.

Bencomo claims to have worked diligently with the prosecutor to prepare an indictment of [the narco-trafficker] Santillan but did not indict him for the first murder. This is further indication that the prosecutors were attempting to conceal Ramirez [Peyro's] involvement in the first murder. I believe it was never the prosecutor and ICE's intention to arrest Santillan for the first murder because they continued sending the informant to Juarez where additional murders took place. Moreover, when the prosecutor [initially] indicted Santillan in November 2003, she did not charge him with the first murder. Fielden knew the murders were taking place and they took no action to prevent them. DEA was never consulted during this time.

Bencomo knew of the first murder and the caliber of the Juarez Cartel they were investigating. It stands to reason that other murders would follow. By the informant's modus operandi, ICE would have reason to expect that others would be killed. As the record shows, Ramirez [Peyro] was acting as an agent of the U.S. government.

The agents attempt to justify their actions by claiming that all of this happened in Mexico. The murders were being supervised, however, by an informant sponsored by the U.S. government. It is startling to say the least given [ICE El Paso Special Agent in Charge] Gaudioso's experience and training that he allowed the operation to continue after Ramirez [Peyro] admitted to committing murder while working for ICE.

The ICE officials, including Raul Bencomo, Curtis Compton and Giovanni Gaudioso, make no efforts to stop Ramirez [Peyro] from participating in the murders. The several management reviews of Bencomo, Compton, [ICE Associate Special Agent in Charge Patricia] Kramer and Fielden show a total disregard for human life and disrespect for the rule of law in Mexico. The evidence indicates that ICE officials and Ms. Fielden made no efforts to arrest the suspects and "take down" the case. This allowed an additional 13 murders to take place [which includes the related murder detailed in the DEA timeline that was carried out in Juarez by order of Mexican state police commander Miguel Loya after the House of Death was exposed]. According to the DEA review, the ICE agents and the prosecutor's office went to great lengths to protect this homicidal informant. Gaudioso allowed the prosecutor Fielden to make operational decisions regarding Ramirez [Peyro]. The operation was only stopped after the attempted murder of a DEA agent and his family in Ciudad Juarez, Mexico.

Under DEA and Department of Justice guidelines, a federal agent has an affirmative duty to prevent a premeditated murder or bodily harm that could lead to death. The federal agents knew that the informant and the Juarez Cartel had specifically targeted specific individuals for execution. After review of the evidence, the federal agents made no attempts to prevent the murders from occurring.

The actions of Raul Bencomo, Curtis Compton, Giovanni Gaudioso, Patricia Kramer and Juanita Fielden show deliberate, reckless, or callous indifference to the constitutional rights of the victims and their survivors. The victims and their families [include] legal residents and citizens of the United States protected by the Constitution. The fact that the crimes committed by Ramirez [Peyro], the confidential informant, were only halted after the apparent targeting of two DEA special agents [in a traffic stop] is unprecedented in my 30 years of law enforcement.

Phillip E. Jordan
October 6, 2006

Dispatch 9
August 25, 2007

Frank Montalvo, the federal judge in El Paso hearing the civil litigation brought by the families of the House of Death victims, essentially adopted the government's arguments wholesale in ruling on the case in late summer 2007.

He dismissed the families' claims against the United States government as well as the claims against individual government agents, including Assistant U.S. Attorney Juanita Fielden and ICE supervisors Giovanni Gaudioso, Patricia Kramer, Curtis Compton and ICE agent Raul Bencomo.

The families of the House of Death murder victims filed their joint lawsuit in December 2005 in federal court in El Paso, Texas. They accused the government and certain of its agents of constitutional violations and negligence stemming from actions, or lack of actions, which resulted in their loved ones being tortured, murdered and buried in the backyard of a house in Juarez, Mexico. Judge Montalvo ruled, in essence, that the families could not establish legal claims under federal and state of Texas negligence statutes because either those laws didn't apply to the murder victims since the crimes occurred in Mexico, or, in the alternative, because the government owed no duty to protect the victims from the acts of third parties, such as the Juarez-based criminal cell that operated the House of Death.

From the judge's August 20, 2007, ruling:

Pursuant to the FTCA [the Federal Tort Claims Act], there is no subject matter jurisdiction for claims "based on the exercise or performance or the failure to exercise or perform a discretionary function or duty [in this case, preventing murder] on the part of a federal agency or employee of the government.

The judge also dismissed the claims against the individual ICE agents and Fielden because he determined that the families had failed to establish a proper claim that their constitutional rights, or those of the murder victims, had been violated. Montalvo points out in his ruling, that "public officials (such as ICE agents and U.S. prosecutors) are entitled to "qualified immunity" for their actions on the job unless they violate "clearly established statutory or constitutional rights of which reasonable individuals would be aware."

"None of plaintiffs' [the victim's] allegations, even if true, sufficiently establish constitutional liability on the part of any of the individual defendants [the ICE agents or U.S. prosecutor]," Montalvo states in his ruling.

It is key here to note that Montalvo comes to his conclusions in this case even in light of assuming all of the families' allegations are "true." This is a quite amazing revelation about the nature of our law with respect to murder and law enforcement. The major allegation in this case, which is supported by the government's own documents, is that an informant (Guillermo Eduardo Ramirez Peyro, alias Jesus Contreras, or simply Lalo) who was **on the payroll of ICE** (paid nearly a quarter of a million dollars for his service while claiming he's still owed some $400,000) **assisted and in some** cases participated in the murders of at least a dozen people at the House of Death in Juarez, Mexico, between August 2003 and mid-January 2004.

The lawyer representing the families of the victims also alleges (and immigration court testimony by the informant himself supports this) that ICE agents were made aware of the murders, sometimes in advance of the killings, yet continued to send the informant back to the House of Death time and time again over the course of five months — after receiving approvals from high-level officials at ICE headquarters as well as from the Department of Justice.

From the informant Ramirez-Peyro's **under-oath testimony** in U.S. Immigration Court:

Government attorney: Did you tell your — the ICE officers that you were aware that Mr. Santillan [the boss of the Juarez Cartel narco-trafficking cell] had ordered the deaths of people associated with the cartel [the victims at the House of Death]?

Ramirez Peyro: Yes.

Government attorney: Did you tell them before, right before it happened?

Ramirez Peyro: Yeah, several occasions. For example, in one occasion in Chicago, and Santillan talks to me, so I could send the boy there to open the house [the House of Death in Juarez] and me being in Chicago with the agents from ICE, and they knew because I authorize for them to hear my phone conversations. And besides that, I told them what's going on, and in El Paso they [ICE agents] were listening to my phone calls.

The whole bloody affair came to an abrupt end when the killers — Mexican cops on Santillan's payroll — nearly assassinated a DEA agent and his family. At that point, ICE officials and the U.S. Attorney's Office in San Antonio chose to finally arrest Santillan and pull their informant, himself a former Mexican cop, out of the field. So, even granting that all of this is true, Judge Montalvo still determined that the families' case has to be dismissed because the ICE agents and the U.S. prosecutor overseeing the case committed no foul under existing law.

In other words, even though the government employed the killer, and knew he was committing murder, neither the government nor its agents bear any liability for the deaths of the victims.

From the judge's ruling:

The record reflects the often-cited carne asadas [at the House of Death] were gruesome murder "parties" conducted by vicious men and women. [Note, no women associated with the Juarez Cartel were ever accused of involvement in the House of Death murders. It was men killed and men doing the murdering.]

Considering the record as a whole, this court concludes that, with or without Ramirez [Peyro's] involvement, this is how these types of groups operate.

... Even assuming the defendants [the ICE agents and prosecutor] had foreknowledge of the murders occurring in Mexico, the court concludes the only arguable duty, if any, on their part would have been to notify Mexican law enforcement.

However, the court concludes the evidence fails to show how any of the defendants played a part in creating the circumstances leading to the murders or did anything to render the plaintiffs [the victims] more vulnerable to such circumstances.

ICE officials did, in fact, inform the Mexican government of the first House of Death murder, but recall they claimed their informant had only "witnessed" a murder in Juarez — when he, in fact, supervised and participated in that murder. So, it is clear from that **written communication** from ICE to Mexican federal officials that the truth in this case was being concealed from the Mexican government.

ICE officials also informed Mexico City and Juarez DEA commands about the first **"murder incident"** at the House of Death, but ICE agents did not provide DEA agents with sufficient information to identify the location of the house in Juarez. In addition, ICE officials in El Paso, with support from a federal prosecutor there, refused to allow the informant to assist DEA with locating the house because they claimed it would jeopardize the safety of their informant — Ramirez Peyro.

Had the DEA been furnished with the location of the House of Death and if the Mexican government had been made aware that the informant participated in the first murder, could it not be argued that actions might have been taken by DEA or the Mexican government to prevent future murders at the House of Death, or does that not matter?

Apparently not, according to Judge Montalvo's interpretation of the law and oracle-of-the-future analysis. It appears there's nothing wrong, at last in a legal sense in the U.S., with the government employing an informant who participates in murder in another country while on a federal agency's payroll, particularly if government officials claim omniscient powers of future vision and argue the murders are going to happen anyway. After all, people are killed every day in the drug war, so why should it matter?

To be fair to the judge, the case presented to him by the families' attorney, Raul Loya of Dallas, arguably could have been wrapped in a better package. It might be that Dallas attorney Loya was simply outgunned by the array of lawyers lined up against him — by the government's stable of esquires and the attorneys for the individual defendants. It seems clear that the evidence he mustered to the families' cause, based on the judge's own admonishment, was, to some degree, lacking in legal fine tuning.

More from Judge Montalvo's ruling:

> The court here takes the unusual step of issuing the following admonishment to plaintiffs' counsel Mr. Raul Loya. Throughout their filings, plaintiffs [the House of Death victims represented by Loya] make numerous factual allegations which are not supported by the documentary evidence claimed.
>
> In deciding the instant motions, the court checked every single allegation against the documentary evidence and found numerous discrepancies. The court cautions plaintiffs' counsel that it will not tolerate misleading statements and sanctions will result for any further such conduct.

In the wake of new evidence that surfaced only days prior to the judge making his ruling (and which he did not consider as part of his ruling), however, it is clear that there is now some reason to believe that the government might have been less than forthcoming in its own pleadings in the case. That is a factor which also must be considered in passing judgment on Montalvo's ruling.

To date, the government and its agents, for their part, contend that they did not know, nor could they have foreseen, that the informant would be involved in future murders at the House of Death after the first murder. Apparently, they were ignorant of what the judge presumed in his ruling is a given, that "this is how these types of groups [narco-traffickers, whom the ICE informant worked for at the House of Death] operate."

At a minimum, ICE agents most certainly were aware that the informant Ramirez Peyro was charged with overseeing the burial of the bodies at the House of Death, given they actually allowed him to return to Juarez after the first murder to pay the gravedigger. In some cases, the informant **even purchased lime** in advance of the murders to aid in decomposing the bodies he was to bury, a fact **memorialized in an ICE memo** penned right after the initial House of Death murder of Mexican attorney Fernando Reyes. You would think that might have made someone at ICE at least a bit suspicious about their informant's activities at the House of Death. And recall, one of the informant's helpers at the House of Death later **told the DEA** that the informant was present for at least five of the murders at the House of Death, **DEA documents** show.

In all of this, though, we should consider that what might be most lacking in our justice system is a fundamental, horse-sense notion of fairness and truth. Instead, it seems, justice in this nation leans in favor of the party that can marshal to its side the most money, power, influence (and expensive lawyers) all aimed at twisting the truth through a stovepipe of legal sophistry.

* * *

Judge Montalvo is arguably a judicial product of the George W. Bush administration. He was appointed to the bench in 2003 by President Bush and at the time was one of only **four U.S. District Court judges in El Paso** — which is part of the federal Western District of Texas. Prior to his appointment to the federal bench, Montalvo served as state of Texas district court judge in San Antonio, Texas.

One of his former colleagues in the Alamo City offers high praise for Montalvo in a story that appeared in the *El Paso Times:* "His integrity is impeachable," said State District Court Judge David Peeples of San Antonio. "I think he's a straight-shooter, as straight as they come."

Montalvo is not alone in having connections to San Antonio. Johnny Sutton was based in San Antonio as the U.S. Attorney for the Western District of Texas at the same time that Montalvo was a Texas state judge in the Alamo City. Sutton's office played a key role in the House of Death, given it was responsible for prosecuting the case that was being put together by ICE with the help of their informant Ramirez Peyro. Both Sutton and Montalvo, then, owe their positions to President Bush, whose administration might face great embarrassment, and potential legal liability, if it were determined that the U.S. government or its agents were in anyway culpable in the House of Death murders.

But those facts alone do not prove that Montalvo might be inclined toward prejudice in his handling of the families' House of Death litigation. After all, judges are presumed to be impartial when it comes to matters before their courts. But at least one person took issue with Montalvo's courtroom judgment in a separate case that is related to the House of Death.

Attorney **Mark Conrad**, a former high-level supervisor with the U.S. Customs Service (which has since become part of DHS, and ICE), was twice denied permission by Montalvo to represent a client, ICE employee Renae Baros, in his court. Her case (**Renae Baros vs. Michael Chertoff**, Secretary of Homeland Security) was filed in U.S. District Court in El Paso.

Montalvo refused to grant Conrad *pro hac vice* standing in the court without any explanation. *Pro hac vice* standing is a temporary status granted to an attorney who seeks to represent a client in a jurisdiction in which he is not currently practicing law. Conrad was a member in good standing with the federal Southern District of Texas, but not then licensed in the federal Western District of Texas.

Conrad appealed Montalvo's decision to the U.S. Fifth Circuit Court of Appeals, which then ordered Montalvo to re-examine his decision.

Montalvo did just that, reversing his refusal to grant Conrad standing. Montalvo then removed himself from the Baros case and another judge was appointed.

From Montalvo's January 22, 2007, decision in the matter:

> After carefully reviewing the Fifth Circuit's opinion, the Court finds that it should reconsider its earlier decision regarding Conrad's motion to appear *pro hac vice*.... Accordingly, the Court finds it should allow Conrad to practice before the Court in this case [the Baros case].
>
> ... In addition, to dispel any concerns or appearances that might arise from [my] future rulings in this case, the court recuses itself from this matter. Accordingly, the Clerk of this Court shall immediately transfer this [case] to the docket of United States District Judge Harry Lee Hudspeth....

Now this may all appear to be little more than legal minutia to those who are not attorneys. But in this case, Conrad's request to represent Baros promised to be a bit of a thorn in the side of the government with respect to the House of Death.

Baros' litigation accuses ICE of discriminating and retaliating against her after she reported that an ICE supervisor had harassed her. In her lawsuit, Baros alleges that ICE supervisor Patricia Kramer was one of the major perpetrators of the discrimination and retaliation. And remember, Kramer also was a named defendant in the civil litigation brought by the families of the victims of the House of Death. With respect to another named defendant in that case, ICE supervisor Curtis Compton, pleadings in the Baros litigation allege that he failed to "timely report" information related to the House of Death case and also, in a separate matter, that he engaged in violence in the workplace, misused a government vehicle and made "false statements" to government investigators. In addition, a former ICE internal affairs supervisor, **testified under oath** that the agency subsequently "re-colored," or whitewashed, Compton's disciplinary record, which resulted in him receiving only a one-day suspension.

These two ICE supervisors helped to direct a U.S. government informant (Guillermo Eduardo Ramirez Peyro) accused of assisting and even participating in the torture and murder of a dozen people found buried at the House of Death in Juarez in early 2004. Compton was a group supervisor with ICE at the time. The other ICE supervisor now in the spotlight as a result of the Baros case, Patricia Kramer, served as associate special agent in charge of the agency's El Paso office at the time of the House of Death and, as such, was the No. 2 commander in the office — behind Giovanni Gaudioso.

In pleadings in the civil lawsuit lodged by the families of the House of Death homicide victims, Kramer and Compton and their other co-defendants deny any responsibility for the informant's alleged murderous activities. Compton, in an affidavit that is part of the case record, contends that he did not know, nor could he have predicted, that the informant would continue to assist in the murders after ICE became aware of his participation in the first murder in August 2003.

From **Compton's affidavit** in that case:

> I was not aware of any of the [House of Death] killings described in the [lawsuit brought by the victims' families] prior to the events taking place. Moreover, to my knowledge, no one at ICE or the United States Department of Justice was aware that the murders would take place prior to their occurrence.

Prior to recusing himself from the Baros case, Montalvo was sitting in judgment for both the House of Death families' and Baros litigation and should have been very well aware of the Kramer connection to both cases from the legal pleadings. Conrad, as part of his legal work on the Baros case, later brought to light damaging allegations related to Kramer and Compton that have a direct bearing on their House of Death accounts.

Given the revelation in the Baros lawsuit that ICE supervisor Compton has a past track record of making false statements to law enforcement agents, Compton's credibility with respect to his claims of ignorance in the House of Death murders might now be deemed suspect. Likewise, as a result of the Baros lawsuit, now in question is the veracity of Kramer's House of Death claims. According to a **federal judge's ruling** in the Baros case, Kramer committed a violation of ICE rules related to a criminal investigation that was serious enough for an ICE commander to recommend her removal from the agency. And given the agency whitewashing allegations raised in the Compton case, it is hard for us to really know if anything ICE tells us officially about the House of Death is the unvarnished truth.

In any event, it is clear that **Conrad's prowess** as an attorney helped to reveal some disturbing allegations about two of the ICE agents who were central to the House of Death. (**Conrad passed away** in 2017, at the age of 67, after serving for 27 years at the now-mothballed U.S. Custom Service, retiring as special agent in charge of Internal Affairs. In early 2003, **U.S Customs was merged** into the then recently created Department of Homeland Security — with the investigative agents at U.S. Customs becoming part of ICE.)

Judge Montalvo (and the government's attorneys) likely would have known from the Baros pleadings that Conrad would be in a position to probe into the records of key ICE players in the House of Death case and potentially expose information harmful to the government's efforts to bury the House of Death. That has to be considered when assessing Judge Montalvo's treatment of Conrad and his denial, absent explanation, of Conrad's application for pro hac vice standing in the Baros case.

Again, this does not prove any quid pro quo arrangement between Montalvo and Bush administration officials, but as a public servant employed by the citizens, Montalvo also should not be given a free pass from scrutiny with respect to his judicial actions — particularly if they create an appearance of a conflict of interest. And clearly, the government's lawyers were concerned about Conrad's ability to cause them heartburn over the House of Death, given that in the Baros pleadings themselves, the government's attorneys advanced the following argument in seeking a protective order to prevent Conrad from questioning ICE commanders Kramer and Compton about their disciplinary records:

From the government's motion for a protective order in the Baros case:

> ... Kramer and Compton are named defendants in a civil lawsuit [filed by the families of the victims of the House of Death] the basis of which arose during their tenure in El Paso. ...To the extent that any disciplinary history may exist, there is a likely possibility that this information may unfairly be used in an effort to undermine Ms. Kramer's and Mr. Compton's legal rights in the lawsuit....

The government attorneys even invoke *Narco News'* coverage of the House of Death case as a source of concern on that front. More from the government's pleadings in the Baros case:

> Curtis Compton and Patricia Kramer have been the victims of unfounded negative publicity. In particular, [Baros] testified in her deposition that she acquired negative information about Curtis Compton from a web site known as "*Narco News.*"
>
> Additionally, there have been several stories in various media outlets where either Kramer or Compton have been cast in a negative light. To the extent that any disciplinary history may exist as to either Curtis Compton or Patricia Kramer, the potential exists that if it is disclosed, it will make its way into these media outlets and be used for purposes of further harassing and embarrassing both Compton and Kramer. ...

Baros' attorneys, including Conrad, have a different take on the matter, as one might expect. Baros' lawyers claim that the disciplinary records are critical to demonstrating that the leadership of the ICE office in El Paso is blinded by racial prejudice, particularly with respect to Latino women — such as Baros. Kramer and Compton played important roles in creating that hostile and discriminatory working environment, Baros' attorneys argue in court pleadings.

From Baros' court pleadings responding to the government's motion for a protective order:

Ms. Kramer's disdain toward women in general in her office and towards Hispanic women led to 10 Hispanic females filing a Congressional complaint that led to an internal investigation of Ms. Kramer's discriminatory practices.... That investigation was conducted by Senior Special Agent Steven Cooper.

The Plaintiff [Baros] has asked for this document in discovery and is entitled to it since it will bolster [her] claim of gender and racial discrimination. ... [Baros'] attorney has also developed information that Ms. Kramer referred to those who died in the so-called House of Death matter in a derogatory manner when she stated, "They're just Mexicans." ...

Kramer's alleged comment is explored further in a deposition filed as an exhibit in the Baros case. That **deposition** (or testimony) was provided by ICE Supervisor Joseph Bosarge, who worked in El Paso between 2000 and 2002. Bosarge claims in his deposition that Kramer pressured him to improperly deny a promotion to ICE special agent Anita Trujillo, who worked under Compton's supervision in the agency's El Paso office. Bosarge revealed the following in his under-oath testimony under questioning by Houston attorney and former federal prosecutor Ron Tonkin:

> Tonkin: Are you saying Ms. Kramer discriminated against Ms. Trujillo because she's Hispanic?
>
> Bosarge: I don't know what reason she [Kramer] discriminated against her [Trujillo], but she surely discriminated against her.
>
> Tonkin: On what basis?
>
> Bosarge: Well, probably because she [Trujillo] had made [discrimination] allegations against Curtis Compton, who is Ms. Kramer's right-hand man.
>
> Tonkin: So, in order to protect Curtis Compton, she's [Kramer's] going to come down on Anita Trujillo?
>
> Bosarge: Absolutely.

Bosarge claims in his deposition that Trujillo had accused Compton of improprieties in his handling of informant files and reports of investigation. Compton, in turn, tried to turn the blame for those problems back on Trujillo. ...

More from the deposition:

Bosarge: There was — what I had been told by Ms. Kramer was that, essentially, Anita [Trujillo] had lied in an affidavit for a Title III [wiretap], was one of the issues. And I guess her and Mr. Compton worked on that together a lot.

And the other issue I had is that when I was in charge of the informant file, I had done — when I first moved here I did a very thorough inspection, because it hadn't been done on these files, and I found numerous discrepancies in payments and a lot of stuff that wasn't documented. One of the issues that I found was an informant file that hadn't been witnessed by a supervisor that needed to for the amount [of the payment]. And I brought this to the attention of management, and it was another dispute over Curtis' [Compton's] word against her [Trujillo's] word on the informant file.

... And then I believe there were other — you know, the scuttlebutt in the office was that they didn't like each other because Curtis was having affairs with women in the office, and Anita was friends with them. I mean, I don't know. That's all just hearsay on my part.

... When I showed up in El Paso [in 2000] I would look at [investigative] reports, and a lot of agents were doing, you know, really poor reports. And [the] U.S. Attorney's Office had made such an issue of our poor report writing that they had come in and brought two U.S. Attorneys in on two occasions to tell them what to do in the reports and how to do sufficient stuff. ... Because the reports were horrible. ...

Bosarge makes it clear in his deposition that ultimately Trujillo was "exonerated" with respect to the charge that she had falsified the Title III affidavit. Conrad, who also served as Trujillo's attorney, at the time said, "Anita Trujillo was cleared of the Title III affidavit allegations."

"ICE looked at it, and there was nothing to it," Conrad added. "It was a false allegation. ... The government has in its possession documents that exonerate Anita. Those documents show that she was not responsible for any of the inaccuracy in the [ICE] reports."

But it appears, according to Bosarge's testimony, that Kramer was intent on using the unfounded allegations against Trujillo to undermine her credibility with respect to her discrimination claims.

More from Bosarge's deposition: "She [Kramer] was saying that Anita wasn't going to be credible because of her lying on an affidavit. ... She just said, 'Don't worry about it, you know, Anita's - it's going to come out, whatever's on Anita.'"

Kramer was scheduled to testify at Baros' trial. Conrad says she failed to appear, however, and therefore never took the stand under oath to defend her actions before the jury.

The allegations related to Compton's past credibility issues are spelled out in even more detail in an excerpt from a legal deposition that is attached to Baro's court pleadings as an exhibit. The deposition was taken in January 2007 and is related to yet another legal case that was pending before the **U.S. Merit Systems Protection Board.**

In the deposition, Kenn Thomas, a former ICE program manager and later the special agent in charge of ICE's Office of Professional Responsibility, or internal affairs, in San Diego, testified directly about Compton's past disciplinary issues.

Following is an excerpt from the Thomas deposition – in which questions are addressed to Thomas by Baros' attorney, Conrad, who represented a separate client in the MSPB case:

> Conrad: All right. We'll kind of switch gears a little bit. You already indicated, correct me if I'm wrong or misstate this, you indicated earlier that Anita Trujillo had problems with Curtis Compton?
>
> Thomas: Yes.
>
> Conrad: Again, for the record, are you aware that Anita Trujillo is also a client of mine?
>
> Thomas: Yes, I am.
>
> Conrad: ... I just want to make it absolutely clear in my mind, was Curtis Compton honest, candid, forthright in the answers he

responded during the [ICE] management inquiry involving Anita Trujillo [related to her allegation that Compton harassed her in the workplace]?

Thomas: No.

Conrad: I'm sorry?

Thomas: No.

Conrad: And was he less than candid more than one time in that investigation?

Thomas: Yes, he was.

Conrad: Are we talking about a dozen times, three or four, to the best that you can recall?

Thomas: I recall substantiating a false statement allegation that included four or five examples.

... Conrad: Do you know what the charge was [for Compton in relation to ICE's investigation of his alleged misconduct]?

Thomas: There were two files. There was one substantiated violation from what you're referring to as the House of Death. I don't know what the actual case title is. That had to do with failure to timely report [information]. Then there were the allegations that I substantiated [with respect to Trujillo's case] when I was in OPR [the Office of Professional Responsibility, or ICE internal affairs] that had to do with violence in the workplace, misuse of a government vehicle, time and attendance violations, and false statements. The two cases were lumped together.

Thomas then goes on to testify that ICE officials actually "re-colored," or whitewashed, the final internal affairs report on Compton and, based on that, gave him only a one-day suspension. From Thomas' deposition:

I know that in Compton's case he received a one-day suspension based on the two red books [internal affairs investigations]. ... Patty Kramer was proposed a severe discipline and chose to retire. ... What I substantiated [in Compton's case] was a hostile work environment, misuse of a GOV [government vehicle], something to do with violations involving time and attendance, dereliction of duty and false statements.

What showed up on the action memo [the final ICE report] was conduct unbecoming and something else. So that case was entirely re-colored, and the discipline was delved out based on that.

Baros' court pleadings describe in more direct language what ICE did in the Compton case as follows: "As referenced earlier, Mr. Thomas flatly stated that the Agency (ICE) 're-colored' the results of the serious misconduct (including false statements) and labeled it 'conduct unbecoming.'"

The Thomas deposition also includes the following interrogatory that certainly seems to, at the very least, leave the question very much open as to whether ICE and its agents are being straight with us about their roles and actions in the House of Death mass murder in Juarez.

> ... Conrad: Mr. Thomas, are you aware of any discussions within the agency [ICE] as to taking disciplinary actions against the people involved in the House of Death, the concern being the liability of the agency in that matter if they took actions?
>
> Government's Attorney: Objection! That may be privileged communications if an attorney was present.
>
> Conrad: All right. ...

Adding to the note of concern on this front is the fact that Judge Montalvo issued his ruling dismissing the families' claims in the House of Death litigation on August 20, 2007, only six days after Conrad filed pleadings in court for the Baros case that exposed the troubling allegations about Kramer and Compton. This coincidence in the timing of the judge's ruling assured that the new evidence could not be further explored in the House of Death families' civil lawsuit.

Whatever you make of these latest revelations, it must be conceded that the Baros case itself is not centrally about the House of Death — even if some of the players involved are intimately acquainted with that bloody tragedy. The pattern of alleged discrimination and lack of candor revealed in Baros' court pleadings with respect to Compton and Kramer, however, clearly could be viewed as damaging to the U.S. government's claim that it is in no way complicit in the House of Death mass murder.

In any event, the judge in the Baros discrimination case, Senior U.S. District Judge Harry Lee Hudspeth, on August 15, 2007, issued a ruling on the Department of Homeland Security's motion for a protective order that might be seen as taking the wisdom of Solomon to its extreme in that it actually does cut the baby in half. In that ruling, the judge agreed that Compton should not be required to testify about or otherwise have his disciplinary record entered into evidence in the Baros case. The judge determined that Compton's "trials and tribulations" are not relevant to Baros' claims in her case.

With respect to Kramer, however, the judge determined that the government should produce certain portions of the Cooper report (which examined the allegations of the 10 Hispanic females in the ICE El Paso office who accused Kramer of discriminatory behavior in a letter to Congress). "The plaintiff [Baros] is entitled to those pages of the [Cooper] report which refer to her complaint and complaints," the judge ruled.

As far as the allegations in the Baros lawsuit that Kramer "falsified government documents to improperly pay government informants," government attorneys, in response, submitted documents to the judge in the case for his private inspection. We do not know the content of those documents, however.

On August 20, 2007, Judge Hudspeth issued a ruling (excerpted below) focused on the allegations against Kramer.

> ... The defendant [the government] has now produced for the court's inspection a report of an [ICE] internal agency investigation which occurred in late 2004 [while the House of Death criminal case against Santillan and his cohorts was still being prosecuted]; a memorandum signed by Acting Special Agent in Charge Jesus Torres; and a settlement agreement to which Kramer was party.

The 2004 investigation and the Torres memorandum dealt with allegations that Kramer, whose title was Associate Special Agent in Charge in the El Paso [ICE] office, had failed to comply with certain agency rules and policies in connection with one particular criminal investigation [not described].

The Torres memorandum proposed her removal from the service. Neither the report of investigation nor the Torres memorandum accused Kramer of "the falsification of government documents." ... One of the terms of the settlement agreement was that the proposed [forced] removal was rescinded. The other terms of the settlement are not relevant to this case.... [By the time of the ruling, Kramer had retired from ICE]."

Based on the new revelations that surfaced in the Baros case, at a minimum, there now appears to be reason to be highly suspicious of the "We knew nothing" defense advanced by the U.S. government to date in defending its decision to send their informant back to the House of Death repeatedly on a mission of murder. For his part, Baros' attorney, Conrad, declined to comment on his client's case beyond what is in the court record. **Baros' case** went to trial in October 2007, and a **jury returned a verdict** finding that ICE Associate Special Agent in Charge Kramer did retaliate against Baros for "her complaint of sexual harassment against a supervisor."

Among the allegations that surfaced in the Baros litigation are the following:

- Kramer demonstrated a callous indifference to the House of Death murder victims by referring to them as "just Mexicans."

- Kramer violated agency rules and regulations related to a criminal investigation and faced termination from her job — but the recommendation that she be fired was withdrawn as part of a settlement agreement, and she subsequently **retired from ICE in the fall of 2005.**

- Kramer's treatment of certain ICE employees led 10 Hispanic females in the ICE El Paso office to file a Congressional complaint that led to an internal investigation of Kramer's alleged discriminatory practices.

• Compton allegedly failed to "timely report" information related to the House of Death case and also, in a separate matter, reportedly engaged in violence in the workplace, misused a government vehicle and was accused of making "false statements" to government investigators.

• In addition, an ICE internal affairs supervisor testified under oath that the agency subsequently "re-colored," or whitewashed, Compton's disciplinary record, which resulted in him receiving only a one-day suspension.

A National Public Radio story broadcast in 2010 indicates that Kramer felt "ICE's handling of the House of Death case tarnished her good reputation."

"Several sources have said that Kramer was forced to take early retirement," the NPR story added. "When reached by NPR, Kramer declined to characterize her retirement from ICE."

Kramer's alleged comment referring to the House of Death murder victims as "just Mexicans," however, assuming the court pleadings revealing that disparaging remark are accurate, suggests that tarnished reputations are not all that is at stake in this case. Antipathy toward people of color also appears to be tarnishing the path toward justice for the House of Death victims and their families.

Dispatch 10

August 13, 2007

Even if it could be shown beyond a shadow of a doubt that the government, or its agents, knowingly **broke the law** in the House of Death mass murder, and are still working to cover up that fact, I suspect there would be some arcane legal theory that could be stretched over the **truth to project** the illusion of justice.

That underlying truth, though, is hard to sidestep, despite all the government's legal rationalizations to date. The truth is that an informant, employed by the U.S. government and under the supervision of federal agents and U.S. prosecutors, assisted and participated in mass murder in Juarez, Mexico.

Over the many years of covering the House of Death mass murder, I have experienced many emotions, both high and low, and entertained numerous thoughts and theories about what this tragedy says about our country and its relentless, hopeless drug war — and the future of our democracy. The one constant in all of it that I have come to see is both truth and lies in life, like water from an underground spring, constantly feed the lake above, even when the lake appears constant, unchanged on the surface.

The **judge's ruling** in the lawsuit lodged by the families of the House of Death outlines a major premise of the U.S. government's defense in that litigation that is provably inaccurate, but which the judge failed to address in his ruling — likely because the evidence revealing its inaccuracy was not considered as part of the case.

The following is the judge's summary of the government's position in the lawsuit:

In general, the defendants [the government] contend plaintiffs [the families of the House of Death victims] simply reiterate the allegations of former DEA Special Agent in Charge Sandalio Gonzalez ("SAC Gonzalez"). SAC Gonzalez was upset after the identities of his two DEA undercover agents in Juarez were disclosed and lives jeopardized when they were confronted by corrupt Mexican law enforcement working for the [Vicente Carrillo Fuentes organization].

Gonzalez suspected that [the informant] Ramirez Peyro had disclosed the agents' identity while working for ICE. Gonzalez challenged many of the defendants [federal agents named in the lawsuit] when he learned ICE agents allegedly failed to share information with the DEA because of a mistrust of DEA officials.

With this backdrop, Gonzalez, by all accounts a non-witness to the relevant facts of this complaint, wrote [in his letter] of his understanding of the events which, in his personal opinion, led to the compromise of his agents' identity and how that scenario could have been avoided.

Defendants [the government] submit that Gonzalez' unfounded conclusions supply the basis of the plaintiffs' [the families'] baseless amended complaint.

The memo Gonzalez wrote, which the government dismissed as the "opinion" of a disgruntled DEA employee, was, in fact, an accurate rendering of the facts of the situation, according to two high-level DEA employees who testified to that fact under oath. That testimony was provided in December 2006 by DEA Chief of Operations Mike Furgason and Michele Leonhart, then the deputy administrator of DEA. They were deposed as part of Gonzalez' lawsuit against the Department of Justice filed in federal court in Miami in which he claims he was subjected to discrimination and retaliation, in part, due to his decision to write the House of Death memo.

The fact that Furgason concedes in his testimony that **Gonzalez' letter** was accurate on the facts is a powerful statement on the extent of the House of Death coverup. In fact, Leonhart's acknowledges in her testimony that the details of the House of Death (as outlined in Gonzalez' letter) were so serious — of a "life and death" nature, she said — that they were brought to the attention of the highest law enforcer in the land, the U.S. Attorney General.

After Gonzalez penned his memo in early 2004, however, high-ranking officials within ICE (and the Department of Homeland Security of which it is a part) and the Department of Justice (for whom Sutton worked) went to great lengths to bury the paper trail on the House of Death and to keep the story out of the media spotlight. Those efforts included suppressing the final report of a **joint DEA/ICE internal probe** of the House of Death fiasco, which was conducted in February 2004. To this day, that so-called joint assessment report investigating the House of Death case, called the **JAT report,** remains buried at both agencies. That's despite multiple efforts over the years by multiple parties, including me, to seek the release of the full report through the Freedom of Information Act.

I did manage to ferret out a small portion of the JAT report, however, through a FOIA request lodged with **the U.S. Merit Systems Protection Board.** Although that snippet of the report is far from the complete picture, its contents do offer a glimpse of the extent of the investigation targeting the Juarez Cartel at the time.

Portions of the JAT documents released were redacted, but I was able to fill in the missing text where possible [in brackets], based on a review of other public documents and interviews with sources.

MEMORANDUM

TO: [John Clark] ICE Director of Investigations

[Michael Ferguson] DEA Chief of Operations

FROM: [Redacted] SAC ICE Buffalo, New York

[Rodney Benson] ASAC, DEA Boston Field Division

SUBJECT: Joint Assessment Team Report

Pursuant to a directive from DEA Chief of Operations [Mike Ferguson] and ICE Director of Investigations [John Clark], a Joint Assessment Team (JAT) composed of ICE and DEA personnel was sent to El Paso, Texas, and Mexico City, Mexico, in order to review ICE and DEA activities/events pertaining to investigations targeting [the Juarez Cartel and Heriberto Santillan Tabares], et al. This review also included events pertaining to the evacuation of DEA special agents and support personnel assigned to the DEA [Ciudad Juarez] Residence Office, which occurred on January 14, 2004.

This review commenced on February 10, 2004, and ended on February 19, 2004. In connection with this review, the JAT conducted 44 interviews of DEA, ICE, United States Attorney's Office and Department of State personnel in El Paso, Texas, and Mexico. In addition, the JAT conducted investigative and confidential source file reviews and reviewed several hundred recorded conversations in connection with the ICE and DEA [redacted] investigations....

SUMMARY OF INTERVIEW with DEA El Paso Field Division [Special Agent in Charge] Sandalio Gonzalez

Date: February 11, 2004

Place: DEA [El Paso Field] Division

Synopsis of Interview

Pertaining to Operation Sky High: SAC Gonzalez was aware that [Operation Sky High] was an ongoing multi-agency operation including DEA, FBI, ICE, USAO (U.S. Attorney's Office) and Mexican authorities targeting elements of the VCF organization [the Juarez Cartel] in Mexico. According to Gonzalez, this multi-agency operation was initiated by DEA [El Paso].

Over the years, there has been some concern from U.S. law enforcement agencies regarding the sharing of information with Mexican authorities. Gonzalez stated that he stressed that DEA would not share another agency's information with Mexican agencies without permission from the agency providing the information. Gonzalez stated that the FBI and ICE did not want certain information passed to the Mexican authorities. Gonzalez stated that the [Heriberto Santillan Tabares] investigation was a joint investigation between DEA and ICE and that the FBI had very little involvement with this investigation. Gonzalez recalled the March 2003 controlled delivery of 29 kilograms of cocaine that was received by the ICE CS [confidential source Guillermo Eduardo Ramirez Peyro] from [Santillan].

* * *

That controlled delivery was part of an evidence-gathering operation monitored closely by U.S. law enforcers that played out months in advance of the first House of Death murder. Santillan was not taken down then, however. Instead, his bloody criminal enterprise was allowed to continue with the help of ICE informant Ramirez Peyro.

DEA commander Gonzalez' letter to ICE and Sutton complaining about the handling of the House of Death case, and his related filings with oversight agencies like the **Office of Special Counsel** and **MSPB**, are so controversial because they allege — with many supporting facts — that government officials were grossly negligent and, in the worst case, potentially criminally culpable. Gonzalez' **pleadings in his Merit Systems Protection Board case**, filed in July 2005 — less than six months after penning his House of Death letter — offer a glimpse of what ICE and Sutton's office were facing.

"The murder of a human being in the Republic of Mexico, knowingly misrepresenting facts to Mexican federal law enforcement officials with jurisdiction over the crime of murder in Mexico, and obstructing the investigation of a threat against the lives of a DEA agent and his family are clear violations of human rights, law, rules or regulations, and constitute gross mismanagement of resources of criminal investigative procedures," Gonzalez alleges in his MSPB pleadings. For that bit of truth-telling and rocking the boat, Gonzalez faced retaliation and was ordered by his superiors at DEA to remain silent. He was eventually pressured into retiring early from DEA.

As to the merits of former DEA commander Gonzalez' lawsuit? Well, the Department of Justice, under **U.S. Attorney General Alberto Gonzales**, ultimately agreed to cough up $385,000 in U.S. taxpayers' money to settle the whistleblower/discrimination lawsuit that Gonzalez filed against the government in federal court in Miami. That lawsuit was Gonzalez last best chance to get some justice after exhausting the agency **administrative-appeal process.**

The case did go to a jury trial, resulting in a verdict **in December 2006 favoring Gonzalez.** The government initially indicated it planned to file an appeal in the case, but in a July 2007 **settlement** reached with Gonzalez' attorneys, DOJ lawyers agreed to **drop the appeal and pay the piper** — in this case, Gonzalez. The U.S. government's willingness to abort its appeal and pay through the nose — which is a concession that it did, in fact, discriminate against Gonzalez — is yet more evidence that Gonzalez' claims about the House of Death coverup are on the mark. Gonzalez claimed in **pleadings in his legal case** in Miami that DEA had retaliated against him for a variety of reasons, including:

- His participation in activities exposing DEA's discrimination against Latino agents and other employees.

- For the letter sent to ICE's Gaudioso and DOJ's Sutton decrying the government's role in allowing an ICE informant to participate in murder at the House of Death in Juarez — a decision that nearly led to the assassination of a DEA agent and his family.

- For an earlier act of whistleblowing on his part in which he demanded that DEA investigate alleged law enforcement corruption and a missing 10 kilos of cocaine in a **case gone awry in Miami** in the late 1990s.

Gonzalez claims further that the coverup of the House of Death murders goes to the highest levels of DOJ and DHS, adding that DEA Administrator Karen Tandy initiated the retaliation against him at the behest of President Bush's friend, U.S. Attorney Sutton. But not surprisingly, little attention was paid in the halls of U.S. power or in mainstream media to Gonzalez' revelations and legal victory.

Given those dynamics, one has to wonder how many more houses of death have been spawned along the U.S./Mexico border as a result of the ugly trifecta of unchecked homicidal informants; U.S. government inaction (or even tacit approval) of that activity coupled with whistleblower attacks and retaliation; plus, tired media narratives echoed by self-aggrandizing experts who refuse to jettison their cartoon notions of the war for drugs.

Part II

Deportation Battle

Dispatch 11

June 28, 2009

Heriberto Santillan Tabares was arrested in El Paso, Texas, on January 15, 2004, after being lured across the border by a U.S. government informant, Guillermo Eduardo **Ramirez Peyro**, on the pretext of a meeting. His arrest was carried out the day after Santillan's enforcers executed a traffic stop targeting a DEA agent and his family in Juarez.

The informant, as part of law enforcement's plan, is pulled over by an El Paso squad car while driving his car on a pre-designated street — with Santillan as a passenger. ICE agents then swoop in and arrest Santillan and the informant on outstanding warrants. The arrest of Ramirez Peyro, of course, is a ruse designed to cloak his role in Santillan's arrest.

The same day, **DEA documents** show, another of Santillan's associates, a Mexican state police commander named Miguel Loya Gallegos (Santillan's nephew), orders the execution of an individual he believed stole from the cartel. The man is shot dead at point blank range while seated in his pick-up truck in Juarez. The attack, carried out by two plainclothes Mexican cops, also seriously wounds the passenger — who was shot in the mouth and neck. Loya allegedly shows up at the murder scene to "investigate" the crime.

Over the prior five months, at least a dozen other people had been tortured and murdered by Santillan's gangster-cop crew and then buried in the backyard of a house in Juarez. The informant Ramirez Peyro helped supervise and participated in at least one of the murders at the house, brought other victims to the house, and was present for a number of other executions — including at least two murders in which he delivered the victims to Mexican state police commander Miguel Loya Gallegos and his men to be murdered.

Ramirez Peyro claims he reported his activity to his ICE handlers — often in advance of the "carne asadas" at the House of Death. An affidavit sworn under oath by an assistant U.S. attorney in El Paso, Texas, and testimony in a federal civil lawsuit filed by DEA commander Sandalio Gonzalez confirm ICE and the Department of Justice, at the highest levels, were made aware of the informant's participation in murder, yet sanctioned his continued use.

Within days of the arrest of Santillan in El Paso on drug and murder charges, the informant Ramirez Peyro also became a protected witness and was relocated to San Antonio, Texas, along with his family, where ICE put them up in an apartment. Santillan was slated to be put on trial in San Antonio, where the office of U.S. Attorney Johnny Sutton was prosecuting his case.

ICE took Ramirez Peyro to San Antonio, in part, to hide him from operatives of the Juarez Cartel who surely wanted to kill him for being a rat. Within weeks of Santillan's arrest, Ramirez Peyro's role as an ICE informant had been exposed through media reports, both in the U.S. and Mexico. Even though his real name was not used in those reports, it would have been clear to Santillan, and others associated with him, who the informant was in this case.

Despite this reality, Ramirez Peyro claims his ICE handlers suggested he find a job in San Antonio. And he did, as a security guard, working under his real name, he says, at shopping center called the Forum — located in Selma, a small northern suburb of San Antonio. ICE also relocated Ramirez Peyro's wife and children to San Antonio. His family was permitted to enter the U.S. from Mexico in January 2004 — a reward of sorts for the informant agreeing to assist ICE with the Santillan lure and arrest.

While in San Antonio — and several months after he was officially deactivated in March 2004 as an ICE informant — Ramirez Peyro claims that ICE agents sought his assistance on yet another drug-smuggling case they were working in the El Paso/Juarez area. The case focused on an allegedly corrupt U.S. customs inspector.

A federal agent familiar with the House of Death case, but who asked not to be named, alleges Ramirez Peyro "caught wind" of a case being developed against an alleged corrupt U.S. law enforcer through another informant he knew who also was embedded in a Juarez Cartel criminal cell — separate from the Santillan criminal cell Ramirez Peyro had infiltrated that led to Santillan's arrest. That other informant was working undercover, of course, in a case against a cell, "headed by an individual with the last name of Laredo," the federal agent claims. And Ramirez Peyro wanted in on the investigation because he knew he'd "get a big paycheck," the agent adds.

The informant Ramirez Peyro was essentially attempting to piggyback on an existing "controlled-delivery" operation (a monitored illegal-drug sting] targeting another dangerous criminal cell affiliated with the Juarez Cartel, not realizing all of the operation's details. And again, as in his arrest for smuggling drugs in New Mexico, all this was being done, according to the agent, without the knowledge or permission of his ICE handlers.

One of the crucial operational details Ramirez Peyro allegedly was unaware of was the fact that the ICE sting operation he sought to attach himself to, which targeted a corrupt U.S. customs inspector, had been called off month's earlier, the agent claims. The sting had been cancelled based on information provided by the U.S. government informant embedded in the Laredo criminal cell. That scenario created the conditions for more extreme violence, given "Laredo" wanted vengeance against Ramirez Peyro because he knew by then Ramirez Peyro was an informant, and Laredo realized Lalo had assisted ICE in arresting his brother as part of a 2001 corruption case involving yet another U.S. customs inspector, **Raymond Monroe Allen II** — who in 2002 pleaded guilty in U.S. court to drug-smuggling charges.

The federal agent who spoke with *Narco News* says he assumes Laredo's people continued working with Ramirez Peyro on the money drop — a payment for another supposedly corrupt U.S. customs inspector (separate from Allen) — in order to set him up for assassination. Ramirez Peyro, however, continued to believe he was somehow helping to set up Laredo for arrest by ICE. Those dynamics, assuming the federal agent's account is accurate, set the stage for a tragedy to unfold on the day a money drop was arranged at Whataburger fast-food restaurant in El Paso.

"So, he [Laredo] was trying to get revenge, because by that time people [the cartel] knew he [Ramirez Peyro] was a snitch," the federal agent says.

In the agent's version of events, it's still not clear how Ramirez Peyro, without ICE's knowledge, made the 550-mile journey to El Paso in far West Texas from San Antonio in South Texas — where he was allegedly under the protection of ICE agents. (ICE incompetence and/or negligence might explain it, though.) Nor is it clear how Ramirez Peyro happened to show up at a Whataburger fast-food restaurant on August 25, 2004, again without ICE's knowledge, on the very night of a bloody murder playing out in the establishment's parking lot, which took the life of an FBI informant. Although, it appears, and Ramirez Peyro now agrees, those bullets were meant for him.

What's clear, based on an **internal memo dated March 12, 2004,** is that the director of ICE's Office of Investigations had approved the deactivation of Ramirez Peyro as an ICE informant well ahead of the informant's journey to El Paso in late August 2004, which ended with a murder at the Whataburger fast-food restaurant.

Memorandum For: John P. Clark, Director, Office of Investigations

From Paul M. Kilcoyne, Deputy Assistant Director, Investigative Services

Subject: Deactivation of Confidential Informant SA-913-EP [Ramirez Peyro]

This memorandum serves to inform you of the deactivation of Confidential Informant (CI) SA-913-EP. The Special Agent in Charge

(SAC) in El Paso initially documented SA-913-EP on July 17, 2000, and has had a continuous relationship with the CI [confidential informant] since that time. Under the direction of the [ICE] SAC El Paso, SA-913-EP provided information concerning narcotics and cigarette smuggling from Mexico into the United States that resulted in numerous seizures and arrests. To date, the SAC El Paso has paid SA-913-EP monetary awards totaling $224,650....

On June 28, 2003, SA-913-EP was arrested for his/her involvement in the smuggling of 102 pounds of marijuana into the United States near Las Cruces, New Mexico. Prosecution of the case was declined by the United Sates Attorney's Office. On that same date, the case was presented to the Las Cruces, New Mexico, District Attorney's Office, and SA-913-EP was arrested and booked into the Dona Ana County Jail for state narcotics violations. The charges remained pending until December 2003, at which time they were dismissed as a result of SA-913-EP's assistance in the ... [Santillan] investigation.

Although the Source [Ramirez Peyro] remains a critical witness in a number of ICE cases, further and/or continued use of the Source [Ramirez Peyro] is not anticipated at this time.

Based on the facts outlined above, I hereby recommend that the SAC El Paso deactivate SA-913-EP.

It's important to note again that **the ICE memo** from headquarters deactivating Ramirez Peyro as an ICE informant was drafted some five months prior to Ramirez Peyro leaving San Antonio and heading to El Paso. It's possible ICE re-activated Ramirez Peyro for a short time for that trip, or that he was asked to assist with the operation informally (not as registered informant) in some way that is legal or at least on the line, or that he was clued into the ICE operation via his sources and, as the federal agent source claims, was willing and able to grift himself into the operation with the hope of scoring a potential payday — even after being deactivated as an informant.

Or it's possible Ramirez Peyro cooked up his own deal to make a fast buck. Some law enforcers speculate that the Whataburger money drop was not a law enforcement operation at all, but rather a clandestine deal gone bad that involved shady cartel characters and real estate that Ramirez Peyro had title to in Juarez that he had sold off in an effort to earn some extra cash.

A darker subplot might exist as well, and that would be that some of Ramirez Peyro's U.S. government handlers actually set him up to be killed by the Juarez Cartel — or at least turned a blind eye — because Ramirez Peyro had become a serious thorn in their side due to his participation in murder under their watch. And that potential was not ruled out completely by federal agents who spoke with *Narco News*. Although there remain many unanswered questions — in Mexico and with the drug war generally that is the norm — the federal agent who spoke on background says one big motivator as to why Ramirez Peyro left San Antonio for El Paso is clear.

"Lalo wanted to go see his fiancé in El Paso, and she had threatened that if he wouldn't come back that she was going to go tell people he was a snitch," the federal agent claims. "It was big mistake on the agency's part putting him back with his ex-wife in San Antonio, with his fiancé and all that, so it was just a big mess."

The informant, however, insists there is no mystery as to why he flew from San Antonio to El Paso in late August 2004. Ramirez Peyro says it's because he was involved in a sanctioned ICE sting operation with the full knowledge of his ICE handlers. "I set up the deal from San Antonio [while supposedly under ICE's protective custody and working at an area shopping center]," Ramirez Peyro said. "It took me two months to find someone to do it [to agree to bring a load of drugs from Juarez to El Paso to snare the allegedly corrupt customs inspector] because I didn't want to deal directly with cartel people."

Ramirez Peyro said once the deal was in motion, and he got the go-ahead from ICE, he purchased an airline ticket and flew, by himself, to El Paso, arriving in the Texas border city on Monday morning August 23, 2004. "I took a cab to my girlfriend's apartment [in El Paso, leaving his wife, from whom he is separated but still legally married, and kids in

San Antonio]," he added. "I wasn't worried about getting killed because no one knew I was there."

Other than his ICE handlers, supposedly, that is.

The plan was simple, in theory. A driver was to bring the merchandise, marijuana, by van across the bridge from Juarez to El Paso. Another individual was to bring across the money to pay off the corrupt customs inspector for passing the load through the checkpoint. In this case, according to Ramirez Peyro, part of the money was sent in advance of the drug delivery, and the balance was to be delivered at a Whataburger fast-food restaurant in El Paso.

"I was told to remain in the background," Ramirez Peyro said, "just to coordinate the different people."

The final leg of the sting was set to play out the evening of August 25, 2004, at the Whataburger hamburger joint near the border in El Paso. Ramirez Peyro said he sent his friend, Abraham Guzman, to pick up the money. "He was an informant for the FBI, but he was loyal to me," Ramirez Peyro said of Guzman, who was 27 and the father of a two-week old baby boy.

In fact, according to Ramirez Peyro, Guzman had helped him out in the past as well. "About two weeks before, he had picked up money from a house I sold in Juarez and deposited it in my bank account," Ramirez Peyro claimed.

(Some law enforcers, on background, contend the money from such a house sale was not likely to be deposited in a U.S. bank account, where a record would be created for taxes or where it might be subject to seizure. Rather, they claim, that cash is very likely what was really being delivered at the Whataburger money drop that late summer evening.)

Whatever the truth is, it's clear Guzman did not profit from it in the end. He found himself at the Whataburger near downtown El Paso at about 11 p.m. waiting in a purple Lincoln Navigator for a bag of money to be delivered.

"... The owner of the [cartel's] merchandise [the marijuana] was supposed to deliver the money to Guzman [at the Whataburger] to pay the corrupt inspector," Ramirez Peyro recalled in a later interview with me.

Instead, Guzman ended up on the receiving end of four bullets to the face and chest delivered by a Juarez Cartel assassin. Ramirez Peyro says he was in a white Pontiac car with his girlfriend driving toward the Whataburger when they heard the gun pops that ended Guzman's life.

"We heard the shots and turned around," Ramirez Peyro said. "I then called [Raul] Bencomo [his ICE handler]."

Ramirez Peyro said he and his girlfriend then met with Bencomo in the parking lot of an El Paso supermarket. "I got out of the car and got into Bencomo's car, and we talked," Ramirez Peyro said. "My girlfriend then took me to a hotel, and she went to talk with Bencomo. I don't know where they went."

Ramirez Peyro said he later learned that ICE agents took his girlfriend to retrieve her children from her apartment, and she was then delivered to a separate hotel. Ramirez Peyro said that was the last he saw of his girlfriend. He added that he phoned Bencomo after arriving at his hotel to let him know where he was staying. Then, at about 2 a.m., Ramirez Peyro said ICE supervisor Curtis Compton showed up at the hotel and hauled him down to ICE headquarters in El Paso, where he was confronted by a cadre of agents as well as Assistant U.S. Attorney Juanita Fielden.

"They asked me why I was in El Paso," Ramirez Peyro claimed. "They said I was not supposed to be there, and I was put into custody." An August 2005 **ruling by an immigration judge** in Minnesota, states the following: "After the shooting of [alleged FBI informant] Guzman, Lalo and a female friend stayed in separate hotels as ICE agents provided round-the-clock surveillance, worried that cartel leaders, on learning that the wrong man was killed, would try again. There is a report that states the [informant Ramirez Peyro] had violated his agreement with

ICE by escaping from a safe house and going back to the drug business."

So, it appears, Ramirez Peyro's version of the Whataburger incident, and ICE's version, together, don't add up to the whole truth. That is the nature of the drug war. At any given time, no one really knows whose deal is going down around them and whether they are on the right or wrong side of it — often with lethal consequences at stake. Journalist and author Chuck Bowden once explained to me that the only thing one can be sure of in the magic land of Mexico is your own death — and at that point it won't matter.

In the wake of Guzman's murder, Ramirez Peyro claims that at least three other people connected to the botched sting operation were killed by Juarez Cartel assassins — including the driver of the van who delivered the marijuana across the border on the front end of the deal, the driver's son, and the individual who set up the supposed drug deal with Ramirez Peyro.

Not long after those murders, ICE arrested Ramirez Peyro "to return him to the U.S. Marshal's Office," court records indicate, given he was a protected witness. He was shortly thereafter brought before a federal judge, where a U.S. government prosecutor argued he had to be returned to protective custody — specifically, a prison this time. "Fielden claimed that ICE didn't have the resources to keep me safe," Ramirez Peyro said. "I argued [in front of the judge] that I could not be put in prison, to keep me under house arrest, that I needed to be with my family."

Ramirez Peyro also claimed the Mexican government was trying to blame him for the murders that happened in Mexico as a result of the botched Whataburger money drop. They were seeking to "put a warrant on me," he said. Had Mexico been successful in that effort, Ramirez Peyro insisted it would have been a death sentence for him. Once returned to Mexico, he would have been turned over to the cartel assassins by corrupt elements within the Mexican government — most likely cops.

As it turned out, Ramirez Peyro wound up in prison, in the U.S. He alleges that result was due to an act of blackmail carried out by Fielden. "She told me either I agree to stay in jail, or we will deport your family," Ramirez Peyro alleges. "So, I had no choice but to agree."

In May 2005, some nine months after the Whataburger murder, Ramirez Peyro faced another serious threat. The Department of Homeland Security initiated deportation proceeding against him. He now faced the prospect of being forcibly returned to Mexico by his former employer, the U.S. government. Crucially, only a few weeks earlier, then-U.S. Attorney Johnny Sutton cut a deal with Santillan, the boss of the House of Death, agreeing to drop all murder charges against him in exchange for a guilty plea on narco-trafficking-related charges.

That same month, May 2005, Sutton also announced the U.S. would not pursue a criminal charges against Santillan associate Miguel Loya Gallegos. The plea deal with Santillan was struck within weeks of me making public via *Narco News* the letter penned by DEA commander Gonzalez — obtained via a Freedom of Information Act request. Gonzalez' explosive missive, now public and on the Internet, exposed in vivid detail Ramirez Peyro's and the U.S. government's roles in the House of Death carnage.

After deportation proceedings were initiated, Ramirez Peyro was sent directly to jail and held in solitary confinement for his "protection," though he did not see it that way. He dug in for a fight against the U.S. government and its effort to send him back to Mexico, where he says certain death awaits him at the hands of the "cartel," which, Ramirez Peyro insists, has its roots deep inside the Mexican government.

"It doesn't' take too much for the cartel to figure out it [a drug sting] is a set-up" Ramirez Peyro said of the Whataburger fiasco. "It would not be the first time. Most of the time when that happens, all the people involved get killed."

Dispatch 12

October 11, 2007

In the spring of 2005, Guillermo Ramirez Peyro found himself cut off from the world inside a U.S. prison cell, where he was kept in isolation for his own protection — and seemingly to also protect the interests of the U.S. government.

The U.S. government was seeking to deport Ramirez Peyro back to his homeland, Mexico, because he is an "illegal alien." Ironically, that same U.S. government previously found his Mexican citizenship to be an advantage for its purposes, evidenced by the fact they employed Ramirez Peyro as an informant for nearly half a decade — and paid him a quarter of a million dollars for his services.

After being jailed, Ramirez Peyro made a number of startling revelations, including advancing accusations that the Mexican government was an active player in the narco-trafficking world. In fact, Ramirez Peyro's accomplices in the House of Death murders were Mexican police officers who worked for Santillan — and by extension were part of the Juarez Cartel criminal network. The informant claimed that if the U.S. government was successful in deporting him to Mexico, he was certain to be tortured and murdered by the narco-traffickers he betrayed. He argues further that the Mexican government will not protect him, as the U.S. government contends, but rather will help to deliver him to his doom.

The Department of Homeland Security launched deportation efforts against Ramirez Peyro in May 2005. The government's lawyers argue that the informant has no recourse in forestalling deportation, despite the fact that he betrayed powerful members of the Vicente Carrillo Fuentes drug organization to assist U.S. law enforcers. The Minnesota-based federal immigration judge in Ramirez Peyro's case, however, disagreed with DHS' contention and in August 2005 granted

Ramirez Peyro relief from deportation under Article III of the United Nations Convention Against Torture, or CAT.

Attorneys for DHS appealed the immigration judge's ruling to the Board of Immigration Appeals (BIA), a DOJ-captive immigration appeals court that is under the control of U.S. Attorney General [Alberto Gonzales at the time], who has the power to appoint the board's members and overrule or modify its decisions.

Perhaps predictably, the BIA sided with DHS and reversed the ruling of the U.S. Immigration Court judge in Bloomington, Minnesota, where Ramirez Peyro's immigration case was heard. That reversal forced the informant, with the help of Texas-based immigration attorney Jody Goodwin, to take his case to the **U.S. Court of Appeals for the Eighth Circuit** — which has jurisdiction in Minnesota — in an effort to prevent his deportation.

The U.S. Court of Appeals ruled in 2007 — nearly two years after Ramirez Peyro was locked up — that the informant's deportation case should be returned to the Justice Department-controlled BIA for further proceedings. The BIA, in turn, returned the case back to start — to the original immigration judge — likely hoping that Judge Joseph R. Dierkes would revisit his verdict and find it in his career interest to issue a new ruling that protects the Justice Department's interests in the House of Death case.

Dierkes did not oblige. The government then appealed Dierkes' decision back to the BIA. "If the BIA were to rule against us [again], then we would appeal [again] to the Eighth Circuit [Court of Appeals]," Goodwin said at the time. "Beyond that, would be a discretionary appeal to the Supreme Court."

When does it end?

"Good question," Goodwin added. "The government holds the key to his [Ramirez Peyro's] freedom in my opinion."

Dispatch 13

March 13, 2009

The informant at the center of the House of Death carnage faced a high-stakes court hearing on March 10, 2009, as part of an ongoing appeal process in his immigration case that had now extended over nearly half a decade.

The informant's attorney, Jody Goodwin, appeared before the U.S. Court of Appeals for the Eighth Circuit in St. Paul, Minnesota, that day, pleading her client's case, fighting to prevent his deportation to Mexico, where the informant claimed he would be murdered by the cartel he betrayed, becoming yet another victim of the House of Death.

According to the government's attorney in the appeals court litigation, Tiffany Walters Kleinert, the facts of the case as established by the immigration judge who heard the case originally are not in dispute, and the government did not contest that Ramirez Peyro would, in all likelihood, be murdered if deported to Mexico, probably with the assistance of Mexican law enforcers.

Kleinert also argued before the federal Eighth Circuit Appeals Court, however, that even though Ramirez Peyro faced an almost-certain gruesome death if returned to Mexico, he was still not entitled to protection under the United Nations Convention Against Torture — which prohibits the U.S. from deporting an individual to a country where he faces imminent risk of being tortured by individuals acting on behalf of the state.

Kleinert insisted that even if Mexican law enforcers participate in Ramirez Peyro's murder, as expected, and as they did with the victims of the House of Death, they would not be acting officially "under color of law." Kleinert argued that because the Mexican government, and the president of the country at the time, Felipe Calderon, do not officially condone such corruption and are working to eliminate it, then any participation by Mexican government officials, including law enforcers, in Ramirez Peyro's expected murder would not constitute a homicide "under color of law."

In other words, because any Mexican law enforcer (or soldier) involved in torturing and killing Ramirez Peyro would be acting without the "official" permission of the Mexican government, Ramirez Peyro is precluded, according to Kleinert's argument, from seeking protection under the Convention Against Torture — or CAT.

If the U.S. Court of Appeals agreed with Kleinert, then the U.S. government would provide Ramirez Peyro with a one-way ticket to Mexico, where even the attorney representing the U.S. government in this case agrees he will most likely face the same fate as the House of Death murder victims.

"When you see them doing this, then the fact there's a coverup of the murders [in the House of Death case] should come as no surprise," said former DEA Special Agent in Charge Sandalio Gonzalez, who alleged he faced retaliation from DOJ officials after blowing the whistle on the U.S. government's deeds in the House of Death case. "There is no Department of Justice. There is a government law firm that defends government officials and, in this case, they're going the extra step. They're trying to get rid of the witness [Ramirez Peyro]. Wow!"

Narco News sent an email to the Department of Justice at the time, seeking comment on Ramirez Peyro's case, just to assure that the then-new Attorney General, Eric Holder, was on board with the "under color of law" reasoning. From my email: "I am interested in confirming that a case now before the U.S. Circuit Court of Appeals for the Eighth Circuit is, in fact, on the Attorney General's radar and that the position of the government's attorney (Tiffany Walters Kleinert) arguing that case is supported by the Attorney General."

The Department of Justice did not respond to *Narco News*' query.

The panel of three U.S. Court of Appeals judges who heard arguments in Ramirez Peyro's case on March 10, 2009, was expected to issue a decision within weeks or months. It was an unknown at the time. A number of legal outcomes were possible for Ramirez Peyro in the short-term, but ultimately, and likely sooner rather than later, the courts would have to decide if he could be set free to live in a neighborhood near you.

In the alternative, the court also could allow Ramirez Peyro to be deported and become a dead man walking — awaiting a gruesome death across the border to be delivered with the assistance of Mexican officials and law enforcers who, somehow, will be able to murder him without acting "under color of law." If there is any indication as to how the U.S. Court of Appeals' judges viewed the U.S. government's argument in this case, the following question raised during the March 10 hearing by Judge Michael J. Melloy — directed at Kleinert — appeared to be that oracle:

> Let me ask you a question. ... Do you know going back to our own unfortunate history in civil rights, were police officers not prosecuted under actions taken under color of law when they would stop civil rights workers in the deep South and turn them over to the Ku Klux Klan or participate in murders? I'm thinking of the famous three murders in Mississippi where the police stopped the people under pretense of a speeding violation and then turned them over to the Klan. Do you know, were they prosecuted on the theory that they were performing their duties under color of law?

Dispatch 14

August 4, 2009

The U.S. government's multi-year effort to deport the House of Death informant back to a certain death in Mexico **hit a major roadblock** in the U.S. Eighth Circuit Court of Appeals in the late summer of 2009, yet again — several months after the hearing held before that court in early March 2009.

That federal appeals court in early August 2009 ruled that the DOJ-controlled Board of Immigration Appeals erred in reversing an immigration-court judge's most recent decision to grant ICE informant Guillermo Ramirez Peyro relief under the United Nations Convention Against Torture. The appeals court also issued a sharp rebuke of the BIA's dismissive attitude toward Ramirez Peyro and his work as a U.S. government informant.

The **opinion issued** by the three-judge U.S. Appeals Court panel, published August 4, 2009, says, in part:

> Despite its recognition that Ramirez Peyro "faces a high risk of severe harm upon return to Mexico," and almost certain death, the BIA noted that "violence is an 'occupational hazard' of the illicit drug trade" and admonished Ramirez Peyro for "courting this risk through his own actions."
>
> While Ramirez Peyro may have been involved in illicit actions before becoming an ICE informant, his claim for CAT relief is not based on generalized fears of violence stemming from his involvement in the drug trade, but rather, it is based on the very particularized fear that he will be killed because he worked in concert with the U.S. government to help arrest and convict numerous dangerous international drug traffickers.
>
> In this case, the violence Ramirez Peyro faces, if anything, is an occupational hazard of working on behalf of the U.S. government, and

surely, this is not the type of hazard that we would like to encourage would-be informants to avoid for fear of it being used against them when they seek protection.

... We grant Ramirez Peyro's petition for review, vacate the BIA's opinion, and remand [the case back to the BIA] for proceedings consistent with this opinion.

The Department of Homeland Security had initiated deportation proceedings against Ramirez Peyro in 2005, and his case had been winding its way through the system since then — with an immigration judge twice ruling in favor of granting the now-sidelined ICE informant deferral from deportation under the CAT and the Justice Department-controlled BIA twice ruling against Ramirez Peyro.

So, with the August 2009 opinion issued by the appeals court (which at that point had heard arguments twice in this matter), Ramirez Peyro's case once again was returned to the BIA for review, with new instructions.

Dispatch 15

April 8, 2010

Attorney Jodi Goodwin of Harlingen, Texas, confirmed in early April 2010 that she was in discussions with government officials over former ICE informant Guillermo Eduardo Ramirez Peyro's **release from jail**, but added that she had not received any official confirmation that he was to be set free.

Ever since deportation proceedings were initiated in May 2005 against Ramirez Peyro, he had been locked up in a series of jails in Texas, Minnesota and upstate New York fighting the U.S. government's efforts to return him to Mexico, where he believed he would certainly be murdered for his acts of treachery against the narco-trafficking organization that formerly employed him.

After a nearly six-year battle, however, Ramirez Peyro had finally won a crucial victory in the U.S. immigration courts, where he was arguing that he should be granted a deferral from deportation under the United Nations' CAT because, if returned to Mexico, he would be assassinated by government agents who also are on the payroll of criminal organizations. After ruling against Ramirez Peyro in several prior decisions, the **Board of Immigration Appeals** in late March 2010 finally came down on his side, stating that he "has shown that he more likely than not would be tortured upon return to Mexico, either directly by government agents or indirectly by government agents turning him over to the cartel."

Although the **BIA ruled in his favor** on the major issue, preventing Ramirez Peyro's deportation to Mexico, the board still returned the case to the lower immigration court "for the purpose of allowing the DHS [ICE's parent agency] the opportunity to complete or update identity, law enforcement, or security investigations or examinations, and further proceedings, if necessary, and for the entry of an order. ..."

As a result, it seemed Ramirez Peyro was destined to remain confined for some weeks or months yet in an isolation cell in the Buffalo Federal Detention Center. Ramirez Peyro's pending release from jail, however, also means he will likely soon be living in some bucolic U.S. neighborhood working as a mall cop again, or maybe even a long-haul truck driver.

That's not a particularly attractive outcome for his neighbors, given Ramirez Peyro, by his own admission, played an active part in the House of Death murders in Juarez. That means Ramirez Peyro may well end up committing crimes again.

One law enforcement source told *Narco News* yet another threat with Ramirez Peyro's release from a jail cell is, "a Mexican hit squad coming here [to the U.S.] to do him." There was at least one past attempt on the former ICE informant's life, after all, at the Whataburger fast-food restaurant in El Paso. Ramirez Peyro survived it, but the botched attempt still left a dead man on the pavement.

* * *

UPDATE – 10:42 CENTRAL, April 8, 2010:

Guillermo Eduardo Ramirez Peyro is out of jail.

"He was released," confirms Jodi Goodwin, the attorney who has represented the House of Death informant for some five years in his now-successful battle to avoid deportation to Mexico. Law enforcement sources say Ramirez Peyro was picked up from the Buffalo Federal Detention Center in New York earlier this evening — allegedly by a new attorney who has replaced Goodwin. Those sources also expressed concern that Ramirez Peyro does not appear to have been afforded any official protection.

"The word will already be out to the cartel about his release because of their prison snitches," one law enforcer says. "And these guys [like Ramirez Peyro] always go back to where they ran from, in this case El Paso or San Antonio, where they will surely get to him."

Goodwin would say only that she "can't state whether he [Ramirez Peyro] was picked up by anyone."

"I won't tell you where he is at this point," she adds.

Stonewall

Dispatch 16

May 7, 2006

The staffs of U.S. senators Charles Grassley, R-Iowa, and Patrick Leahy, D-Vermont, appear to have swallowed the **House of Death** Kool-Aid mixed up by the departments of Justice and Homeland Security.

Staff members from both offices were briefed in November 2005 about the details of the mass murder in Ciudad Juarez, the participation of a U.S. government informant in those murders and the subsequent coverup carried out at high levels within the executive branch agencies involved in the House of Death case — including ICE, DEA and the U.S. Attorney's Office for the Western District of Texas in San Antonio and El Paso.

The senators' staffs also were made aware that a DEA agent and his family were nearly murdered as a result of the bungled drug-sting operation and that Mexican state police commander Miguel Loya, the killer in charge of the House of Death assassins, was allowed to escape, in large measure, because of the rift created between DEA and ICE over the informant Guillermo Ramirez Peyro.

The three members of the **National Security Whistleblowers Coalition (NSWBC)** who provided the briefing, however, said neither of the senators, or their staffs, bothered to contact the NSWBC members afterward for additional follow-up information or documentation.

"They have done nothing; zilch; '0'," says Sibel Edmonds, the founder and director of the NSWBC. "I made many follow-up calls. Still nothing. This is outrageous."

The NSWBC, at the time of the briefing in 2005, was a coalition of some 60 whistleblowers who had banded together from a host of U.S. agencies, including the CIA, DHS, DOJ and NSA. Among the NSWBC's members were House of Death whistleblower Sandalio Gonzalez; Daniel Ellsberg, who exposed the Pentagon Papers; Russ Tice, a former NSA intelligence analyst who helped to expose the Bush Administration's illegal domestic-spying program; and Edmonds, a former FBI language specialist and another national security whistleblower who worked at the bureau when John Ashcroft was U.S. Attorney General.

So, it's worth bearing in mind that both Edmonds and former DEA commander Gonzalez caused waves of discomfort within DOJ with their whistleblower disclosures. In addition, the NSWBC itself was by definition an organization that would be seen as threatening to some in power. To make matters worse, according to Gonzalez, one of the staff members present at the briefing in November 2005 was a Department of Justice attorney named Robin Ashton, who had been detailed to serve on Sen. Leahy's staff.

It is a long-standing practice for various executive branch agencies, such as DOJ, to assign employees to temporary positions with Congressional offices. Generally, the executive branch agency continues to pay the detailee's salary while the individual is on assignment. The theory is that the detailees can gain a better understanding of Congress while at the same time help congressional members gain more insight into the workings of the executive branch.

Theory doesn't always work out in reality, however, given DOJ attorneys aren't likely to abandon their loyalty to their bosses at DOJ just because they're detailed to a Senate office for a short time. After all, they have to go back to DOJ after their temporary assignment is completed and continue working under their DOJ bosses, who have sway over their career future.

All three NSWBC members present at the November 2005 briefing — Edmonds; Gonzalez; and professor and national security specialist

Bill Weaver, an advisor to the NSWBC — claim that Ashton was dismissive and not concerned with the allegations and evidence brought to the table at the meeting concerning the House of Death murders and coverup. The reason, they contend, is that Ashton's loyalties are with DOJ by virtue of the fact that her career is tied to that agency.

Weaver claims it was clear from the start of the November 21 briefing that Ashton did not see the House of Death mass murder as a big deal, even after being made aware that ICE agents and a U.S. prosecutor were aware that their informant was participating in the homicides.

"I don't remember the precise words she used," Weaver says, "but her comments were essentially: 'I do not understand the concern. People are killed all the time by drug dealers. We [the U.S. government] did not really do anything [wrong]. We just sat back. If we rush in every time targets broke the law, we would never be able to make cases against the big fish.'"

In reply to Ashton's comments, Gonzalez says he pointed out to her that "people may get killed all the time, but the difference in this case is that the government let their informant participate in the murders."

Ashton is far more than a low-level DOJ attorney. Until August of 2005, just prior to being detailed to Leahy's staff, she served as deputy director of the Executive Office for United States Attorneys (EOUSA). The **EOUSA** deals directly with U.S. Attorneys around the country in providing oversight and support in a variety of areas, including legal issues, personnel, management, budgeting and policy development.

The EOUSA also provides staff and budgetary support for the Attorney General's Advisory Committee of U.S. Attorneys, which plays a key role in determining DOJ policies and programs.

The NSWBC representatives at the briefing claim that Ashton's presence represented a major conflict of interest because two of the major players in the alleged ongoing coverup of the DOJ's role in the House of Death murders are Assistant U.S. Attorney **Juanita Fielden** in

El Paso and U.S. Attorney Johnny Sutton in San Antonio. Sutton, at the time of the briefing, served as the vice chairman of the Attorney General's Advisory Committee of U.S. Attorneys and in late March of 2006 was appointed chairman of the committee.

In a nutshell, the NSWBC members showed up in Washington, D.C., on November 21 to meet with staff representing Grassley and Leahy expecting a fair hearing of the facts and to urge the senators to call for congressional hearings over the House of Death case. At the time, Grassley was the chairman of the Senate Finance Committee and Leahy served as the ranking member of the Senate Judiciary Committee.

Instead of a fair hearing, however, the NSWBC members contend they were put in the position of making their case to a connected DOJ attorney whose future career is in the hands of the very agency leadership accused of perpetuating the coverup.

"While with DEA, I was detailed to another agency, but I knew damn well who paid my salary and who I had to report things to," Gonzalez stresses. "So, the minute I found out who she (Ashton) was, I knew that anything I said would go right back to DOJ."

Conflict-of-interest issues, however, were not limited to DOJ staff detailed to Sen. Leahy's office. Gonzalez points out that he originally met with an investigator with Sen. Grassley's office in late spring of 2004, shortly after it became clear that ICE agents and a U.S. prosecutor had allowed their informant to participate in the House of Death murders. At the time, Gonzalez says, the investigator informed him that an ICE employee was detailed to Grassley's staff.

"And he (the investigator) expressed concern to me," Gonzalez claims, "that anything he said in a staff meeting where that ICE official was present would be reported back to ICE."

Gonzalez adds that when he met with Grassley's staff for the November 2005 briefing, they claimed that the files of the investigator he met with in 2004 contained no information on the House of Death case. That investigator has since left Grassley's staff.

Tracy Schmaler, a press spokeswoman for Sen. Leahy, denies that Ashton was unconcerned with the House of Death allegations and insists that Ashton did her job properly. Schmaler also was seemingly incensed that anyone would accuse Ashton of serving the interests of DOJ while working for the Senator or of being a mole for the agency. She insists that the "burden of proof" should be on the whistleblowers to demonstrate that Ashton's loyalties are with the Justice Department in the House of Death case.

"She (Ashton) never dealt with the (House of Death) case while at DOJ," Schmaler said.

Gonzalez points out, however, that as deputy director of EOUSA, Ashton would have dealt with U.S. Attorney Sutton. Gonzalez adds that it was made clear to everyone at the briefing, including Ashton, that Sutton played a key role in the coverup of his office's role in the House of Death murders.

"In the briefing [that Ashton attended], we made no bones about the fact that we were talking about Johnny Sutton," Gonzalez says.

Schmaler refused to allow *Narco News* to speak with Ashton directly. In addition, though promising to check into it, she declined to discuss what action, if any, had been taken by Leahy's office on the House of Death case.

"Sen. Grassley's office took the lead in organizing the (November 2005) briefing, so they would be in a better position to comment," Schmaler said.

The press secretary for Grassley's office, **Beth Levine,** when contacted, also promised to look into the status of the House of Death investigation in her office but stressed that "just because there have been no hearings, that doesn't mean nothing is going on." Well, if something is going on, it continues to be a mystery, seemingly without a sense of urgency for years now. The first of more than a dozen murders in the House of Death drug-war tragedy occurred in August 2003.

Both Schmaler and Levine failed to get back to me with the promised status update on the case. As a *Narco News* investigative correspondent, I made more than eight phone calls to the offices of Grassley and Leahy over the course of a week seeking information on what was being done, if anything, on the House of Death mass murder case. Neither Schmaler or Levine seemed all too pleased with *Narco News*' persistence on this matter, or our attempts to contact staff members present at the November briefing directly for comment. In any event, not one staff member, other than the press front people for Leahy and Grassley, returned calls.

After evading questions about what was being done by Leahy and Grassley in the House of Death case, Schmaler and Levine each indicated at one point, in separate phone conversations, that they did not have time to talk further and needed to move on to more pressing Capitol Hill concerns. Schmaler yawned and seemed tired or bored during one phone conversation.

It could be that the senators themselves were never made aware of their staff members' apparent lack of concern with a U.S. government informant's participation in mass murder in Mexico. Maybe their staffs failed to brief their bosses on the House of Death case because they were just too bogged down with more uplifting career-enhancing matters than the drug war, where people get killed all the time anyway. After all, dead brown people can't vote — particularly Mexicans, as most of the victims were in the House of Death mass murder.

As far as the ongoing coverup in the House of Death, and the lack of will within Congress to call hearings to investigate, well, that boils down to priorities, after all. And for many career-minded professionals and grizzled politicians, messing with powerful people in the executive branch, some of whom are close friends of the president, may seem like being asked to knock over an outhouse in your own backyard.

"Johnny Sutton is a **well-wired guy**, all the way to the White House," former DEA commander Gonzalez says. "No one is going to go after him. That's the bottom line."

* * *

As the final days of the year 2010 ticked down, the **U.S. Senate confirmed** Michele Leonhart as Administrator of the DEA, and **Robin Ashton was appointed** by **Attorney General Eric** Holder as head of the DOJ's Office of Professional Responsibility (OPR) — which is charged with **ensuring that U.S. Attorneys** are held to highest standards of ethical conduct.

Leonhart, a left-over from the Bush administration, was named deputy administrator of DEA in 2003, where she played a lead role in the House of Death retaliation against DEA commander Sandalio Gonzalez. Leonhart became interim administrator of DEA in November 2007 and later was nominated by then-President Barack Obama to be the new administrator of the anti-narcotics agency — and in 2010 was approved unanimously by the Senate. While leading DEA, Leonhart **broke with the Obama administration's policy on medical cannabis and authorized raids on dozens of medical marijuana operations** in cities where those businesses were legal under state law — and she did so despite **DOJ policy adopted in 2009** discouraging such raids.

Ashton, described in a **DOJ press release** as a "veteran career prosecutor," served as the deputy director for the Executive Office for U.S. Attorneys from 2001-2005, "where she worked closely with the 94 U.S. Attorneys' Offices and provided oversight of the litigation divisions and operational components." Ashton also served as the Executive Assistant U.S. Attorney for Management in the U.S. Attorney's Office for the District of Colombia.

With her appointment in December 2010 as chief counsel and director of **DOJ's OPR, Ashton** was put in charge of a bureaucracy responsible for investigating DOJ attorneys accused of misconduct. At the time, she reported directly to Attorney General Eric Holder.

So, Ashton jumped fast up the DOJ career ladder, rising eventually to oversee the very office charged with investigating alleged misconduct of U.S. prosecutors. That's the case even though Ashton, while detailed to a U.S. senator's office some five years earlier, appears to have played a role — according to members of a national whistleblower group — in stonewalling or at least turning a blind eye toward efforts to propel a congressional investigation into the House of Death murders. That's problematic, given U.S. prosecutors green-lighted the ICE informant who participated in those homicides — the very type of ethically-challenged conduct DOJ OPR is supposed to examine.

That leads to Leonhart's primary role in the House of Death fiasco: carrying out the retaliation against DEA whistleblower Gonzalez. Leonhart's part in the silencing of Gonzalez and his House of Death revelations is outlined in a complaint Gonzalez filed with the U.S. Office of Special Counsel (OSC) — another supposed government watchdog agency that failed to act in the House of Death case.

Again, the pertinent excerpt from Gonzalez' September 2004 OSC complaint, obtained through a Freedom of Information Act request:

> On May 4, 2004, ... the DEA attorney threatened me with a negative performance rating if I did not retire by June 30 of this year (2004).... The Deputy Administrator [Leonhart], who is my first line supervisor and the rating official in my performance appraisal, must approve all matters such as these. Since I did not retire on June 30, DEA carried out the threat. ...
>
> [Leonhart] wrote that my "extreme poor judgment" in writing the [House of Death whistleblower] letter had caused DEA's relationship with ICE and the U.S. Attorney's Office in [San Antonio] to worsen. [Leonhart] also lowered my overall rating from the previous year, despite the fact that the list of accomplishments in this year's rating was far greater than last year's.... I believe that I'm being punished for speaking the truth about a serious matter of public concern that is not publicly known.

As evidence of the veracity of Gonzalez' claims in that OSC complaint, it is worth noting that he emerged victorious in July 2007 with a nearly $400,000 settlement in a civil lawsuit he brought against the DOJ. That lawsuit stemmed, in part, from the retaliation Gonzalez suffered at the hands of brass at DEA and Justice after he brought to light the U.S. government's role in the House of Death mass murder in Juarez.

* * *

For years, hyper drug-war violence and bloodshed have marked Mexico's path and, in particular, Juarez — which recorded some 3,100 homicides in 2010. By comparison, in all of Iraq that same year, during a hot war, 2,505 civilians were killed. A decade later in 2020, following a decline in violence for a time, the murder toll in Juarez again shot up, past 1,600 homicides, even in the depths of a pandemic. In light of that history, the plight of the House of Death murder victims might seem to some in our government, and the public at large, a now-inconsequential matter by comparison.

But as we venture into the future, it is important to note that the escalation of violence in Juarez, since at least 2008, has been encouraged in no small measure by a similar attitude of indifference toward human life and social justice. **Regardless** of how all the **facts** finally sort out in the House of Death in Juarez, the sad truth is that the whole sordid affair — the apathy, the brutality, the buried corpses, the coverup — all of it is just another tragic act in the warped war on drugs along the border.

Evidence of that dysfunction and callousness exists not only in Juarez. In addition to the Juarez Cartel he betrayed, even certain U.S. government officials might not mind waking up to find the informant Ramirez Peyro out of the picture, permanently. All this could have been prevented if the informant had been kept under control from the start, and if more of U.S. law enforcers beyond DEA's Gonzalez — in particular, those overseeing Ramirez Peyro — would have put preserving human life ahead of advancing drug-stat cases and their careers.

Maybe all of this is a reflection of the reality that far too many of those elected to Congress no longer see themselves as representing all the people, but rather are focused primarily on appeasing special interests and other issue extremists to assure they remain in power. From that pedestal of privilege, maybe they do not deem a U.S. informant's participation in the torture and murder of brown people in Mexico worth their time or effort, especially if it means shaking up the status quo in the gravy-train drug war.

We can only hope that they prove my assumptions wrong but hope alone does not bring back the victims or prevent the same cruel acts from playing out again and again without consequence to those calling the shots in this travesty of justice. If any lesson is to be drawn from the House of Death, it is that maintaining the pretense of the war on drugs seems to be more important than human life itself.

And until our so-called leaders and mass media influencers kick their addiction to this deadly pretense, we can be assured that, elsewhere along the border, the players in this game have already put a major down-payment on the next House of Death.

Dispatch 17

May 6, 2008

The House of Death in Juarez became part of a macabre parade of homes early in 2008 when two additional abodes in the Mexican border city grabbed headlines due to their foreboding landscaping features.

Like the original House of Death on Parsioneros, these homes also boast backyards that doubled as graveyards.

In late February 2008, Mexican authorities dug up nine bodies at a home on Cocoyoc Street in Juarez, located less than a mile west of the Parsioneros house. A few weeks later they found at least 36 bodies buried on the grounds of a home on Pedregal Street, located about three miles east of the original House of Death. Mexican authorities told the media that the corpses, which had been in the ground an estimated four to five years, are the byproduct of Juarez's bloody narco-trafficking turf wars.

Sources with ICE told me at the time that all three homes are linked. They contend the bodies found at the houses are tied to an investigation that their agency carried out against a major Juarez narco-trafficking cell headed by Heriberto Santillan Taberas – who, until his arrest in January 2004 was a rising alpha in the Vicente Carrillo Fuentes drug organization that dominated Juarez for decades.

Santillan was sent directly to a federal prison after cutting a deal with the U.S. Attorney's Office for the Western District of Texas, headed by Johnny Sutton, in which Santillan agreed to plead guilty to narco-trafficking-related charges. As a consequence of that bargain, struck in April 2005 (after a multi-year investigation by ICE) all murder charges against Santillan were dropped. Santillan, 67 as of 2021, is slated to be released from federal prison in July 2023, **Bureau of Prison records show.**

A key reason U.S. prosecutors dropped the multiple homicide counts against Santillan included in his initial indictment, law enforcement sources contend, is because of ICE informant Guillermo Eduardo Ramirez Peyro. Had Santillan's case gone to trial in federal court in San Antonio, law enforcement sources say, the role of ICE and the U.S. Attorney's Office (both in San Antonio and El Paso) in allowing their informant to assist in the House of Death mass murder would have been exposed. That could have been politically disastrous for agency chiefs and brass in Washington, D.C., and possibly career-ending, or worse, for some of the shot-callers in the Santillan case.

The newly discovered houses of death on Cocoyoc and Pedregal streets open yet another dark chapter in the hidden history of the U.S. government's role in the original House of Death mass murder. The new tombs raise the total body count from a "mere dozen" at one location to at least 57 at three narcofosas (narco tombs) — all located within walking distance of each other in a city that sprawls for miles along a border between nations and worlds.

There is mounting evidence, beyond what law enforcement sources have told me, pointing to the fact that key officials at ICE and in Sutton's U.S. Attorney Office knew or should have known of these additional torture and murder operations at the houses on Cocoyoc and Pedregal streets. Many of the bodies found at those locations had been in the ground since at least 2003, Mexican authorities **told the media.** That is the same year that the murders were carried out at the House of Death on Parsioneros Street. So, it appears all these homicides happened during the same period of time.

Spain's **EFE News Service** reported the following in English in 2008: "The discovery of the 36 skeletons in 16 graves [at the house on Pedregal street] was made due to an anonymous tip that indicated that mass graves existed at the house, with bodies of people murdered and buried clandestinely by members of the Carrillo Fuentes cartel," the [Mexican] Attorney General's Office said.

The close proximity of the houses to each other (located along a three- to four-mile line that intersects a major Juarez boulevard called Panamericana) means individuals marked for death — or the bodies of those killed elsewhere — could be delivered to any of the homes with great efficiency. And this logistical convenience also leaves open the possibility that additional narco-tombs exist along this same line, since these homemade graveyards do have limited capacity individually. But that coincidence of location alone is not proof that the bodies found at the homes on Cocoyoc and Pedregal streets are connected to the bodies found at the Parsioneros house — the latter all known victims of Santillan's henchmen in murders committed between August 2003 and mid-January 2004.

At the time the original House of Death was exposed publicly in early 2004, however, DEA agents in El Paso and Juarez had reason to believe the Parsioneros narco tomb was not an isolated operation. DEA took a heightened interest in ICE's lone-wolf Santillan investigation after the narco-trafficker targeted a DEA agent and his family in Juarez. After that incident, ICE was forced to reveal the location of the original House of Death to DEA.

A **DEA report** put together in early 2004 shortly after the last House of Death murder reveals that the agency and Mexican law enforcers, at the time, thought there might be at least one other narcofosa (mass grave) in the area based on the activities of and information provided by the ICE informant Ramirez Peyro. Following is an excerpt I prepared for *Narco News* summarizing that **DEA report**. It's worth revisiting here:

> February 3, 2004: The search for bodies at the House of Death is completed. A total of 12 bodies have been found, including the three individuals who were tortured and murdered on January 14, 2004. Mexican law enforcers obtain warrants to search the additional locations. These include two homes thought to be used by Santillan

associate Miguel Loya ... and two suspected safe houses for the Santillan narco-trafficking operation. At the sites, law enforcers find firearms, ammunition and a number of documents.

February 4, 2004: Mexican law enforcers also obtain a search warrant for a ranch near Juarez, where they believe additional bodies are buried. They begin excavating the site. The DEA again asks ICE officials for permission to question the informant [Ramirez Peyro]. ICE finally gives the go-ahead for such a debriefing but informs DEA agents that they cannot ask Contreras [Ramirez Peyro] any questions about the House of Death murders or other criminal activity that has taken place in Mexico. ...

February 9, 2004: The canine units from the Austin, Texas, Police Department arrive at the ranch near Juarez and, along with the DEA and Mexican law enforcers, begin the search for more bodies.

February 10, 2004: The search of the ranch near Juarez is completed. No bodies are found.

So, it does appear DEA and Mexican law enforcement officials did have reason to suspect the 12 bodies found at the House of Death on Parsioneros Street did not represent the full extent of the Juarez Cartel's bloody business. Maybe the informant had already told U.S. law enforcers of other gruesome murder operations in Juarez. Ramirez Peyro has said as much.

"[ICE] was aware these people [in the Juarez Cartel] were ruthless and powerful," Ramirez Peyro told me during a jailhouse telephone interview. "If they say kill someone, you do it, or you get killed. I explained that to Customs [ICE], that those are the conditions I would have to work under, and they [the informant's ICE handlers] said, 'Yes,' and I began to infiltrate the cartel."

The informant said many of the people who were murdered at these death houses in the early 2000s were operating in Juarez without the permission of the dominant Vicente Carrillo Fuentes drug organization.

"Nobody was allowed to work cocaine in the city, and if they did, they would be killed," Ramirez Peyro said. "We [ICE through the informant] had infiltrated the most powerful criminal organization in the country, and they kill people as part of their work. There's no way to avoid it."

ICE and the U.S. prosecutors in El Paso and San Antonio working the Santillan investigation understood that reality, according to the informant. Ramirez Peyro told me at the time that there were a "number of death houses" in Juarez that he became familiar with as part of his work for ICE.

"ICE knew about these houses where they were torturing and killing people," Ramirez Peyro said from a prison telephone. "I would report on these houses in debriefings [with ICE] but they never asked me where the houses were. I had the addresses, but ICE never asked me for the addresses."

The informant said U.S. law enforcers and prosecutors didn't seem to care about the murders since they were happening "on Mexican soil." The revelation that ICE and U.S. prosecutors were made aware that there were multiple death houses in operation while the informant was working for them is important because the informant has since been accused of helping to facilitate some of the murders — with the U.S. government's knowledge.

Ramirez Peyro explained that the leadership of the Juarez Cartel as well as the top leadership from the other major narco-trafficking groups in Mexico, "have good relations with the Mexican government."

"I'll even give [Mexican President Felipe] Calderon the benefit of the doubt in his war against narco-traffickers, but the problem is, to do it effectively, he would have to bring in people from another planet," Ramirez Peyro said in offering his take on Calderon's military assault on drug traffickers launched in Juarez two years into his six-year presidential term, which started in December 2006. "That's because many of his commanders, in the military and police, along with politicians, are already corrupted. ... The Juarez Cartel, military, and law enforcement, [they] are all the same people."

Another dynamic that was playing out in Juarez by 2008, some four years after the House of Death, was the rise of the Sinaloa Cartel and its violent efforts to take over the Juarez plaza — and other major border plazas as well. Some media at the time even reported the plaza turf wars might be part of a broader clandestine, government-backed drug war strategy agreed to tacitly by the U.S. and Mexico and designed to weaken both criminal syndicates, so they could be more easily rolled up or controlled after the carnage. If that's the case, it was a horrible strategy that failed miserably. Such theorizing is common in the narco-trafficking world, where appearances can run deep and evidence points in many directions. Like the Juarez Cartel criminal organization, the Sinaloa Cartel, led by Ismael "El Mayo" Zambada Garcia and the since-jailed Joaquin "El Chapo" Guzman Lorea, has its own network of corrupt law enforcers, military commanders and politicians, and is continually wooing new collaborators — on both sides of the border.

One thing did seem clear, however. As Juarez approached the end of the first decade of the 2000s, any *Pax Romana* that might have existed between the Juarez and Sinaloa criminal organizations had long since been extinguished by bloodshed. That reality, Ramirez Peyro said, explains why he would be doomed if deported to Mexico, given he would be seen by both criminal organizations as an enemy — and a traitor. In all likelihood, Ramirez Peyro reasons, he would be picked up by Mexican police "and it is Mexican law enforcement that does the killing for the cartels."

The ramp-up in violence in Juarez at the time couldn't be missed. It was like a war zone, with more than 1,600 murders in 2008 alone — a trend that amplified further the following year. Shootings were so frequent that they weren't even tracked in any coherent way. This hyper violence plays out even with the presence of a massive Mexican military force in the city, which Ramirez Peyro said makes perfect sense, if you consider the true dynamics of how the narco-business works in Mexico.

"The [leadership] of the Juarez Cartel is not worried about the military," he said. "They are tipped off when something is taking place and simply lay low. What they [the military] is doing is combating the competition of the cartel."

That competition can be another cartel, as in the case of the Sinaloa/Juarez cartel turf war. Or, according to Ramirez Peyro, it can be fueled by desperation and poverty, leading more independent operators to turn to the narco-trafficking business as an opportunity to overcome their plight, despite the grave risk.

"Regardless of the danger, they are willing to take a chance of having five good years of life rather than a whole life of poorness," Ramirez Peyro said in an interview. "What has increased in the last few years is the competition [from multiple players] as a result.

"… There is this permanent war against narco-trafficking, and the U.S. is spending a lot of money to combat it, but nothing is changing. Things are the same as they were 20 years ago, only more ruthless now."

* * *

We do not know for sure whether ICE and DOJ agents, prosecutors or officials were made aware of the murders at the houses on Cocoyoc and Pedregal streets in Juarez as they were being carried out in the early 2000s. But the informant Ramirez Peyro claims they were at least aware that multiple death houses existed during that period, when the Santillan House of Death case was still underway.

It's worth mentioning here that any ambiguity on the facts also can be by design. The whole point of obfuscating the truth, and by extension justice, is to assure uncomfortable facts stay buried. But with the House of Death, the bodies so far refuse to stay buried. We are now up to nearly five dozen corpses — tortured and murdered human beings — potentially linked to the House of Death mass murder. You have to wonder at what point, at what body count, it starts to matter to anyone who has the power and position to ask with consequence: "Why did this have to happen?"

Blood in the Streets

Dispatch 18

December 15, 2006

Yet another body turned up on Juarez' bloody streets in late fall of 2006, long after Santillan's arrest and the shuttering of the House of Death by Mexican authorities. Still, it was one more murder linked to that dark house.

This Christmas gift appeared intended for ICE agents. The Associated Press wrote about the incident at the time, indicating that on November 23, 2006, a body was dumped in broad daylight in a well-traveled park in Juarez.

The dead man, now a gruesome corpse, had a finger planted in his mouth and two business card plastered to his forehead. One of those calling cards was clearly legible. It bore the name of ICE agent Raul Bencomo, the informant Ramirez Peyro's handler. Law enforcers explained to me that the severed finger left in the mouth of the corpse was a message from the killers that the victim was a snitch, or finger-pointer, who has now been silenced by the cartel.

The corpse is just another ugly drug war statistics from Mexico. Although this victim's fate is now known, the fate of many, many more drug-war victims in Mexico remains unknown to this day. The Mexican government as of the start of 2020 estimated that some 61,000 people have been "disappeared" under the cloak of the nation's narco-violence. For these victims' families, it is a fate worse than death in many ways. Their loved ones have simply vanished without a trace and are presumed dead in most cases.

A significant share of that toll — some experts contend the figure is actually as high as 120,000 — has occurred since 2006, a year that marks the start of a bloody new era of narco-violence in Mexico. That bloodshed was sparked by the all-out war declared on drug cartels and organized crime by then newly elected President Felipe Calderon — who also had access to billions of dollars in U.S. help and firepower supplied through the **Merida Initiative** enacted in 2007.

It's important to make clear that the disappeared figure doesn't include homicides, which are tallied separately and have increased in Mexico from nearly 9,000 in 2007 at the start of Calderon's war on the cartels to some 36,000 in 2020, the first year of the coronavirus pandemic. The murder count over the entire **14-year period** — the beginning of 2007 until the end of 2020 — totaled roughly 352,000, according to **Mexican government data,** and reached an estimated 386,000 by **the end of 2021.** To put those figures into perspective: The homicide rate in Mexico in 2018, the most recent year comparable data was available, stood at 29 murders per 100,000 lives. In the United States that same year, the **homicide rate stood** at five murders per 100,000 lives.

"The mainstream narrative consistently ignores the primary role of the state in the massive and constant numbers of homicides and disappearances in the country, characterizing the violence as a cartel war, and portraying the Mexican military and security forces as fighting violent criminals, rather than perpetrating many of the worst crimes — with the complicity and help of U.S. money and advisors," Dr. Molly Molloy, a border specialist and emeritus professor at the University of New Mexico in Las Cruces, wrote in June 2021 to readers of her Frontera-list email service, which tracks media reporting on Mexico.

* * *

U.S. Attorney Johnny Sutton **announced in spring 2005** that his office had reached a plea deal with Heriberto Santillan Tabares, As part of that plea agreement, Sutton said his office was dropping all murder charges against Santillan, who pleaded guilty to "conducting a criminal enterprise [drug trafficking]" and accepted a 25-year prison sentence in the bargain.

At the time, Sutton — the chief federal prosecutor for a good swath of Texas, based in San Antonio — justified dropping the murder charges against Santillan with the following words to the public: "All of the murders were committed in Ciudad Juarez, by Mexican citizens, including law enforcement officials, and all of the victims were citizens of Mexico. While much of the evidence relating to the murders is from Mexico, Sutton said his office would share with Mexican authorities any evidence developed in the United States."

It turns out that Sutton's claim simply isn't true, according to Guillermo Eduardo Ramirez Peyro, the U.S. government informant at the center of the House of Death mass murder. In fact, the first murder victim to be buried at the House of Death was a U.S. citizen, Ramirez Peyro insists.

This homicide, allegedly involving an El Paso man, predates the dozen murders that Ramirez Peyro helped facilitate with, he claims, the knowledge of U.S. law enforcers between August 2003 and January 2004.

In August 2005, Raul Loya, a Dallas attorney representing the families of House of Death murder victims Luis Padilla and Fernando Reyes, among others, claimed he was looking into charges that the informant, known then by the codename Jesus Contreras, was involved in the kidnapping and murder of an El Paso resident in the fall of 2002.

Loya claims the family of the man— named David Castro — asked him to investigate the case. Castro was a truck driver and a U.S. citizen living in El Paso who found himself sideways on a valuable drug load — just one of the thousands of illicit cargo loads moved each year from Juarez into the United States. As a result, Castro owed money to the wrong people.

Castro was abducted in Juarez in late September 2002, according to those familiar with the case — including federal agents, family, and the ICE informant Ramirez Peyro. Castro was then murdered after the money he owed a player working for a cell of the Juarez Cartel was not delivered in time. His body has not been found.

Attorney Loya says Castro's family is convinced their loved one was abducted with the participation of the informant Ramirez Peyro sometime after meeting the ICE informant at an auto-dealership lot in El Paso. At some point after arriving at the El Paso car lot, Castro was transported across the border to Mexico. A demand was later made for ransom, which the family could not afford to pay. Castro was then murdered, the family alleges — according to their attorney, Loya. The FBI supposedly did get involved with the case; however, Loya says the family claims the FBI was not able to do much because the victim by then had already been taken across the border — where U.S. law enforcers have no authority or arrest powers and must rely on cooperation from Mexican authorities to pursue sanctioned investigations.

Loya stressed that David Castro was a U.S. citizen, and his disappearance is disturbing. His allegations are serious, but, in the summer of 2005 when Loya first aired these charges, all leads seemed to come to a dead end. After all, Mexican law enforcers were not likely to investigate Castro's disappearance because the police in Juarez at the time were controlled largely by the Juarez Cartel. And U.S. law enforcers and prosecutors involved with the House of Death case had no incentive to investigate Castro's disappearance and likely murder if their informant was implicated in the murder while he also remained key to prosecuting pending career-boosting drug- and cigarette-smuggling cases. Nobody likes a big turd dumped in their backyard by a neighboring canine — and that's basically what Castro's disappearance and possible murder represented to many law enforcers on both sides of the border. Unfortunately, his murder was, and remains, an inconvenient truth.

Still, the allegations around Castro's disappearance raise even more serious questions about what Homeland Security agents and U.S. prosecutors knew and when they knew it in the House of Death mass murder. A critical document that brings us inside the House of Death tells us, however, that U.S. law enforcers should have been aware by at least mid-February 2004, less than two weeks after the twelfth body at the House of Death was dug up on January 29 of that year, that their informant played a major role, by his own admission, in David Castro's disappearance some two years earlier. The document is a debriefing of the informant Ramirez Peyro carried out under oath on February 12, 2004, by an assistant legal attaché for the Attorney General's Office of Mexico.

In that debriefing, the informant Ramirez Peyro describes the kidnapping and murder of an individual named "David Castro" that matches the known details provided by Dallas attorney Loya of David Castro's disappearance in Mexico in September 2002 — a period when Ramirez Peyro was an active ICE informant and a rising player in the Juarez Cartel. Ramirez Peyro also confirmed over the course of multiple interviews conducted with him some years later that the person disappeared in Juarez that fall day in 2002 was the same David Castro. From the debriefing document:

> Regarding David [Castro] in the year 2002, David and I were seeing about a transaction, and we went to Ciudad Juarez to check out some merchandise consisting of 400 pounds of marijuana....
>
> ... We met Chito on the Avenue of the Americas. ... Chito asked him [Castro] if he remembered that he owed him some money from a drug load which he had given him to sell and which he had agreed to pay for. Later he tried to collect but David did not want to pay. When they met, David began to argue. Chito was with six other guys, and he told me, "Go to hell. This is none of your business." ... I later found out that [Castro's wife] went to the FBI to report the kidnapping.

So, again the trail of blood in the House of Death appears to touch yet another soul. Still, the coverup within the Justice Department and Homeland Security continues.

* * *

Grace Castro was David's wife of a dozen years prior to separating in 2000, some two years before he vanished on a trip to Juarez. After their marriage fell apart, Grace says she believes David got sucked into the drug business and eventually found himself in deep water.

"Once he knew he was in that far," she said, sobbing, "he stopped talking to us and seeing our [three] kids. ... We still don't have answers on what really happened. What am I supposed to tell our kids? They deserve to know."

Grace Castro was among the parties to the civil lawsuit filed against the U.S. government and several ICE agents individually over the House of Death murders — a case dismissed in 2007 over jurisdictional issues (the murders occurred in Mexico) as well as the fact that the individual ICE agents named in the lawsuit, according to the judge, "are immune from liability under the doctrine of qualified immunity."

Grace Castro says she became aware that her ex-husband, a U.S. citizen, had been kidnapped after "his divorce attorney filed a motion in court withdrawing from the [divorce] case because ... he [David] had been reported kidnapped in Mexico."

"I thought it was BS," she added. "I called the FBI, and they told me they did have a report of him missing, but they couldn't investigate because it happened in Mexico. And two years later [in 2004], they finally told me they think David was killed in Mexico."

But there is a big hole in this story that frustrates both Grace Castro as well as Yvonne Lozoya, David Castro's girlfriend at the time of his disappearance, leaving both of them grasping for more answers. And that is the story of Castro's body. Ramirez Peyro insists he was buried in the backyard of the House of Death in Juarez, which eventually became a tomb for at least a dozen more bodies — victims who crossed Santillan and the Juarez Cartel in one way or another.

"I tell ICE that he [David Castro] was buried at this house [at 3633 Parsioneros in Juarez], but they did not know where the house was, or nothing else, and they didn't ask questions about it," Ramirez Peyro said in an interview. "Well, it worked like this: Sometimes they would bring a body to the house already dead, and yes, sometimes they bring the people alive, and they killed them there."

At the time of Castro's abduction, Lozoya says she was living with him, in El Paso, raising their young son. The day Castro made his doomed trip to Juarez, Lozoya recalls dropping him off at a used-car lot in El Paso, where Ramirez Peyro was waiting for him.

The informant operated a used-car lot in the city as a side business, he confirms. It was dealership Ramirez Peyro allegedly opened with 20 cars obtained (apparently without ICE authorization) from an individual in Chicago who needed to pay off a debt owed to the Juarez Cartel, according to a federal agent familiar with the House of Death case who asked not to be identified.

Together, in late September 2002, Castro, then 36, and Ramirez Peyro, then 31, walked across one of El Paso's three international bridges into Juarez to conduct some business. Lozoya says the story she got from Castro that day was that he was going to pick up a Harley-Davidson motorcycle in Juarez, which he planned to drive back to El Paso that same day.

Ramirez Peyro concedes there was more to Castro's trip than a Harley ride. He also was working to recruit Castro as a driver for a drug load. Ramirez Peyro's job for the Juarez Cartel criminal cell included coordinating marijuana shipments into the United States, and for that he needed drivers, he explained.

After waiting a day for Castro to return from Juarez, Lozoya says she became concerned and called the El Paso Police Department to report him missing. The El Paso police brought in the FBI. Ramirez Peyro says he was then asked to brief the FBI on what he knew about Castro's abduction. He also says he was concerned that the FBI's involvement in the case would lead to a bad outcome for Castro.

Lozoya claims the FBI did listen in on the several calls Castro made to her while he was being held hostage in Juarez. On one of those calls, she says, Castro said his captors were demanding an $80,000 ransom.

"I remember he said, 'Bring over the money,'" Lozoya recalled. "But there was no money."

Some three weeks after Castro's abduction in late September 2002, Ramirez Peyro's concern about the FBI's involvement in the case proved prescient.

"After the incident [Castro's kidnapping], I went to the El 16 Bar [in Juarez] to meet with Chito, who explained to me that [since] he could not cross over into the United States, and [because] David Castro had not wanted to pay the debt... that was why he had kidnapped him," Ramirez Peyro said in his statement to the Mexican government. "Several days later, I found out that the FBI had went to visit the wife and children of Chito in El Paso, and they alerted Chito, and that is why he decided to kill David."

The FBI did not respond to a request for comment on Castro's case.

From Lozoya's point of view, David Castro's disappearance is the result of his entanglement with the informant Ramirez Peyro. He would not have been kidnapped in Juarez in late September 2002, and then murdered, had he not gone to Juarez with the informant that fateful day.

"The government just wanted to catch the big fish [in the Juarez Cartel] and they ignored everything in between," Lozoya said. "David's killer is still out there."

Grace Castro adds: "No one deserves to die like that, and we're left behind to put the pieces together."

Ramirez Peyro offers a more chilling perspective on the House of Death murder victims in Juarez:

"ICE monitored my phone calls and knew hours ahead that murders were going to happen [resulting in bodies being buried at the house on Parsioneros]," the informant claims. "They don't really do nothing. It wasn't happening on U.S. soil, and so there was nothing we can do, so they just listen to it, but didn't show no interest in that."

***

The story of David Castro is among a series of revelations that Ramirez has helped to illuminate during the course interviews conducted with him between 2007 and 2014 while he was being held in various prison cells in Minnesota and later New York. Ramirez Peyro admits to being present at the House of Death for a total of at least three murders. Another witness, one of Ramirez Peyro's helpers, claims that the informant was present for at least five murders, according to the DEA timeline document.

Now, Ramirez also concedes that he played a role in the kidnapping and murder of David Castro in the fall of 2002. Ramirez is quick to point out, though, that he does not consider himself responsible for Castro's death. It is clear, however, that while acting as a paid informant for ICE, Ramirez did put into motion the events that led to Castro's kidnapping and appear to have led to his murder and eventual burial at the House of Death — something that U.S. Attorney Johnny Sutton, ICE and the Department of Justice, to date, have failed to acknowledge. This is important because U.S. government officials, via court pleadings, have only conceded so far that the first murder they were made aware of involving the House of Death was that of Mexican attorney Fernando Reyes. After the informant Ramirez reported that murder in August 2003 to his ICE handlers — and the fact that he had participated in the slaying — high-level ICE and Justice Department officials approved Ramirez' continued use in the investigation against Mexican narco-trafficker and Juarez Cartel cell leader Santillan.

In the wake of that fateful decision, the House of Death claimed at least 11 more victims — all buried in the backyard of the house on Parsioneros. Enabling that carnage was U.S. law enforcers' decision to continue the Santillan investigation even after Sutton's office had enough evidence to indict him months prior to the murder of the first House of Death victim, Fernando Reyes. That fatal flaw in judgment ultimately led Santillan's assassins to target a DEA agent and his family in Juarez for assassination, a fate they barely escaped. Now we have reason to believe the first victim buried at the House of Death was not Fernando Reyes, a Mexican citizen, but rather El Paso resident and U.S. citizen David Castro. That's contrary to claims by Sutton and other U.S. officials that all of the victims found buried at the House of Death were Mexican citizens — the excuse used by Sutton publicly to dismiss murder charges against Santillan.

Assuming Ramirez Peyro is telling the truth, then Sutton's public claim that "Mexico has a superior interest in prosecuting those responsible" for the House of Death murders is misleading at best. In the worst light, it is an outright lie — and represents another effort to derail justice in a bid to conceal the U.S. government's role in the House of Death murders.

These latest revelations bear repeating, with more context. Ramirez Peyro claims that Castro, as a truck driver, in the early 2000s assisted a Juarez narco-trafficking cell headed by an individual nicknamed Chito. As part of his informant work for ICE, Ramirez Peyro says he approached Castro in 2002 seeking to entice him to transport illegal drugs and cigarettes for "his people." Ramirez Peyro, at the time, had already infiltrated Santillan's cell of the Juarez Cartel as an ICE informant. He also was key to a then-pending investigation the feds were pursuing in a separate case against a 35-year-old cigarette smuggler from Sunland Park, New Mexico, Jorge Abraham, who was ultimately arrested in February 2004 — shortly after Santillan was arrested in El Paso.

Abraham reached a deal with Sutton's office in April 2005, and he agreed to plead guilty to one count of being part of a conspiracy to smuggle cigarettes. That same month Sutton announced a plea deal with Santillan in which all murder charges against him were dropped. Abraham, for the crime of depriving Uncle Sam of millions of dollars of sin taxes, was sentenced in December 2004 to five years in federal prison and ordered to pay $6 million in restitution. He had been facing

92 counts of cigarette smuggling, wire and mail fraud that collectively carried a potential sentence of 300 years.

U.S. Attorney Sutton, who authorized the plea deal, told the media at the time: "These criminals deprived the American people of millions of dollars owed in taxes. While the rest of us are working hard and paying our fair share, these cheaters did not pay one cent."

Sutton neglected to mention the pressure he was under to cut deals with Santillan and Abraham in order to minimize the damage done by an individual former DEA commander Gonzalez described as a **"homicidal maniac"** — ICE informant, Ramirez Peyro. An expose on Abraham's case published in 2008 by the **International Consortium of Investigative Journalists** — disclosure, I was interviewed on background for the story — had this to say about Sutton's plea deals with Abraham and Santillan:

> The real thanks should have gone to Lalo [the informant Ramirez Peyro], who by then was about to be exposed in the sordid, high-profile drama at the drug cartel safe house in Juarez [the House of Death].
>
> Tainted by the murders, he was no longer a credible witness against Abraham. Unwilling to put Lalo on the stand, prosecutors agreed to settle short of trial. ...

David Castro, of course, had no hint that Ramirez Peyro was an ICE informant when he went with him to Juarez in September 2002. In fact, it appears he assumed Ramirez Peyro was a fellow associate in the illegal smuggling business. Ramirez Peyro, in a phone interview focused, in part, on the Castro missing-person case, said the following:

> What happened is I met him [Castro] to set up a drug deal. ... One day [in September 2002], I said let's go to Juarez to check out some merchandise [which was a 400-pound load of marijuana]. I suggested that we walk across the bridge [from El Paso to Juarez] to save time when we come back [avoiding the vehicle traffic and law enforcement on the bridge].
>
> When we were in Juarez, we ran into Chito, who was with a group of people, and we both knew him, so we said hello. At one point [during

the conversation] Chito said, "What about my money?" David owed Chito money from a [past drug deal]. And then the men grabbed David, and I said, "wait," and they said, "Get the fuck out of here; we're taking him [Castro]."

Ramirez claimed Castro, at that point, told him to "not worry," that he had the money and everything would work out. So, Ramirez recounted, he returned to El Paso and informed his ICE handlers of the kidnapping.

After his disappearance, Castro's then-significant other, Yvonne Lozoya, contacted the El Paso police to report David Castro missing — resulting in the FBI being brought into the matter as mentioned previously. Ramirez Peyro claims the FBI then contacted Chito's wife and children in El Paso. After that, Chito got wind of the fact that the FBI was involved, and sometime after that Ramirez Peyro said he learned that "they did kill him [Castro]."

"The FBI knew Chito was the kidnapper, but they couldn't do anything because the kidnapping happened in Mexico," Ramirez Peyro added.

Whether the FBI was aware that Castro was subsequently murdered is not clear. Ramirez Peyro said he did inform his ICE handlers of that fact, however, and also that Castro's body was ultimately buried at the House of Death. He said he made his ICE handlers aware of these facts about David Castro prior to the murder of Mexican attorney Fernando Reyes in August 2003.

Ramirez Peyro added that Chito and Santillan were business acquaintances, with each being the alpha wolves of narco-trafficking criminal cells in Juarez. He also claimed that after David Castro was killed, one of the individuals who worked with Santillan and Ramirez Peyro, a man named Alex Garcia, offered to bury Castro's body at the House of Death on Parsioneros Street in exchange for a payment — a seven-year-old Ford pickup truck.

"At that time, Alex (Garcia) and me were working together," the informant Ramirez Peyro said in an interview. "After meeting up with [Chito] one time in a bar [in Juarez], I talked with him and he said Alex [Garcia] had contacted him about getting rid of the body [Castro's body]. His body was buried at the house on Parsioneros."

When Santillan ordered the murder of Fernando Reyes, Ramirez Peyro said Alex Garcia proposed to Santillan that he bury Reyes' corpse at the Parsioneros house as well. "Then, from that point on, they started to use it as the House of Death," Ramirez Peyro said.

* * *

A January 29, 2004, story in the Mexican newspaper *El Siglo de Torreon,* founded in 1922, reported that the owner of the House of Death at 3633 Calle Parsioneros in Juarez was an individual named "Juan Ernesto Chavez Ocampo," who rented the property to "Erika Mayorga Diaz."

"Her husband, [Alejandro] Garcia Cardenas, confessed to having participated in the executions [at the House of Death and elsewhere] since January 2003 under the direction of Humberto Santillan Tabares and a commander of the Chihuahua Judicial Police [Miguel Loya]," a translated version of the *El Siglo* report states.

In the Mexican press accounts of the list of victims unearthed at the House of Death in early 2004, there is no mention of David Castro. In addition, U.S. officials have never stated publicly that a U.S. citizen was among the victims found buried at the Parsioneros house. In fact, the only known victim from the U.S. was a young man from the El Paso-area named Louis Padilla — who was not a U.S. citizen, though he was a legal U.S. resident at the time of his murder.

Yet there was one grave at the House of Death that contained no body, only human clothing. "The PGR [Mexican law enforcement] also located a hole which contained a pile of clothing," the DEA timeline report on the House of Death states in an entry marked "Monday, January 26, 2004." Within two weeks of that date, the final body buried in the backyard of the House of Death had been located by authorities, but not Castro's corpse. That lone grave site, however, with only a pile of clothes in it — located only feet from a dozen other graves, all with dead bodies buried in them — raises a logical next question: Was a body of one of the House of Death victims relocated for some reason and, if so, why?

We may never know now, some two decades after Castro vanished, joining the ranks of the tens of thousands of other human beings who have been disappeared in Mexico. Had Ramirez not sought to draw Castro into a smuggling deal to advance his informant work for ICE, then it is arguable that Castro might still be alive today. ICE, according to Ramirez Peyro, was made fully aware of Castro's kidnapping and alleged murder by a Santillan business acquaintance, Chito, and of his subsequent burial at the House of Death months prior to the murder of Fernando Reyes in early August 2003.

Ramirez Peyro also played a role in Reyes killing — physically assisting with the murder. If we accept that Ramirez Peyro kept his U.S. law enforcement handlers in the loop on Castro's fate, it also means that U.S. Attorney Sutton's office should have been aware that the U.S had a "superior interest" in investigating that crime, the murder of a U.S. citizen, and bringing the killers to justice. That interest in justice, however, is outweighed by the ugly reality that investigating David Castro's disappearance and alleged murder in Mexico would have inevitably led to unwanted scrutiny of ICE informant Ramirez Peyro and his role as a mole inside the Juarez Cartel, his enabling of Castro's kidnapping and later as a participant in the House of Death mass murder.

In the face of those hopeless dynamics, we can expect that Castro's disappearance and his body will remain buried in the shadows of the corrupt drug war along the border, where the truth of your death is only known to you at the moment the bullet hits the bone, but the truth of your corpse can and often is disappeared.

Dispatch 19
January 30, 2012

One victim of the House of Death killers, who says he survived being shot by Santillan's assassins — a bullet ripped through his mouth and neck — has stepped out of the shadows to shine more light on the Juarez narco-trafficking organization and its grip on the city.

This individual, who was interviewed at length, asked that his real name not be published because he claims that he is still being pursued by "the cartel." In addition, this individual, whom we will call Juanito, has reason to fear the "migra" in the United States will once again deport him, despite his long history of saying the pledge of allegiance in U.S. school classrooms.

Juanito was born in Mexico, he concedes, and is now living somewhere in the United States, without proper papers. Juanito also says, however, that he came to this country with his family at the age of 6 and grew up here, until he was deported more than a decade ago after a run-in with the law.

Finding himself stranded in Mexico after his forced exit from the United States, and with no family or way to make a living in Mexico, Juanito says he saw no other option but to continue to walk the path of an outlaw in the business of drug trafficking, not as a major player, but as a worker — moving cars to locations where they were needed, loading and unloading the cargo of the trade and assisting with all the other manual labor that goes with keeping a sales and distribution business in motion.

Juanito's transgression against the law, which led to his deportation at the turn of the century, resulted from youthful indiscretion, a decision in his early 20s, after visiting friends in Mexico, to drive a car back across the border packed with marijuana, the stuff of parties and play in a broad swath of consumer America. He did 30 months in a U.S. prison for that act, he says, and then got a one-way ticket back to Mexico courtesy of Uncle Sam, soon winding up in Juarez, separated from his family, who had long ago left the motherland and settled in the U.S.

If Juanito's story is accurate, then what he saw and experienced during his time in Juarez, as the House of Death was playing out, could make him a key witness against a group of assassins operating under the cloak of Mexican law enforcement who remain at large, according to multiple sources, with some still likely active in the trade.

The House of Death assassins who confronted the DEA agent and his family on the streets of Juarez in early 2004, based on **law enforcement records** obtained by *Narco News*, apparently did not realize, or care, whether that agent was, in fact, a U.S. law enforcer — possibly assuming he was a rival trafficker, or a crooked cop, either of which would have meant that mercy from harm was not likely in the cards had help not arrived.

That is evidenced in ICE informant Guillermo Eduardo Ramirez Peyro's official statement to the Mexican government — provided to Mexican authorities in Dallas on the morning of February 12, 2004, under threat of perjury. It details his role in and knowledge of the House of Death and related murders. At the time of the statement, the informant was still undercover and using the code name, Jesus Contreras, as an alias. Mentioned in his testimony is a law enforcer referred to as Homer Glen, which is the first part of the name of the DEA agent (last name McBrayer) — whose vehicle was pulled over by Santillan's henchmen in Juarez. The DEA agent who arrived at the scene later to assist him used an alias, Rene Ramirez.

Other background that matters: Ramirez Peyro, according to an official **DEA timeline of events**, had convinced Santillan that he was associated with a corrupt U.S. customs inspector in El Paso, which made it possible for him to obtain U.S. law enforcement intelligence for Santillan. That, of course, was a convenient lie concealing Ramirez

Peyro's actual work as an ICE informant who was providing U.S. law enforcers intelligence on the cartel.

Following are some excerpts from the informant's statement to Mexican authorities that evidence Santillan's violent intensions for the DEA agent and his family:

> The last execution I know of was on January 13 of this year [2004]. Santillan asked me to have the house ready because he was going to have some "grilled meat." Later, at 10:00 in the evening, he told me to hold off, to start early in the morning.
>
> So, then at around 8 in the morning [on January 14], he spoke with me and told me to send someone to the house to be waiting. So, I sent my buddy Jose Jaime Marquez, who went to open the door of the Parsioneros 3633 house. Later, at around 1 p.m. [as victims were being tortured at the house] Santillan spoke to me and asked if I knew John Brown, who was a U.S. customs inspector. After checking, I told Santillan no.
>
> Later, at around 6:00 p.m. on January 14 of this year [2004], Santillan called me again [after his men had detained the DEA agent and his family on the streets of Juarez] and asked me to find out if there was an inspector whose name was Homer Glen and [he asked for information on] a Rene Ramirez, because apparently the latter was part of the three letters. I believe that what he [Santillan] was referring to was that he was part of the Drug Enforcement Administration.
>
> He told me that the reason that he wanted me to investigate that information was because Homer Glen had a safe house in Ciudad Juarez, and they [Santillan's killers] wanted to blow it up.
>
> After investigating, I informed him that they weren't customs inspectors but rather appeared to be part of the DEA. ... We agreed [Santillan and the informant] to meet the next day in El Paso, and he told me that a family from the town where [House of Death victim] Omar Zepeda lived had asked Vicente Carrillo Fuentes as a favor to take revenge for [something] Omar had done [to the family], and that was the reason they kidnapped [Omar and] two more people [on January 14, 2004].

> While they were torturing these people [at the House of Death], one of them said that they had drugs at Homer Glen's house and that was why Santillan set up a surveillance of Homer Glen's house [where DEA agent Homer Glen McBrayer lived in Juarez with his family].

The **timeline of events prepared by DEA** detailing events leading to their agents being evacuated for safety reasons from Juarez adds the following about Santillan's presumed intensions that day, January 14, 2004:

> Further details reflected that [Juarez Cartel] associate Loya Gallegos [a Mexican state police commander] was attempting to identify a stash house in the vicinity of [DEA agent McBrayer's government living quarters in Juarez] and had initiated surveillance in that area.
>
> It is suspected that information pertaining to the stash house was obtained through the alleged abduction, torture and killing of three unknown males earlier that day in Juarez.

* * *

One of those murder victims, the informant later told *Narco News*, was U.S. resident Louis Padilla. And that brings us back to Juanito, and his place in the House of Death slaughter.

I did check out Juanito's story, as best as can be done in the netherworld of the narco-trafficking jungle. The level of detail in his story, and his consistency in recalling that detail, makes it difficult to believe he is making things up. In addition, key events he outlines do coincide with details revealed by my sources and in U.S. government documents that have surfaced in the House of Death case, including a **DEA timeline of events**, the informant **Ramirez Peyro's official statement to the Mexican government**, and U.S. court records.

In fact, in the DEA timeline, Juanito's story is mentioned in the context of a shooting that occurred on January 15, 2004, the day Santillan was arrested in El Paso and **the day after the DEA evacuated all of its agents from Juarez**. From that timeline report:

Two males in a white pickup truck were shot after being stopped by two subjects reportedly acting as police officers. The targets were stopped upon departing the gated residential subdivision identified as ... in Ciudad Juarez. The subjects were asked for identification by one of the two alleged officers who approached them. Immediately upon identifying the driver, one of the suspects fatally shot the driver in the face and head with a 9-mm handgun.

The SOI [a DEA source inside the Mexican state police in Chihuahua] reported that Miguel Loya Gallegos directed the killing of [Rodolfo] Renteria Cervantes due to the loss of a 4,000-pound load of unspecified drugs. The other occupant of the vehicle ... was shot in the mouth and neck. He remains in critical condition in a hospital and has not been able or willing to give a statement.

So, Juanito's story, it seems, merits telling. It began with an email from Juanito: "Am the survivor of the 01 15 2004 [shooting] were Rodolfo Renteria Cervantes was murder. I got shot on the face. need too talk about some things that I know about the cartel."

In 2003 and 2004, when the House of Death was oozing blood, Juanito claims he worked for Renteria Cervantes, a bit player in the narco world who was not part of the ruthless House of Death criminal cell controlled by Santillan, ICE informant Ramirez Peyro and state police commander Loya Gallegos. Juanito contends this was an era when anyone running drugs through Juarez had to pay financial tribute to Vicente Carrillo Fuentes and the Juarez Cartel for that privilege or face a savage penalty — with the House of Death, and others like it, serving as the court of justice for administering that penalty.

Renteria Cervantes made a fatal error on that front by purchasing some "cheap" marijuana from a supplier, Juanito claims, and selling a portion of that payload in Juarez itself. It turned out, Juanito contends, that one of the reasons the marijuana was so inexpensive was because it was likely stolen from the Juarez Cartel, a crime punishable by death. And it was Santillan's cell of the cartel that supplied some of the enforcement power — through Loya and police under his command. These Mexican cops served as the enforcers and sicarios charged with carrying out the ultimate penalties. And they were extremely efficient at their jobs. Juanito told me the following during one of our telephone interviews — for which I had to use a disposable phone as a security precaution to guard against the outside chance my regular phone was being monitored:

> We were at Rodolfo's [Renteria Cervantes'] house [on January 15, 2004]. And that same morning me and his son went out to get something to eat, some barbacoa. And we saw a car parking on the street; we saw a red car. Then we went back into the house, and I told Rodolfo that there's a car, "I don't know, like mysterious."
>
> And he said, "You're just scared."
>
> So, we ate breakfast and everything, and he gave me the keys to the truck, and I said, "Nah," because I didn't want to go with him. I had other things to do, but he said, "Nah, you drive." And I said, "No you're driving."
>
> So, I threw the keys back to him and we went to the truck. We went down the street like three houses, and we saw those guys come, walking to us, to the truck and they said they were police, and they asked for his name, and Rodolfo said, "No that's not my name." They said, "No, I know it's you."
>
> The first thing they say is get out of the truck. So, he [Rodolfo] got out, and I got out, and then this guy one of the two Mexican state cops, not in uniform, but each with badges, was pointing the gun at me in the head, and I heard the shots [near me], something going boom, boom, like that, and I turned my head around. That's when they shot me in the face.
>
> So, one shot him [Rodolfo] and the other one shot me. [And then Juanito's shooter walked over to Rodolfo and put a second bullet in his skull for good measure.]
>
> And I know the names of those cops.

That knowledge, it seems, is critical, in terms of Juanito's standing as a witness to murder; to being a key to apprehending the individuals involved in the aborted assassination of the DEA agent and his family;

and to explaining why Juanito is still on the run, still fearing retribution from the "cartel."

In the wake of the shooting, presuming Juanito was dead, the shooters left the scene, and an ambulance appeared shortly after, called by Rodolfo's family, who had heard the shots that killed him. Juanito was rushed to the hospital, with the police coming to investigate the crime scene after the ambulance had departed. Among the cops appearing at the crime scene, and seen laughing, Juanito says he later found out, was the chief sicario at the House of Death, state police commander Miguel Loya Gallegos.

Juanito said he spent about 20 days in a coma in the hospital in Juarez. When he woke, Mexican police were at his bedside, asking him to identify his shooters. He says he told them the cops' names, and even identified them via photos. That's when things began to go even further south for him, he says. The police kept returning to the hospital, pressing him for more information, but Juanito says it was clear to him they were far more interested in knowing how much he knew, and whom he knew, than they were in apprehending suspects. From an interview with Juanito:

> They show me some pictures [of cops], and I said, "Oh, this is one, and this is the other one."
>
> They said, "Are you sure."
>
> And I said, "Man I could see their faces. I know it's them." ... Then they went outside and came back and started asking if we were working for who and all that, you know. ... And after that they wanted to take pictures, and I said, "I don't want you guys to take no pictures" ... and they said, "OK," and they left.
>
> That same night, the nurses was putting a diaper on me. ... I heard somebody calling my name, you know, and the nurses closed the door and started almost screaming. And they called the cops, but they [the cops] said they couldn't find the guys who come inside at night [at the hospital] asking for me, but they said they had some machine guns with them.

[The doctors at the hospital] said I need to call the cops, so I can get protection day and night because I was putting people in danger. I said no, because they're the ones [the cops] who probably want me dead because they know I know the people [who also were Mexican police] that did this to me.

Juanito says, at that point, less than six days after emerging from a coma, he, with the help of his family and friends, left the hospital and moved into a safe house in Juarez for several weeks, where he continued to receive health care from some brave nurses.

"After that, they took me to Durango, Mexico, to hide over there and see how things go," Juanito says.

Juanito's family, now living in the U.S., had purchased some property in Durango, where Juanito hid out, living in the community under the radar for some two years. But eventually, he said, "Some people from La Linea found me. [La Linea, "The Line," is another name for the Mexican cops who provide extreme services for the Juarez Cartel.]

Juanito said one day some people showed up in Durango asking questions about him, and because it's a small community, he got a heads up about the strangers, who were driving a truck with Chihuahua state plates — the Mexican state where Juarez is located. The next day, Juanito says, he found an abandoned truck parked near his family's property in Durango, "with an AK 47 in it, and it was full of blood and human brains." Juanito adds that the air had been let out of the tires of the truck, so it couldn't easily be moved, and that there was a report of human body parts being found along a roadside about 10 to 20 miles away.

"So, I got out of [Durango] and went back to Juarez and found a coyote and then I [crossed the border]," Juanito says. "I move to [the U.S.] ...."

He found work doing construction jobs that paid pretty well and lived in his new home for several years, near his family. Then, Juanito says:

> One day my dad is outside [his house] and a stranger shows up asking, "Is your son here." My dad said, "No, he doesn't live here." And he [the stranger] said, "He owes me a car...."

> There was another visitation after that, a knock on the door at night. And yet another time, as his father was walking to his house, "a guy got out of a car and started following him," Juanito recalls. ... My dad asked him if he was following him, and he [the stranger] said, "No. I'm looking for your son. He owes me something, and I need to fix things with him."

> My dad called me then, crying, saying, "They're still looking for you." That's when my dad sold that house and I moved [out of the area too], Juanito adds. Not even my family knows where I am living now. ...They [the cartel] know I saw a lot, a lot of faces of people.

Juanito adds one more detail to his story that might go a long way in explaining at least one of the thousands of unsolved murders in Juarez in recent years — if, in fact, the murder is even recorded anywhere in the public record.

> The reason why I am more afraid for my life [now than ever, even in the United States] is because the place where I was hiding out at [in Juarez] after the hospital, the ones [who] was helping me ... in May of 2010, she got killed. They followed her and shot her. It seems they are stopping by all the places where I been. Her name was Lorena Ojeda. ...

It could well be the Mexican state cops who allegedly shot Juanito in the face and killed his compadre, Rodolfo Renteria Cervantes, may be the source of Juanito's current nightmare. The names of those cops, Juanito alleges he told Mexican law enforcers at the time of the shooting, are **Erick Cano Aguilera and Alvaro Valdez Rivas**. One of those names, Alvaro Valdez, shows up in a statement ICE informant Ramirez Peyro gave to the Mexican government concerning the House of Death. The other, Erick Cano, appears in a DEA timeline of events chronicling the House of Death case.

Alvaro Valdez is identified in **Ramirez Peyro's statement** as allegedly being one of the two Mexican cops who, along with Ramirez Peyro, restrained and murdered Mexican attorney Fernando Reyes at the House of Death in early August 2003. And a **DEA timeline** of events documenting the House of Death chronology, again, obtained through a Freedom of Information Act request, details Eric Cano Aguilera's alleged connection to the House of Death:

> Investigation to date reflects that the referenced telephone calls and traffic stop [of the DEA agent and his family] were, in fact, overt acts within a conspiracy between Santillan..., [Mexican state police commander Miguel] Loya ... and others. [The goal was] to identify and execute those responsible for the unauthorized transit or loss of approximately 4,000 pounds of marijuana.
>
> It is suspected that the conspiracy involved the kidnapping and torture and murder of three individuals on January 14 [2004, including Texas resident Luis Padilla], which resulted in the subsequent identification and murder of a fourth subject.... This fourth subject is identified as Rodolfo Renteria Cervantes. ...It is further suspected that the traffic stop of [the DEA agent and his family] on January 14, 2004, [in Juarez] was a misdirected attempt by co-conspirators to identify and locate Renteria Cervantes and/or a related [drug] stash house location.
>
> ... Investigative Note: One of the subjects [involved in the traffic stop of the DEA agent] subsequently identified himself ... as David Rodriguez. The CJRO [DEA's office in Juarez] later determined the true identity of this subject as Chihuahua State Judicial Police Agent Erick Cano Aguilera....
>
> ... Cano Aguilera was subsequently identified by the CS [confidential source, the ICE informant Ramirez Peyro] as a participant in the murders occurring at the residence [the House of Death].... The [Mexican] state of Chihuahua posted U.S. $10,000 rewards for information leading to the arrests of the fugitive state police officers, Miguel Loya ... Erick Cano Aguilera [and] Alvaro Valdez Rivas....

If the details of Juanito's story are on the mark, his fate ahead, and the odds of his story ever being heard in a court of justice, seem rather bleak, given the bloody reality of the House of Death case, according to U.S. law enforcers who spoke with me on a not-for-attribution background basis.

"His [Juanito's] story is plausible," explains one former federal law enforcer. "If anyone [in power] really tried to do something with the House of Death case, he [Juanito] would be a witness.

"But it seems everyone has forgotten about the murders and the targeting of the DEA agent," the law enforcer adds. "All they did is work to cover up the government misconduct. They didn't care that someone tried to kill a DEA agent or that a U.S. informant was involved in all these murders."

So, where does someone like Juanito turn to plead his case for justice, for his life? To the halls of government? It seems he is a man without a country, without a home, caught on the devil's bridge, facing grave consequences if he crosses in either direction.

Similar to ICE informant Ramirez Peyro, Juanito appears to be another part of the "blowback" from a failed war on drugs now more than half a century old. On any given day, that pernicious war could place any one of us or our loved ones in the crossfire — even as it continues to reward corruption and dysfunction on both sides of the border with impunity. And worse, this tragic war on drugs serves as a training ground for the next generation of cartel capos and sicarios.

"Lalo [Ramirez Peyro] would tell us 80 percent of the story, and 80 percent was true, but he just neglected or forgot to tell us the most important parts," a federal agent close to the House of Death case revealed. "He had been working for us for such a long time, I mean this guy was a sharp individual.

"We were our own worst enemies because we let him into the office, and he would see how the operations worked," the agent added. "We always said if he [the informant Ramirez Peyro] doesn't work for us, and he goes back to Mexico, he's going to be the next one of the cartel leaders."

The Informant Interviews

"One last bit of worthless advice from me. Things in Mexico make more sense if you realize no one can wear a white hat and survive." — journalist and author **Charles Bowden** (1945-2014)

To better understand the **point of view of ICE informant Guillermo Eduardo Ramirez Peyro** when it comes to the House of Death murders, I conducted a series of jailhouse interviews with him in July 2009 and again in late June and early July 2014. For those interviews, I regularly used the nickname he embraces, Lalo.

All of the interviews were conducted by telephone because attorneys, jailhouse rulers, and other government officials, including ICE, precluded the press from visiting Lalo in-person while he was incarcerated fighting deportation and later facing criminal charges. Most of his time in jail was spent in solitary confinement — for his own protection but also, in part, to keep him away from the media.

In addition, even getting phone access to the informant for interviews was quite challenging, given Lalo could only be contacted initially through his attorneys — and they generally did not see it in their client's interest to provide even phone access to me, an investigative journalist, and only did so after Lalo insisted. All calls had to be initiated by Lalo through the prison phone system, which meant all of our calls were recorded by prison officials, and the prisoner paid by the minute for phone-use time. Consequently, each interview session was interrupted by dial tones about every half hour or so, with Lalo calling me back to continue the interview after each interruption.

In the chapters to follow, then, are excerpts and explanations gleaned from those interviews with ICE informant Lalo, some of which were aired in 2009 on the **Expert Witness Radio** show on Pacifica Radio in New York City — hosted by a former deep undercover DEA agent, Mike Levine, along with his co-host and the show's sound technician, musician Mark Marshall. In addition to the informant interviews conducted in 2009, while Ramirez Peyro was in jail in Minnesota fighting deportation, are excerpts from later jailhouse interviews conducted while he was imprisoned on another matter in Missouri in June 2014. Still other excerpts appeared as part of court litigation or, in one case, the excerpts come from a handwritten letter penned by the informant while in jail.

Dispatch 20

June 4, 2009

Lalo was a wired-up torpedo inside the cartel. He carried a tape-recorder provided to him by his handlers and his phone was monitored by ICE. In addition, his ICE handlers provided him with a phone that he gave as a gift to Heriberto Santillan Tabares — Lalo's narco-trafficking boss. It, too, was tapped by ICE, Lalo said, allowing ICE agents to listen in on Santillan's calls and in-person conversations.

As a result, Lalo said his ICE handlers, and the prosecutors they worked with, were fully aware that people were being murdered at the House of Death on Parsioneros in Juarez, sometimes in advance of the murders.

"I would get a call to come [from El Paso or to contact someone else] to open up the house [in Juarez] for a carne asada," Lalo said. "And I know at least five or six times those calls were being monitored by ICE."

Lalo said as part of his work for the Juarez Cartel, he was not required to be present at every murder carried out at the Parsioneros house, but he was required to "check on" the activities and "to take charge if there was a problem." In addition, Lalo said some bodies were delivered to the Parsioneros house for burial as a result of murders that took place elsewhere.

Lalo explained that the leadership of the Juarez Cartel, along with the leaders of other major narco-trafficking syndicates at the time — such as the Sinaloa, Tijuana and Gulf cartels — work with each other and with the government "all the way up to the president's office."

Lalo explained his assessment in a jailhouse interview **recorded in July 2014:**

Even after the arrest of Chapo [Guzman, former head of the Sinaloa Cartel] it's well known the way it is in Mexico. In order to get control of the situations over there, you need to have the law enforcement and the military on your behalf. That's the only way.

That way, they make their money. Their [law enforcers and politicians'] salaries is preposterous [very low] over there, so they're going to be corrupt one way or another. Now, not necessarily are they going to push for the same cartel or same criminal organizations, because that also is part of the situation [in a corruption-for-sale market]. Everyone needs to make money.

But things is against me. That is for sure. I am sure all of them is going to be in agreement that I need to be killed. Because they need to set the example that no one should help the U.S. government. It's what I did. Working for U.S. government is like betraying all the people there.

Under the top "cartel" leadership exists what Lalo terms the "control groups" that oversee operations for the various drug organizations in major markets, or plazas, such as Juarez. These control groups take orders from the criminal organizations' top leaders, among them, for a time, the Juarez Cartel's **Vicente Carrillo Fuentes** or the Sinaloa Cartel's Joaquin "El Chapo" Guzman-Loera — both now in jail and since replaced by other cartel leaders. And there are many others unknown at the apex of the narco-trafficking business in Mexico and the U.S. The control groups are headed by sub-bosses — an individual known in Juarez in the early 2000s as "No. 1," for example, Lalo explained.

Under the control groups are a host of criminal "cells," or gangs — such as the group that was headed by Santillan. "The members of these cells don't know who the other cells are," Lalo said. "The cell leadership just reports to the control group in the city. So, it is the control groups who give the orders."

In addition, according to Lalo, these cells don't work exclusively with one narco-trafficking organization. They may do a job for the Juarez organization one time and later do work for the Sinaloa organization, he said. "It's not exclusive," Lalo added. "It all depends on who their customers are. A cell does not belong to one [narco-trafficking organization]. The only exclusive [relationship] is between the control group [and the top cartel leadership]."

The various deadly cells supporting these criminal syndicates are all in constant motion then, like electrons jumping from one nucleus to another in a cloud of unstable atoms. The leaders of these rackets also face persistent existential threats internally from ascendant rivals and externally from honest and corrupt law enforcers. **Carrillo Fuentes** was arrested in 2014, for example, and **Guzman** two years later for the final time — after previously escaping Mexican jails twice.

Prior to their fall, however, the two criminal organizations Carrillo Fuentes and Guzman led (the Juarez and Sinaloa cartels, respectively) were actually cooperating with a third cartel, the Gulf Cartel, to ensure all benefited from drug-trafficking routes in a particular precinct. Lalo explained how that mutual-benefit deal worked in his 2005 statement to Mexican authorities:

> In the city of Acuna [located across the border from Del Rio, Texas] Jesus Fernandez Calderilla and Jose Luis, or JL, are the ones who operate in this region, but since Osiel Cardenas [Guillen, head of the Gulf Cartel, who was arrested in Mexico in March 2003 and later jailed in the U.S.] felt the [illegal narcotics] traffic had stopped, they wanted someone strong to control the precinct, so they could start trafficking drugs again.
>
> I proposed this to Santillan (affiliated with the Juarez Cartel at that point) and he proposed it to Ismael Zambada [or El Mayo, co-leader of the Sinaloa Cartel] that his son Vicente Zambada [also arrested in Mexico, in 2009, and later jailed in the U.S.] should be in charge of that precinct. So, I went to see the location to see how they worked, and it was agreed that they would start working there in January of this year [2004].
>
> ... Regarding the house that I've mentioned as "Big Brother," it was used as a guest house for the bosses when they came to visit Juarez. This house was occupied on different occasions by Sadam, Luis Portillo [Juarez Cartel control group leaders, the latter the head of the

Juarez "precinct" and referred to as No. 1] and one of [Sinaloa Cartel leader] El Mayo Zambada's operators, whose name is Jorge.

This house was used for board meetings or to devise work plans regarding drug trafficking and executions of people.

Despite the flux, treachery and internecine bloodshed that often marks cartel relations, the narco-trafficking business still thrives. Lalo said his boss, Santillan, was part of a criminal cell that reported to a "control group," which directed numerous other cells that also operated death houses. "So there were many [death] houses," Lalo said. "At some point, they would leave those houses and move to other houses [to carry out the torture and murders, often disposing of the bodies at the houses]. So, there are a lot more of them [than just the House of Death on Parsioneros Street]."

Lalo said Santillan was under the direction of the "control group," and "he was involved with some of the other houses." Lalo stressed that he made his ICE handlers aware of the extent of this death machine, but they chose not to act on the information or to inform the Mexican government. Instead, U.S. Justice Department and ICE officials at the highest levels **sanctioned** the continuation of Lalo's activities even after they were made aware of his participation in murder at the Parsioneros House of Death.

Lalo reminds however, that at the same time he was working as an informant on the Santillan and Juarez Cartel case, he also was working for ICE as an informant in a separate cigarette-smuggling case. Pulling the plug on either investigation too soon could have compromised Lalo's cover because his identity would likely have been revealed if either case went to trial while the other was still an active investigation. That, in turn, would have jeopardized the ongoing investigation.

As it turned out, likely as one consequence of DEA commander Gonzalez' missive exposing the U.S. government's enabling of the House of Death murders, Lalo was never called to testify in either the Santillan or cigarette-smuggling case. That's because U.S. Attorney Sutton chose to accept plea deals in each case – assuring that Lalo would not testify in court and that the role played by ICE and the U.S. Attorney's Office in propelling the Juarez carnage would not be examined in the light of day through public legal proceedings. And the sad truth of it is that none of this needed to happen in the first place. Instead, the carnage at the House of Death was allowed to continue despite the fact that Sutton and the prosecutor under him handling the case had enough evidence to arrest Santillan several months prior to the first House of Death murder.

"Why ICE [and Sutton] did not shut down the operation, I cannot say," Lalo said in an interview. "They gave me the order to continue."

Dispatch 21

August 18, 2008

In 2008, after Mexican troops and federal cops were deployed to Ciudad Juarez, the city became a major battleground in the drug war, with an average of about 100 murders a month — a total of 780 corpses as of mid-August by one count.

But like most figures in the drug war, there is nothing certain about that number. It might well be higher, with more bodies out there, hidden, still waiting to be counted. The paranoia that existed back then in this Mexican city just across the border from the placid U.S. community of El Paso is hard to describe, or at least words failed me after visiting Juarez in the spring of 2008 — when Mexican troops had only recently arrived in the city. I came to understand a much deeper dimension of the war for drugs.

Drug-war journalist and author Chuck Bowden, in one of our many email conversations over the years, described the mayhem gripping Juarez as the first decade of the new century neared its end like this:

> Just as it is essential for major media for [the] drug lords, etc., to be controlling this violence, the notion that the violence can come from many groups and have no real on-and-off button is, well, not conceivable to them. But it is to me.
>
> ... I understand the problem and I share it, and I think it is this: What we are seeing in Juarez does not fit our old models .... It is something new and what makes us blind to it and what makes us terrified of it is simply that no one is really in control. Think Baghdad where all sides flounder in explaining the killing, including Al Qaeda with its vision of restoring an older world.

In other words, the old script of "cartels" battling it out over turf does not explain fully the carnage in Juarez. Bowden's words have helped me to see things a bit clearer. He is right, I think. There are many causes for the extreme bloodshed in Juarez. But at its core is the drug war and the breakdown of civil society that it eventually brings to all who are sucked into its void. In that world, which was the city of Juarez in 2008 and beyond, you are either a hunter or someone's prey. No one is exempt from that street rule of survival.

The House of Death murders took place in 2003 and early 2004, just as the 2000s were getting underway during the presidencies of George W. Bush in the U.S. and Vicente Fox in Mexico. The House of Death in some ways, however, sets the stage for the extreme violence that was to follow in the borderlands. Felipe Calderon was elected president of Mexico in late 2006, promising to wage a war on the cartels. He succeeded in greatly escalating the bloodshed in Juarez after sending the military and a contingent of federal police into city starting in the spring of 2008 under "Joint Operation Chihuahua." That's when Juarez became an urban war zone — with the bloodshed in full public view, no longer hidden behind the walls of a House of Death.

But even four years into the new century, as a U.S. government informant assisted narco-traffickers and Mexican cops in carrying out the torture and vicious murders of a dozen or more people, the signs of the breakdown of civil society were all there in front of us. And those horrors continue to haunt our justice system, fueled by what is in reality a war over who will control the flow of banned drugs.

The informant Lalo was paid nearly a quarter of a million dollars by U.S. taxpayers for his informant work for ICE, which included a gig overseeing the House of Death for the Juarez Cartel. The hunter who ordered the murders at the House of Death, Santillan, employed an assassin squad composed of Mexican cops led by a Mexican state police commander, Miguel Loya Gallegos. Their prey were tortured first to maximum agony prior to death if brought to the house. If lucky, they were killed elsewhere, though even that was no guarantee of a fast exit from this life. One corpse delivered to the house was completely wrapped in black plastic bags, another had a rope still around the neck. Both were stored under a staircase at the House of Death for a time, until they could be disappeared. Ultimately, a dozen bodies were found buried in the backyard of the House of Death at 3633 Parsioneros — a dead-end street in a seemingly sedate residential neighborhood in Juarez.

It is in that context that a letter was penned by the informant in 2008 — written with a pencil while he was still confined to a prison cell in Minnesota fighting deportation. The letter details, from Lalo's point of view, the events leading up to the House of Death murders. It is written in Spanish and was later translated into English.

Lalo's prison missive recounts the initial stages of his efforts to infiltrate the Juarez Cartel — and Santillan's narco-trafficking cell in Juarez in particular. Among the revelations in his prison letter that some may find surprising is that Lalo grew up in an upper-middle-class family as the son of well-educated professional parents who worked as civil engineers in Mexico. After taking a stab at college, Lalo went to work in the late 1990s as a federal highway patrol officer in the state of Guerrero in southern Mexico for about a year before he was fired because he had problems getting along with his boss. Lalo later moved into the drug business full-time. Lalo says that was a natural career move, given he had already made numerous connections in the cartel world while he was a cop and through his work for a relative's construction business in Mexico.

Once in the narco world full-time, Lalo found himself overseeing the distribution of drug shipments for a narco-trafficker based in Guadalajara. Lalo assisted in coordinating the movement of drugs from Colombia into Mexico for that narco-trafficker. After gaining experience doing that job for a while, Lalo made his way to Juarez to begin his work for Santillan — and ICE.

Lalo's prison letter itself is noteworthy because of his central role as a U.S. informant in the House of Death case, but it is important to stress that the veracity of all Ramirez Peyro's claims in the letter shouldn't be assumed. Where there's overlap, however, they are consistent with prior claims he has made in testimony provided to

Mexican officials and in U.S. immigration court and are not inconsistent with information contained in public documents obtained through the Freedom of Information Act or courthouses.

In the case of the House of Death, what we do know as fact is that 12 bodies, most broken and contorted from brutal torture, were found buried like garbage in the backyard of a typical middle-class home in Juarez.

* * *

The letter penned by Lalo only references a year once (2000), so the timeframe of these events can only be estimated, although they all appear to have played out between 2000 and 2002 based on month and seasonal references in the letter. At that time, Lalo was working as a paid informant for the U.S. Customs Service. The agency predates ICE and can trace its roots to 1789.

Customs carried out its vast mission as part of the U.S. Treasury Department from 1875 through the start of the 2000s. That all changed after September 11, 2001, however, when Customs as a stand-alone agency was dissolved. The 9/11 terrorist attack led to the speedy enactment of legislation in late November 2002 creating the Department of Homeland Security and ICE. The first murder at the House of Death — in which Lalo was a participant — occurred in early August 2003, while he was employed by ICE, which was then a new agency that had been created out of the remnants of other dismantled federal agencies, including the U.S. Customs Service.

Because ICE was so new at the time, its agents had something to prove, but it also had its own internal dysfunctions to contend with. There were tensions between Customs investigators who were folded into ICE and their counterparts from the Immigration and Naturalization Service — which, like Customs, also was dismantled to create DHS.

In that context, Lalo, and the cases he could help ICE make, seemed to be the kind of lift the agency and its law enforcers could use.

He was a meal ticket to netting "narco-kingpins"; racking up dope-bust and arrests stats; making other agencies, like DEA, look a step behind ICE in taking down the "drug cartels"; and in the process generating budget-boosting headlines that make the politically appointed agency heads and their bosses look good in the public eye.

Lalo's prison letter, an excerpt

(Information contained in [brackets] in the letter to follow has been added for context and clarity.)

> He [Santillan] also told me that [agents] from the DEA were also on the payroll [of the cartel] and that when the operatives [law enforcement] were coming, they warned them ahead of time, so they could leave the area for a while. Then when the [DEA] operatives come, there is nothing happening, and they leave empty-handed — like they did at Amado [Carrillo's] sister's wedding.
>
> He [Santillan] also said that they [the cartel-compromised DEA agents] had told them about the crybabies [snitches] and that they had already killed two of them from Torreon. Santillan told me that a lady [snitch] who used to clean one of the houses ... that they sent a guy to her house dressed like a worker from the water company, and when the lady opened the door, he shot her.
>
> He [Santillan] also told me that he had traveled all over the country orchestrating and escorting the cocaine shipments that were coming from South America. I asked him that since he made good money and had his farm and all, if he was thinking of retiring. He said no — once in the mafia, there was no way out, given they thought it would be considered treason.
>
> I really had nothing to say. I only told him ... that in Juarez I was only involved with the ones who brought [illegal] cars, as an intermediary or a packer. Santillan asked me to help him get smugglers, packers, grocers/sellers [bodegueros], truck drivers, really to hire everybody necessary [for a narco-trafficking business]. He told me he already had everybody, but it was always good to have more options.

So, then, once in Juarez, he agreed to call me, and I went to El Paso to talk to [Raul] Bencomo [the U.S. Customs turned ICE agent who originally recruited and served as Lalo's "handler," or main contact, while he was an ICE informant]. I asked [Bencomo] if there was anyone in his office who would be interested in what we were working on with Santillan, that he should talk to his bosses, and that they should be more competent, because in the cases I'd done before [with ICE], they had left me with a lot of problems. And this [the Juarez Cartel] was the big leagues, so they had to be smarter. And I told him everything Santillan had told me on the way.

After talking with his superiors, Bencomo told me that, yes, they were interested in the Santillan case, and that they would do everything they could so I wouldn't get burned. I told him that the best thing for the moment would be to begin to hire truckers because that way we could take the drugs somewhere else and give them [U.S. law enforcement] more time to seize them, and that way they wouldn't suspect me. I also reminded him, "No DEA," given the things that Santillan had said [about corrupt DEA agents].

At that same time, they [some of Lalo's other Juarez drug-smuggler contacts] offered me a crossing with a corrupt [U.S. Customs] inspector, which I discussed with Bencomo. And he told me that he was again interested that I become involved in that case too. ...

[Bending the Rules]

We finally had a case [referring to the Santillan investigation], but since I had to become involved in the activities in Mexico, [Bencomo's supervisor in El Paso] Curtis Compton said that they would have to wait for Washington [D.C.] to get permission to use me as an operative/informant [inside Mexico]. That for the moment, we couldn't do anything, just that I should take note of everything that was sent through [illegal drug shipments].

To which I made him [Compton] see that it wasn't just taking notes, that as he well knew the operation was very complicated and involved various criminal groups who were synchronized down to the slightest detail, and that it would be impossible for me to just stand to the side now that I was [a key player]. Everything would fall apart if I distanced myself, with the additional risk of my [criminal] associates undermining the relationship with the corrupt U.S law enforcer because we knew they were lazy and not very bright, their lack of credibility besides.

So, we agreed that I would keep coordinating everything so that when the permission came from Washington, we would have everything on a silver platter. At the same time, as the business with the corrupt inspector [is happening], I keep meeting with Santillan because he kept asking me to go. And he talked with some of my associates and me about how things were done in the cartel.

And he [Santillan] even told us to be aware of anyone selling cocaine or saying that they had connections with the cartel, to investigate it immediately and, if necessary, take appropriate action. And that we should be ready to support the operations that would soon take place — that being blowing up the houses of people [violently assaulting or murdering them] who in some way had affected the cartel's interests. We exchanged phone numbers with his nephew, [state police] Commandant Loya, and given Santillan was not always in Juarez, anything that came up we would take care of directly amongst ourselves. As always, I told all this to the OIUSC [Office of Investigation, U.S. Customs — which in March 2003 became part of ICE.]

Dispatch 22

October 12, 2006

The House of Death informant Guillermo Eduardo Ramirez Peyro, Lalo, on August 11, 2005, gave testimony under oath in his deportation-removal proceedings held before an administrative judge in a U.S. Immigration Court in Bloomington, Minnesota. The transcript of that testimony — not made available to me until more than a year later — can only be described as startling in parts and puzzling on other fronts.

At this point in history (August 2005) — as Mexican citizen and now-former ICE informant Ramirez Peyro takes the stand in Minnesota — the president of Mexico is Vicente Fox of the conservative National Action Party, or PAN. Fox's six-year term in office ended November 30, 2006. Felipe Calderón, also of the PAN, succeeded Fox as president and shortly after launched an all-out war on the narco-mafias — or at least some of them.

From Lalo's 2005 immigration-court testimony, we get a clearer idea of who might want to kill him, and why it doesn't matter to the Mexican government, or seemingly even parts of the U.S. government — based on the resources and years spent by U.S. agents and lawyers trying to deport him back to Mexico to face the cartels he betrayed.

Testifying is the informant, Ramirez Peyro. He is being questioned by his attorney, Jodi Goodwin and the attorney for the U.S. government, Kevin Lashus.

[Part I]

Goodwin: What will, what will happen to you if you are returned to, to Mexico?

Ramirez Peyro: Well, they, they will kill me, or they will torture me and then will kill me.

Goodwin: Who will?

Ramirez Peyro: Yeah, the police, the cartel, the government, it's all the same people.

Goodwin: Why do you say it's the same people?

Ramirez Peyro: Because the police works for the cartel.

Goodwin: How do you know this?

Ramirez Peyro: During the three years of working as a investigation [a U.S. government informant infiltrating the Juarez Cartel], I recorded and I showed that, that the police is under the order and to service the people from the cartel, inclusive this are recordings where I would record the conversations that I would have with [cartel cell leader] Santillan, and he would explain to me the arrangements that they would have with militaries with high executives, high-level government people.

Goodwin: The, the arrangements that the cartel had with the military?

Ramirez Peyro: They were militaries, with politics — politicians and with the police. That's for sure that they are under the orders.

Goodwin: And when you say the police, are there many levels of police?

Ramirez Peyro: Yes, there is three levels, federal, state and municipal.

Goodwin: Which ones are under the control of the cartel?

Ramirez Peyro: All three of them.

Goodwin: You indicated that you have recorded some conversations with Santillan where he explained arrangements that were made with military and politicians. What, what specific arrangements did he tell you about politicians?

Ramirez Peyro: No, that he didn't precisely, himself, well, the cartel [the Juarez Cartel] had arrangements with people that were close to President Fox [of Mexico]. He explained to me that President Fox took, took the position to arrange, consult with the cartel from Juarez to — which it, which it means that he was going to attack the, the enemy cartels being from Tijuana and from the Gulf, and then the cartel from

Juarez would be operating with this court, you know, without the government being —

Goodwin: This is —

Ramirez Peyro: — on —

Goodwin: — what —

Ramirez Peyro: — top of them.

Goodwin: This is what Santillan told you?

Ramirez Peyro: It's one of the long conversations that we did have. Also, when I did go to Colombia to make arrangement with the Colombians, the plan was to come by sea, and the Mexico's Navy, the ships, they're the ones that would get the drugs in the, in the sea — marina — ocean borders, you know, of the national territories. They, yeah, they kept close to what you call ground, firm ground, and the PGR [Mexico's office of the attorney general, whose employees are supposed to pursue narco-trafficking investigations and prosecutions] then would fly this drugs to the — to Juarez, the city of Juarez.

Goodwin: So, from the source of the drugs through the distribution, were all these arrangements made with different government parts?

Ramirez Peyro: That's, yeah, that's the purpose, to make arrangements with them so they won't have any losses. So, they invite them, you know, to take part of the vehicle [narco proceeds], and that way they avoid a war....

[Part II]

Lashus: All right. Other than the [Juarez] cartel, who else would be seeking [to kill] you, either here in the United States or anywhere else in the world?

Ramirez Peyro: Well, the government of my country.

Lashus: Okay. And that's including Vicente Fox's entire government?

Ramirez Peyro: Yeah, and even if Vicente Fox is ready to leave and, if he does leave, the militaries and the policemen, they still are the same people.

Lashus: All right. And why do you think that Vicente Fox would be looking for you?

Ramirez Peyro: No, no, not the president. I mean he's very busy, he's got allied occupation.

Lashus: I'm, I'm generalizing. Why would anybody with his government seek to harm you?

Ramirez Peyro: Okay. Just to show, to show the rest of the people that you shouldn't show evidence against the narco traffic and if you — if somebody does that — you'll end up dead.

Lashus: So, you, you believe the Mexican government seeks you in retaliation for your assistance in the Santillan case?

Ramirez Peyro: Of course, yes.

[Part III]

Lashus: All right. You testified that you are manager for drug distribution in Mexico.

Ramirez Peyro: Yes.

Lashus: And I also know that you were involved in the management of transporting drugs from Mexico to the United States.

Ramirez Peyro: When?

Lashus: When you were working for ICE.

Ramirez Peyro: Oh, yes, yes.

Lashus: And again, we're talking hundreds of thousands of pounds. Marijuana and cocaine. And hundreds of thousands of dollars.

Ramirez Peyro: I'm, I'm sorry. Not, not hundreds of thousands of pounds, but really thousands of pounds.

Lashus: Okay. Thousands of pounds of cocaine and marijuana and also cash. You had, you had to transport, manage the transportation of the money?

Ramirez Peyro: Yes, sir.

Lashus: Were you involved in any harming of people?

Ramirez Peyro: Yes, yes. I did have the supervision that the bodies would be buried. Yeah.

Lashus: Were you involved in actually harming the bodies?

Ramirez Peyro: No. No, the assassins ... the ones that do the killing were the policemen.

Lashus: ...But, but my question was you were not involved in the killing of those people [at the House of Death].

Ramirez Peyro: I repeat. And if involved means that I was present, yes, I was. If involved means that I hit him, and I asphyxiate him, then that's not.

Lashus: ...You bought the duct tape?

Ramirez Peyro: Yes.

Lashus: You bought the lime [for the dead bodies]?

Ramirez Peyro: Yes.

Lashus: You bought the hydrogen peroxide?

Ramirez Peyro: No. That was bought by Santillan.

Lashus: ...What's not clear is whether or not you held Fernando's [the first House of Death murder victim's] legs down while he was being murdered. Because you told us that you did not.

Ramirez Peyro: I didn't hold him. When they grab him, they told me, lay him down. But they had him, one from one side and the other one from the other side. The only thing I did was grab hold to pull his legs so he could lay down. It was not necessary. ... And, and that was also clear.

[Part IV]

Lashus: Did you tell your — the ICE officers that you were aware that Mr. Santillan had ordered the deaths of people associated with the [VCF] cartel?

Ramirez Peyro: Yes.

Lashus: Did you tell them before, right before it happened?

Ramirez Peyro: Yeah, several occasions. For example, in one occasion in Chicago, and Santillan talks to me, so I could send the boy there to open the house [the House of Death in Juarez] and me being in Chicago with the agents from ICE, and they knew because I authorize for them to hear my phone conversations. And besides that, I told them what's going on, and in El Paso they were listening my phone calls.

[Part V]

Lashus: All right. You're concerned about those police who are corrupt that work for the [Juarez] cartel. Is that right?

Ramirez Peyro: Well, that was part of my worry —

Lashus: Well, and —

Ramirez Peyro: — my concern.

Lashus: — you're worried about, you're worried about the cartel using the legitimate government to enforce an order to kill you.

Ramirez Peyro: Yes.

Lashus: But you know that, I mean, it's against the law to assassinate people in Mexico.

Ramirez Peyro: Yeah, but I also know that they don't live up to the law in Mexico.

Lashus: Because they're —

Ramirez Peyro: Don't —

Lashus: — corrupt?

Ramirez Peyro: — comply with the law. And personally, that's a sad reality of my country.

Lashus: ...At the beginning of your testimony you today, you said that the [Juarez] cartel, the police and the Mexican government is all the same group.

Ramirez Peyro: Yes, unfortunately, yes.

Lashus: You don't think that there is any legitimate enforcement of the drug laws in Mexico?

Ramirez Peyro: No, unfortunately, all the police organizations in Mexico, they are corrupted.

Lashus: But you're not — Santillan was talking about the army. He's talking about Fox. We're talking about everybody.

Ramirez Peyro: Yes, yes.

Lashus: So, there's no legitimate enforcement of the drug laws in Mexico?

Ramirez Peyro: Well, what they [politicians and law enforcers] do is they associate themselves with a cartel, in this case, with the cartel from Juarez, and in effect they do attack the rest of the cartels [that compete with the Juarez Cartel].

Lashus: So the —

Ramirez Peyro: There is persecution — prosecution against drugs. I mean there is, which [is against] the cartels that are not affiliated with the government.

Lashus: It's selective enforcement?

Ramirez Peyro: Yeah. They have to decide, I mean, they [government players] can't associate with every one of them [every cartel].

... Goodwin: Did ICE allow you to continue with your investigations of the, the Juarez Cartel after you had already told them about people being killed?

Ramirez Peyro: Yes, of course, yes.

Goodwin: So, they knew about the murders, but the investigation still continued?

Ramirez Peyro: Yeah, I was informing them as I was getting to know things.

Dispatch 23

July 6, 2009

Narco News in July 2009 published a short story promoting an upcoming radio show in New York City focused on the House of Death informant. The story announced that the radio show planned to air an exclusive interview with the House of Death informant, Guillermo Eduardo "Lalo" Ramirez Peyro.

At the time, Lalo was sitting in Sherburne County Jail in Elk River, Minnesota, awaiting the outcome of the U.S. government's efforts to deport him. At that point, he had been locked away in jail cell for nearly five years — since the Whataburger-murder fiasco in El Paso in the fall of 2004.

The long-running radio show, co-hosted by retired federal agent Mike Levine along with Mark Marshall, was broadcast weekly and focused in large measure on issues and personalities related to law enforcement, national security, organized crime and corruption. From the *Narco News* story announcing the radio show:

> The House of Death will once again be broadcast over New York City airwaves, as well as over the Internet, for your listening elucidation. Mike Levine, a former deep-cover DEA agent and author with a long-running radio show on Pacifica Radio, offers the details in a promotion below:
>
> EXPERT WITNESS RADIO SHOW
>
> Monday, 7/6/09, WBAI, New York City: 99.5 FM; beginning a 4 p.m. [Eastern] or live on the internet at: http://www.expertwitnessradio.org
>
> HIGH-LEVEL U.S. GOVERNMENT INFORMANT SPEAKS
>
> If you have been following the House of Death series [nine radio episodes; plus dozens of stories on *Narco News*] you know that "Lalo,"

the top-level Homeland Security [ICE] undercover informant who was outed by journalist Bill Conroy and retired top-level DEA supervisory officer Sandy Gonzalez, as being an integral part of the Juarez Cartel's murder machine — facilitating and taking part in the torture deaths of more than a dozen people ... and the attempted murder of a DEA agent and his family — while on the U.S. government payroll and with the knowledge of his U.S. government handlers, is now [in the process of] being deported to Mexico where he will most certainly die.

Bill Conroy, the only journalist in America to follow this story has recently been able to tape-record his jailhouse interviews with Lalo, which we are bringing to the WBAI airwaves today in the first of a two-part mind-blowing series. ...

Listen and hear Lalo himself describe:

1. Details of some of the murders in which he was a participant

2. The close involvement and knowledge of Mexican government and police officials in the murders.

3. The attempted murder of a DEA agent and his family stationed in Mexico.

4. How Lalo recorded at least one murder and turned it over to his ICE handlers.

5. How Lalo was instructed to continue his activities but to cease recording the murders.

6. How the Mexican government was notified of the ongoing House of Death murders and refused to take action.

7. How at least one of the murders was committed by a high-level Mexican police official in Lalo's presence, and how the Mexican police took part in and/or actually committed most of the murders.

8. Evidence that the entire operation was overseen by the United States Attorney's office. And MUCH, MUCH, MUCH more.

And there's another twist in story, of course. The informant also reveals in the interview the identity of yet another alleged U.S. government informant: El Paso resident and House of Death victim

Louis Padilla, who was among the last victims murdered at the House of Death.

In the following interview excerpt, aired on WBAI radio in New York City, the informant Lalo describes what happened to two individuals — Paisa and Chapo — who were deemed to be unsuccessful at their cartel jobs.

> ... These guys we were just working with, one ... he was in charge of a unit smuggling drugs onto U.S. soil. So, they start failing, and I tell them I rather don't work with them because our organization [the Juarez Cartel] is very serious and, at some point, I'm going to have troubles myself. These people are professional and have the police working for them, so I don't want no troubles.
>
> They said they want to stay working, and they produce good things for about a week and then they fail again, so I just told Santillan and Comandante Loya I definitely don't want to keep working with these people. So Santillan told me, "You know what ... let's meet tomorrow and just have some talk with them."
>
> So, the next day I went over there to Juarez [from El Paso] and ... this guy, Paisa, arrive with this other guy [El Chapo], his compadre, and when they approach me, I was in my suburban [automobile]. I said, "What's going on with this guy [El Chapo]? What he have to do with us?"
>
> He [Paisa] said, "He's my compadre." And I ask him, "Do you want to stay with us?"... and [he] said, "No, I want to stay."
>
> [El Chapo, or "shorty," is a common nickname in Mexico, and the individual with Paisa was not Joaquin "El Chapo" Guzman, who, at the time, was a leader of the Sinaloa drug-trafficking organization.]
>
> I call Santillan ... and he said why don't you come to the House [of Death] just to talk. So, I said, "All right." And we went to the House. Then Santillan arrived, and then 15 state police agents, among them Comandante Loya. ... So I explain to these guys [Paisa and Chapo] the situation that I already told them, that they can't mess with us. If they don't feel respect for me, they better feel respect for the organization

[the Juarez Cartel] because behind me there was a very big team of people, and they were messing with all of us.

In the meantime, Comandante Loya comes for their IDs, and he leave for the kitchen and starts running their names over several channels. Then Santillan basically repeat what I told to them, and then Comandante Loya repeat it again and, at some point, he said, "You know what? Right now is coming the boss, so you need to cover your head. Just pull up your shirts and put it around your heads."

So, they did it, and he just grabbed them by the neck and put them face down on the floor. They start to put like some kind of duct tape around their head, but one of them started doing noise, so Comandante Loya made signs to someone to pass him a gun with a silencer. So, he shot this guy. And this other one, he heard the shots also and started making noise, so he shot him also.

After Lalo finished describing the murder, former DEA agent and Expert Witness Radio host Mike Levine made the following comment, on air: "What a chilling, holy mackerel! ... For the listeners, what's clear is you had like 15 Mexican state policemen there as part of the cartel, committing the murders, and all of this information going to ICE."

Interestingly, Lalo also describes the same murders — of Paiso and Chapo — under oath in a statement he provided to the Mexican government on February 12, 2004, in Dallas. The pertinent part:

... Another execution that I remember was on November 23, 2003. The municipal police of Juarez seized 70 kilograms of marijuana belonging to commander Miguel Loya that was going to be transported via the Puente Libre (free bridge) in Ciudad Juarez. This seizure caused the deaths of "Paisa" and "Chapo" because Santillan ordered me to have these drug mules meet him in the little Parsioneros house. At that time, Santillan himself arrived along with Dedos Chuecos (crooked fingers); Eric Can; Loya and some others. They were told that the boss was going to arrive, which is why I thought Saddam was going to arrive. I told them [Paiso and Chapo] there that they had to take business with us seriously.

At that point, Loya told them to lift their shirts over their faces so they wouldn't see the boss. At that point, Loya put tape around their head, but they could still breathe, and one of them began to moan loudly so Loya shot him in the head with a pistol with a silencer, but he didn't die immediately. Upon hearing this the other one began to struggle and was shot in the head as well. After they were dead, Alex and I put them under the staircase of the Parsioneros house and later they were buried. These were killed because they were careless with their work taking the drugs across the border.

With these deaths, I warned Manuel Lujan [another Juarez Cartel player] that we were a serious organization as he had hired Paisa.

In another part of the 2009 jailhouse interview I conducted with Ramirez Peyro that was later aired on Pacifica radio in New York, he describes his version of the murder of Mexican attorney Fernando Reyes and what happened after he assisted with that first murder at the House of Death. Recall that the informant's assistance included handing his accomplices a plastic bag to put around Reyes' head. The informant clandestinely tape-recorded the bloody deed for ICE as well.

> ... First, I wasn't holding Fernandez Reyes' legs. I pulled his legs [out from under him]. What happened is Alex Garcia and one of state police trying to take control of his arms, his torso, and other state police try put tape around his head. But Fernandes Reyes was a tall individual. I think he was around 6'3", so this guy who try to put the tape around his head was like 5' 7" or something like that. So, he said we need to lay him [Reyes] down [to finish killing him]. So, I was just looking and the [two Mexican cops] just look at me, saying, "Hey, help us!"
>
> So, I pulled his left leg, like that, so they could put him on the floor. Once he was on the floor, they just got on him, on his shoulders and chest, and continue putting tape around his head while the other [cop] put handcuffs on his hand and behind his back, so they not need Alex [Garcia] or me anymore.
>
> ...After going through everything that happened, they [ICE] said if something like this happens again, don't record it, but now go back and pay the state police and do whatever Santillan told you. Supervise the

people making the hole [the grave] or whatever they have to do and then come back to the office.

So, that's what I did. At 10 at night I arrived back at the House and gave the money to the state police agents [for assassinating Fernando Reyes] and stay there until the other people dig the hole [in the backyard of the House of Death], and then I just come back to the office about 3 in the morning — the office of Homeland Security over there [in El Paso] .. and debriefed what happened.

Later in the interview:

... And the other thing, Alex, he get paid to get rid of the body of this guy [David] Castro [a U.S. citizen], and what he did, he [Castro] is buried there in the backyard [of the House of Death] and that was my belief. I just tell them [ICE] he was buried at the house, but they not even know where or what house, or nothing else. They don't ask for the questions about that.

... Me: Now, there were other death houses besides the Parsioneros house, right? Was Santillan aware of these other houses of death?

Lalo: Yes.

Me: And you made ICE aware of other houses?

Lalo: I report all these situations to ICE, but they don't' say nothing really. ... They don't really do nothing. It not happen on U.S. soil, so nothing we can do, so they just listen to it [my information on other houses where murders happened] but not show no interest in that.

Me: But they knew about the other houses as well as the original House of Death on Parsionaros; the 12 buried there, and some killed there. Was ICE monitoring your calls, and were they aware of the murders ahead of time?

Lalo: Well, it work like this. Santillan used to call me and say, "Hey, send your guys to open the house." [ICE was monitoring both of their phones.] Normally I wasn't there, not even in the city [of Juarez], so I just call Alex and he send someone to open the house. And sometimes I find later what happen, and sometimes they bring body already dead. And yes, sometimes they bring the people alive and they killed them there. We knew [including ICE], like I said, some hours before [the murders were carried out].

The jailhouse interview of the informant aired on the Expert Witness Radio show was interrupted numerous times by a recorded voice issuing the following warning: "All phone calls are subject to monitoring and recording. You have one minute remaining."

Each time the phone call would be automatically cut off. Lalo would then call me back, and the interview would continue, with each new call again starting with a recorded warning: "You have 15 minutes available for this call." And, so, the interview continues – later hitting the airwaves in early July 2009 in the Big Apple:

... My name is Guillermo Eduardo Ramirez Peyro, and I am calling from Sherburne County Jail in Elk River, Minnesota.

I'm absolutely going to be killed by the Juarez Cartel or the Mexican government, which is basically the same thing. In the last years, I have been working over there [Juarez and Mexico] with ICE, and we infiltrated the cartel just to find that the Mexican government at all levels, especially the law enforcement agencies, they are corrupt and being paid by the cartel. And actually, they are the cartel. So, I'm very sure they are going to kill me.

Let me tell you, I start working for ICE in the summer of 2000. In the beginning of 2001, we found a way to infiltrate the Juarez Cartel. Immediately I let ICE know it was a very dangerous organization, that the person who I can start working on [as a target, Santillan], he just let me know how many people he already killed since he working there for the cartel for about a year. I was saying this because I was worried they [ICE] weren't very professional in their covering [protection] of me in the prior cases we were working. That's when I start to do these assignments. It was January 2001, I ask them [U.S. law enforcement and prosecutors, via his handlers], and they said, "Yes, go ahead, and infiltrate the Juarez Cartel."

...The House of Death, everything starts there with the cartel. It was in 2003, and the first thing we start to do over there is I have to go over there with two state police to wait for Santillan and Alex Garcia. They bring an individual named Fernando Reyes. They bring him there so the state police can kill him and bury him there in the yard. Because Santillan wants to steal from Fernando 1,000 pounds of marijuana he already received from him. So, that was how the House started as a place for torture, or just to receive bodies of people who came already dead, just to be buried in the backyard of that house.

I came that day because we have to do that operation, so I start [secretly tape] recording from the beginning, so everything was very clear [as to what happened, for ICE]. First, Alex Garcia explained the plan, and Santillan gave me orders repeating orders Alex gave me. This was about 9 or 10 in the morning. So, I went with the state cops. I didn't want to be over there in the House because I was afraid that I was the one about to get killed because of my work with ICE. We had just busted several different drug loads from the cartel, so I thought they were suspicious of me.

What I did is I put the state police people inside the house, and then I used excuses for me to go out and bring back lime and duct tape, or whatever. I was thinking at some point Alex [Garcia] and Santillan will arrive with this guy Fernando Reyes. Then, they brought him [Reyes] inside the house, and Santillan left, but told Fernando to give me some phone numbers in New York [presumably the U.S. buyers Reyes was dealing with for the marijuana delivery]. So, I was writing the number when these guys with the [Mexican] state police [up to then in hiding in a separate room in the House of Death] jumped Fernando and they controlled him.

At the end, they killed him by asphyxia [suffocating him with duct tape and a plastic bag]. And then Alex [Garcia] said the boss said I should go on break when they are done [murdering Reyes]. So, I left to meet Santillan, who was just around the corner in a little store, and we came back [to the House of Death], so then Santillan [formally] introduced me to the state police officers [who had just murdered Reyes, with the informant's help], and made us exchange numbers, and then everything came back to normality.

... They [his ICE handlers] played the recording [of the Reyes murder] and placed me in another office. Then they brought in an officer from the Sheriff's office from El Paso and another agent from ICE, but one who wasn't in our [case investigation] group, and they work with me on what happen [with the Reyes murder], and we elaborated on what happened and everything. I also know they let everybody know in the ICE office all the way up to the SAC [special agent in charge]. He actually called the Mexican government trying to get this to Mexico City. The answer from the Mexican government [or so his ICE handlers told him] was that they were very busy because they [cartels] just killed 11 [Mexican] federal agents in Nuevo Laredo [just across the border from Laredo, Texas, and about 600 miles southeast of El Paso], so they [the Mexican government] don't really care about one more murder in Ciudad Juarez.

Later in the interview:

...They [Santillan's assassins] just went to that [DEA agent's] house [in Juarez] to see what they can see over there [after being told by a House of Death torture victim that the home was being used as a drug stash-site by a corrupt U.S. customs inspector]. And they saw [DEA agent] Homer Glen come out of the house with his kids [and wife].

[The agent had left work and returned home after his wife called him in a panic because Santillan's men were banging on the door to their home in Juarez.]

And so, they [followed and] stopped them [on the street, the DEA agent and his family]. But at that time, the state police [on Santillan's payroll] did not know that Homer Glen [McBrayer] was a DEA agent. And [Santillan and the Mexican cops working for him] didn't know. The state police thought that they were stopping cartel people.

[And the cops on Santillan's team murdered cartel people frequently.]

... What happened is that Luis Padilla [a legal U.S. resident living in the El Paso area] was a DEA informant. So, I think when he saw all the force used against Omar [Cepeda Sáenz] to get free from these guys [the Mexican cops at the House of Death], and nothing works for them, he [Padilla] just gave this information [the location of the DEA agent's home in Juarez].

I don't know [if it was] with hope of getting deal with people of the cartel, or maybe [Padilla thought] if they go there [DEA agent McBrayer's home] they will find trouble or resistance that would help him get free. I can't really say why, but we know Padilla is the one who provided that address, and they [Santillan's men] went to investigate.

But like I said, nobody knew anything at that time [when] Santillan called and asked me for the [real] names of Homer Glen McBrayer and Rene Ramirez.

Ramirez, like McBrayer, was a DEA agent stationed in Juarez, but Ramirez was a fake name. He arrived at the scene, a street in Juarez, on January 14, 2004, to find McBrayer's car surrounded by three vehicles, one a Mexican cop car. The traffic stop was orchestrated by Santillan's crew using the pretense of a window-tint violation. McBrayer, wisely fearing for his own and his family's lives, called for backup.

The whole tragic series of events started the morning of January 14, 2004, when Santillan's men kidnapped Omar Cepeda Sáenz, along with alleged DEA informant Luis Padilla and a third individual, Juan Carlos Pérez Gómez. All three were brought to the House of Death and meticulously tortured and then murdered.

The informant interview continues:

... I tried to contact Raul Bencomo, and he did not answer the phone, so I called Curtis Compton [an ICE supervisor] and ask him for the [real] names [of the two DEA agents stopped by Santillan's men]. He said he recognized them, and he put a Spanish-speaking agent on it, who called me back and said, "What is going on is that these guys [McBrayer and Rene Ramirez] are from DEA's office in Juarez."

And I said, "You know what, someone [allegedly Padilla] told Santillan that this is a safehouse [McBrayer's residence] owned by a corrupt [U.S customs] inspector, and that they have drugs there, and Santillan is going to shake down that house, so you better let them know they better run from there.

At this time, Santillan believed Lalo had contacts in U.S. law enforcement who were corrupt and could be used to get information, which is why Santillan called Lalo that day, asking him to reach out to those contacts to get the true identities of federal agents McBrayer and

Ramirez — who had only identified themselves at the staged traffic stop as U.S. diplomatic employees.

In a way, Santillan was correct about the informant's allegedly corrupt law enforcement contacts. What he didn't realize at that point, however, was that Ramirez Peyro was on ICE's payroll as well. More from the 2009 interview with the informant:

> ... Then Bencomo called me back and said come to the Homeland Security building [in El Paso] right now. And when I arrive there, the ASAC [Associate Special Agent in Charge for ICE in El Paso], who never talked to me, came and received me and gave me her hand and said, "We really appreciate what you did. You saved these guys' [the DEA agents'] lives."
>
> And I said, "I just passing information on what going on."
>
> We kept in contact with Santillan. We never told him they were DEA agents. We just delayed the response [in providing information on the agent's true identities]. And at some time that night, ICE decide that the next day they had to [finally] arrest Santillan, so I had to bring him onto U.S. soil. That's basically what happen that day.
>
> ... Well, I think the number of murders that actually happen there at [the House of Death] was one, two, three ... so six of them.

Later in the interview:

> ... I was supposed be paid by the case. Once they closed a case, it took several months, a long time, and that was in the beginning. When we got the cigarette case [against Jorge Abraham] and then the Santillan case, because they were very, very long cases — and we were done with cigarette case but can't make arrest because it affects the Santillan cartel case — so ICE start helping me with small payments, like $4,000 every now and then. But they [also said] we going to pay you [for those big cases].
>
> They even owe me on other different cases we did in other places. So, they still owe me that money. They never pay me for the cigarette case, not for the Santillan case, or the other cases, like the cocaine cases we did in McAllen for almost 500 kilos of cocaine, in Los Angeles for 150 kilos of cocaine. They never paid for that. ...

Legal pleadings in Lalo's immigration case indicate that the U.S. law enforcement agencies he did work for or provided information to included ICE, DEA, FBI and ATF. He was paid $224,650 for his informant services, and Lalo claims "that he is still owed about $400,000 for his work," a transcript of an August 2005 immigration court oral decision states. The interview continues:

> ... I [am talking with you because I] just want to get the chance to answer your questions, so you have a first-hand knowledge of what happened. I am willing to take a polygraph. In the beginning, you [in my initial reporting on the House of Death] gave some information that was very tainted information.
>
> You said that it was from anonymous [law enforcement sources]. I want to make clear whatever helps you, things you want help with from me, I am willing to say the truth and not feel I have something to hide. All the work I did for [U.S.] law enforcement agencies, it so ridiculous for ICE to say they don't know something [I told them] or I was mishandled by Bencomo, because the El Paso ICE office knows me, and worked for four years with me, so in that time they knew who I was, and my information was trustful.

The DEA timeline documented the murders at the House of Death but does not provide a list of all the victims unearthed at the "narcofosa" on Parsionaros Street in Juarez. However, according to a February 2004 press report in El Siglo de Durango, the daily newspaper in Durango, Mexico, the victims entombed at the House of Death were as follows, translated from Spanish to English:

> Body number 12 recently discovered inside a narco-grave in Ciudad Juarez corresponds to that of a 46-year-old lawyer Fernando Reyes Aguado; ... Other victims identified include 28-year-old Juan Carlos Perez Gomez; Luis Enrique Padilla Cardona, 27 [a U.S. resident]; and Omar Cepeda Saenz, who disappeared on January 14
>
> In addition, identified were Nestor Edmundo Padilla Garcia, 28, and Jesus Cabral Urias, 27, who were last seen on November 30, 2003, when they left Padilla's house aboard a vehicle.

Ramiro Ortiz Acosta and Óscar Epigmeneo Rodriguez Arzola were also identified. Currently in the morgue of the Forensic Medical Service, there are four bodies that are not identified.

In his statement to Mexican authorities in January 2004, Lalo adds one victim's name to the tally of the unidentified dead. That victim is Cesar Rubio, who was shot and killed "when leaving his house in a Mustang with his daughter." The superseding indictment issued by the U.S. Attorney's Office against Santillan makes clear Rubio was buried at the House of Death on Parsioneros Street, which would account for one of the four unidentified victims.

Of course, there was the 13th body allegedly buried in the backyard of the house and never found — that of U.S. citizen David Castro. The informant interview from 2009 continues:

> ...I grew up in Mexico. I went to school all way to the first year of law school at the university in Mexico, in Durango [where Ramirez Peyro was born]. I then went to the federal police academy and worked there [as a federal highway cop] for about a year. The academy lasts a year-and-half, and then six months of practice on the road, and after that I worked [as a cop] for about a year. Then I went to the academy for Mexican Customs [officers], but they didn't hire me. Then I tried again to start at the police academy [for another position], but I didn't finish. I did like six months and went to work [in the private sector, for a time with a relative's construction company], and later is when I went to Juarez.
>
> In Juarez, I was buying cars and sending them to the center of Mexico to be sold. That's when I started getting a closer relationship with people working in the drug trade [in the Juarez Cartel, after hooking up with Santillan], and started helping them. I didn't really like it, or trust them, and saw they are not very straight. That's when in 2000 I start working for ICE.
>
> ... April 7, 1971, is my birthday. I met my wife in the 1990s, and my first kid was born in 1992 in Durango. My second kid was born there in 1995. They grew up over there. Because of my work, I started getting in a bad relationship with the mother of my kids, and we are not anymore married. We still love the kids and try to be in a friendly

relationship for them, and I support and help her with the payments for the schooling of the kids and their house.

We split up in 1998. No, not at all — she had no idea [what I did, until after Santillan was arrested] and she never asked me things. We were just in a friendly relationship, just for the kids, so I just sent money and used to spend Christmas time with them, and sometimes vacations and whenever I get a chance to see the kids.

In January 2004, I called her [his wife] and told her to get in the car and drive to Laredo [the border crossing], and when you arrive over there, I will tell you what to do. They were met over there by an ICE special agent, and [the agent] crossed them [into the U.S.] and brought them to San Antonio, Texas. They spent three or four days over there by themselves, and that's when ICE let me go over there [to San Antonio], and that's when I explained to my wife [what's going on].

She didn't take it well. She got pissed. And she is still angry with me. She got the worse part of the deal, especially when they put me in jail [after the Whataburger murder]. They [ICE] said they would support them [my family], and they did, but just for about a year. Then, at some point, they told her you need to find a job, and we will give you no more money. They said we are going to give you a permanent residency [status] and you will be OK, but that doesn't happen either. At this time, they are just kind of here illegally, but nobody deports them because they know they are at risk over there in Mexico, but they don't have papers to be here legally.

... We have had some problems recently with the kids. It's very hard for them. This is the part that really pisses me off. It's not fair what [ICE] is doing to me, but less fair and completely wrong what they doing to them. There is no way they can blame them for anything. Right now, she is working but can't even receive credit on her taxes for the kids because they don't have social security numbers, so she can't put them on taxes. It is very unfair to them.

They [the kids] just take it. In the beginning, they were happy to see me and come live [near] me again, but when they put me there [in San Antonio] they understood, because they saw all the agents. The agents told them they are not allowed to be on the internet or for their information to be public. So, they understand the situation. And we were under protection. But now that their mother is working, the only chance they have to see her is few hours daily, and the rest of the time they are by themselves, and now they are teenagers, so that is coming up in their behavior.

The last time I saw my kids, that was in 2004 [five years earlier, at the time of the interview]. They [his children] used to be very good. The biggest one used to be on the football team, and naturally he had a permanent place on the team. The other one was member of national junior honor society, so she was doing very good in school. They both were doing good, but this summer something happened, and they went nuts. My son started getting in fights, but like I said, ICE never answers the phone, and the agent in charge of them never answers the phone [when I call, now from jail].

I had to move my kids out of state [after Texas to New Mexico, and later to California, where they were living with their mother as of 2009] to get away from that kind of thing. All that put lot pressure on me, to be here, sitting [in solitary confinement in Minnesota awaiting a federal appeals court's verdict on ICE's efforts to deport him to Mexico] and getting bad news and more bad news. My parents [live and work] in Mexico. But my three brothers are American citizens. They were born in California. The mother of my kids has lot of family over in California, so I asked my family to help us.

Lalo expressed no faith in the Mexican government, indicating that organized crime is rampant in the nation and has corrupted the government at the local, state and federal levels. That narco-corruption has spread to the point where enforcement of drug laws is selective and based largely on which cartel a particular government official has aligned with because of threats of harm to them or their families, lucrative bribes and payoffs — or both in many cases.

So, government officials and law enforcers who are part of, loyal to or otherwise under the thumb of the Juarez Cartel organized crime syndicate will do what is needed to intimidate, control or eliminate competition, or they and their families will be eliminated by the Juarez Cartel. Contracts in the war for drugs are inked in blood and enforced with violence and death.

More from the 2009 informant interview:

... It would have been senseless to alert the Mexican authorities [about the House of Death murders as they were occurring, or afterward], because they already know about the murders. Actually, they performed the murders. They are the ones who do the killing, and to support this is the case of these two people who were killed there [at the House of Death] because they reported on a [cartel drug] stash house to AFI [the Mexican federal police] and the AFI said, "All right, let us get your information, where you live," and the AFI just call the cartel and told them [about the individuals reporting the crime]. This is usually what happens in Mexico.

[AFI was dissolved in 2012 because of corruption and replaced by the Federal Ministerial Police, or PFM.]

So, the cartel sent the state police, and they picked them up [the duo reporting the drug stash house] and brought them to House [of Death], and they killed them there. That is the way it works in Mexico. So, ICE can't really do anything, because if they call and report on the murders [at the House of Death], what the Mexican police are going to do is they are going to kill everyone who knows about that house. because they know there is a leak to the U.S. government.

But these people [the House of Death victims] were killed because of their relationship with the cartel. At some point, they did something [to cross the Juarez Cartel]. The cartel doesn't need Santillan to go and kill these people. They send the state police. The only reason these people got killed in that House [of Death] is because Santillan was desperately trying to offer some kind of useful work to the cartel. Because on the U.S. side, we were busting everything. All the shipments Santillan was working, we [ICE] were busting.

At some point, he [Santillan] told the No. 1 [for the cartel control group in Juarez], "We can do nothing for you in the U.S." That was another thing. I was desperate to close the [Santillan] case because, at some point, someone was going to think, "Well, who is the only one who has been involved with all of this?" And they [the cartel] were going to say, "I am the one who is busting the shipments."

I was very worried that if the Santillan case didn't stop, and we just kept producing arrests and producing arrests, that eventually everything points at me. But honestly, none of these guys were killed because of the work of Santillan, or my work with ICE. They were killed for other different situations and their own relationship with the cartel.

I agree they [ICE] could have arrested Santillan sooner. In March [2003] we did that cocaine bust [implicating him] or in August [of the same year], when we did that Fernandez Reyes killing. But anyway, Santillan was arrested in 2004, and how many people is the cartel still killing? They are still killing people because that's the nature of the business.

This side of border, [in the U.S.] I agree completely, they [U.S. law enforcers] can do something [about murder]. But on the Mexican side, they can do nothing. First, they have no authority over there [in Mexico] and, second, the ones that have authority [Mexican law enforcers] are the ones who are doing the killing.

That is what the American government at a high level is failing to realize, and that's why this war on drugs is such a travesty.

* * *

A series of follow-up interviews were conducted with Ramirez Peyro in June and early July 2014, after he had successfully gained deferral-from-deportation status under the United Nations Convention Against Torture. The excerpts below are from those follow-up telephone interviews with Lalo, which I also recorded. At this time, he was in jail in Missouri on a separate legal matter.

As mentioned previously, in the case of both the 2009 and 2014 interviews, it was not possible to get the permissions necessary from the multiple players involved to conduct in-person interviews with Lalo at the jailhouses. Following are excerpts from the 2014 telephone interviews with the informant.

... My father and mother, they are both civil engineers. Since I was in middle school, we [two brothers and two sisters, three of them now U.S. citizens) were more like middle upper-class, and we were kind of spoiled, and our cousins. We were like the first generation of kids, or grandkids, from two big professional families, so they can spoil us a little bit. I was attracted since I was in school to become a federal highway police. I had to finish high school for that. But when I finished my high school, there was no current class at that time for the police academy, so I started law school in Durango.

... The police academy was very hard. The problem is my family, no one had ever been in that kind of environment. And with no one there, they just want to take advantage of you and, at some point, I got in trouble with a commander [of the federal highway police], and he got me fired. After that, I went back to my cousin [and his family's construction company]. By this time, my uncle had died, and he left a big construction company for them [his children]. My cousin said, "Hey, come work with us." It was a prestigious construction corporation, one of the best in Latin America. The company doesn't exist anymore. We build bridges, we build housing developments, we build roads and so on.

That's when I started getting approached [by people associated with organized crime]. What happens is some people, some mayors and politicians, they say, "I have this problem, can you help me collect this money, or I have some people giving me trouble, can you help me in checking on them a little bit." And that's how I got into this business. Now you have to keep in mind that in Mexico, the best way to become comfortable [wealthy] for politicians is to become involved in the drug trade. So, they used me and saw I was serious and dependable and not lying like most of the people. That is when I started getting into that kind of [criminal] career, but I was never in the cartel at the beginning, or in a big thing. It was just small things.

... In May 2010, when I was released [from jail after finally prevailing in his deportation case], I could not work because I needed to wait for the ICE to issue my employment authorization, which didn't come until more or less somewhere in October 2010. Then I started working at Target. I work there for 14 months, in [Buffalo] New York. That was just something to start working to learn a little more of the [English] language and then start go to school in order to get my CDL [commercial driver's license]. Once I got that, I started working for Werner Enterprises [a trucking company, where Ramirez Peyro says he drove tractor-trailer rigs across the country and later served as a driving instructor until 2013].

Yes, I did everything under my real name. This is the thing. I'm not in hiding. Everywhere I went I used my real name. In the [job] interview, I told the truth in how I got here, to my bosses and to the human resources personnel that was interviewing me, and I explained the truth and who I was and how I was here and why — because if I want to start a life, I cannot start with lies. I was very honest at the beginning. So, if someone had an issue with that, they better tell me right now, in the beginning. Everywhere I go, and everything I am doing, I say who I am and what my past is, and I take it from there.

No [I'm not living in fear of the "cartel" killing me.] Like I said, I don't care. I think that's up to God. What's going to happen is going to happen. What God wants. I am not in hiding. I was trying to do a review of my life. When I came out [of jail after half a dozen years behind bars fighting the government's efforts to deport him], I was trying to get close to my family. They rejected me.

Later in the interview:

... When I start working with ICE, it was an answer to a prayer. I was kind of lost, desperate. I needed some meaning in my life. I was completely lost. That's when I read about the CIA hiring people in this newspaper. So, I kept praying and praying, and I had a feeling that I had to go ask about it [the CIA hiring] and that's how things started.

[Instead of the CIA, however, when Lalo crossed the international bridge into El Paso to find "meaning" in his life, he was referred to ICE agent Raul Bencomo and a walk-on part as a U.S. informant.]

... I don't know if you are aware, but Durango [a state in north-central Mexico]; Chihuahua [a state on the border]; and Sinaloa [a state on Mexico's west coast] are the golden triangle for drug dealers. The drug route is very narrow. Whatever arrives in Durango goes to Juarez.

... I was never in just one business. I liked to keep myself busy. I worked for the cartel, I worked for U.S. Customs [later rebranded ICE] and I used to have my own business also, a used-car lot [in El Paso]. I was working all the time, even in El Paso. In addition to a used-car lot, I also opened a cell-phone store and a furniture store. So that's what I used to do.

... With cartel, you cannot play with them. First, just to be a member of the cartel, you are targeted [by many enemies]. So, I needed to carry weapons. They said carry and use a gun, because if they catch you alive, it be worse than if you die in a shoot-out. I also know of informants who went and did their jobs, but ICE is very lousy at surveillance, and these guys got killed. But I was the only one to stay alive. My first job [for the Juarez Cartel] they put a gun to my head. So, through all of it, I survived. I am convinced, even if the work was hard, I was doing good. I also see the hand of God at work.

Jorge Abraham [the convicted cigarette smuggler] ask me to kill two people. One of them was a guy I used to work with, and he had sex with his [Abraham's] ex-wife. The other was from New York, and he stole from him. He [Abraham] asked me twice to kill these people. I just played along but did not do anything. I was able to fool him and other mindless guys. But the cartel or Santillan, I had to go all the way and do what they told me to do. Thankfully, Santillan never asked me to kill anyone. I was present when they killed people on two occasions, but he [Santillan] never asked me to kill because, he said, the ones who do the killing [the Mexican cops], know how to divert [police] investigations that come after us.

...I am pretty sure the situation with the cartels in Mexico today is the same [as when I was working for ICE] — even after the arrest [in 2014] of Chapo [Guzman, head of the Sinaloa Cartel]. It's well known the way it is over there. In order to get power [in the narco-trafficking world], you need to have law enforcement and the military on your side. That's the only way. That way, they make their money, too. So, they are going to be corrupted [by the cartels], one way or another [through bribes or the threat of a bullet]. Now, they [law enforcement and the military] are not necessarily going to back the same cartel, or the same criminal organizations. That also is part of the situation. Everyone needs to make money.

But things are now set against me, that is for sure. I am sure all of them [cartel leaders] are going to agree that I need to be killed. Because they need to set the example that no one should help the U.S. government.

Arresting Chapo [Guzman] does not make a difference. It's what I did to everyone there. Working for the U.S. government is like betraying all of the people there

Part III

Career Consequences
Dispatch 24
December 6, 2006

Giovanni Gaudioso served as the special agent in charge of U.S. Immigration and Customs Enforcement in El Paso during the murder spree carried out in Ciudad Juarez with the help of the ICE informant Lalo.

Recall that Gaudioso (along with U.S. Attorney Johnny Sutton in San Antonio) was the recipient of the now-public letter from Sandalio Gonzalez, who was heading up DEA's field office in El Paso when the House of Death murders took place between August 2003 and mid-January 2004.

Gonzalez' February 24, 2004, letter to Gaudioso concerning the ICE El Paso commander's role in the House of Death begins as follows:

> Since our meeting on January 25, 2004, and our telephone conversation on February 14, 2004, I've had an opportunity to digest what you've said as well as to conduct a careful review of the material in this case.
>
> I am now writing to express to you my frustration and outrage at the mishandling of the Heriberto Santillan Tabares investigation that has resulted in unnecessary loss of human life in the Republic of Mexico and endangered the lives of Special Agents of the Drug Enforcement Administration (DEA) and their immediate families assigned to the DEA Office in Ciudad Juarez, Chihuahua, Mexico.
>
> There is no excuse for the events that culminated during the evening of January 14, 2004, and absent a complete and logical explanation of these events, which led to the emergency evacuation of our personnel

and their families in Ciudad Juarez, I have no choice but to hold you responsible for this unfortunate situation.

Well, apparently, the brass at ICE and its parent agency, the Department of Homeland Security, had their own concerns about the House of Death murders and the role Gaudioso might have played in the "unnecessary loss of life." In the immediate aftermath of the Juarez carnage, **Gaudioso was transferred to Washington, D.C.** The East Coast assignment was not a punishment for what DEA commander Gonzalez described as a "mishandling" of a major criminal investigation, however. Instead, the transfer was to buy some time until the House of Death matter cooled down, DHS sources told me at the time. Among the fears was that ICE's role (and the DOJ's) in "mishandling" the House of Death atrocity would gain mainstream media traction. It didn't.

That may seem like a cynical read of the situation to some but, if so, then how can we account for the fact that Gaudioso was subsequently transferred back to Texas to take on another high-ranking position in an ICE field office? The debacle of the House of Death mass murder certainly couldn't have been viewed as a career-enhancing leadership performance for him within ICE. Or was it?

An **internal staff list** dated October 26, 2006, from the ICE office in Houston leaked to me at the time — in late 2006 — shows Gaudioso was then the No. 2 man (deputy special agent in charge) for ICE in Houston — a much bigger and more prestigious law enforcement post than overseeing the El Paso office on the edge of the empire.

DHS sources explained to me then, that yes, technically, going from the rank of special agent in charge to deputy special agent in charge is a demotion, of sorts. Those sources added, however, that Gaudioso — also known as GG — was allowed to keep his Senior Executive Service (SES) pay grade. That fact, along with the cost-of-living increase he received for his move to Houston, the DHS sources explained, means that he actually received a salary bump for his trouble. A **National Public Radio (NPR) report published** in early 2010 **reported that**

Gaudioso had retired by that point but was still serving as a consultant to ICE in Houston.

"GG allegedly was downgraded from SAC to DSAC as punishment with regard to the HOD [House of Death]," one DHS source said, again asking for anonymity. "But if you do the math, he actually received an approximate 10% salary increase with his 'punishment.'"

Now, how many other jobs out there offer those kind of perks?

Based on how the wheels of bureaucracy turn within DHS and ICE, it is not really surprising that an ICE official like Gaudioso, whose past management style allegedly led to the "unnecessary loss of human life," would be put back in the field in a leadership role.

In addition, Curtis Compton, an ICE supervisor who played a key role in the House of Death case, remained on the job as well in the wake of the murders. He later served temporarily as the Acting Assistant Special Agent in Charge in ICE's El Paso field office. Compton was still on the job in El Paso as of 2010, according to the NPR report. The same NPR report indicated that Todd Johnson, another ICE supervisor involved with the House of Death case, as of 2010 also was still with ICE — as a group supervisor in its Dallas office.

Associate Special Agent in Charge Patty Kramer, second in command for ICE El Paso, retired in the wake of the House of Death atrocity, as mentioned previously. That wasn't the fate of Juanita Fielden, the federal prosecutor in El Paso who oversaw the House of Death case. As of 2021, she was still working as a federal prosecutor in another part of state — the U.S. Attorney's Office for the Northern District of Texas, which is headquartered in Dallas. A more recent State Bar of Texas entry lists her as "retired."

* * *

If we are to believe the U.S. government, then justice was served in the House of Death homicides in February 2009, when U.S. Immigration and Customs Enforcement special agent Raul Bencomo was fired from his job.

"The agency established that the appellant [Bencomo] made false statements," legal pleadings related to Bencomo's case state. "... On or about March 31, 2004, you swore in a written interview that on November 25, 2003, you did not conduct a debriefing with confidential informant SA-913-EP [Guillermo Eduardo "Lalo" Ramirez Peyro] because your work group was preoccupied conducting a control delivery of marijuana [a monitored sting operation]. This statement was knowingly false and made with the intention to mislead the agency."

Just because Lady Justice is blind, it doesn't mean she's stupid, however.

Bencomo was the ICE agent who cultivated and directly oversaw, or handled, the informant Lalo. Ironically, Bencomo's official firing date, February 9, 2009, fell within the same week of the month that Mexican law enforcers five years earlier had identified on February 6, 2004, the last of a dozen corpses dug up in the backyard of the House of Death at 3633 Parsioneros Street in Juarez, Mexico.

Bencomo was fired by ICE management in large measure for his alleged failures in promptly reporting the informant Lalo's acts of homicide up the chain of command. Prior to his official termination, Bencomo had been on ICE's payroll (the taxpayers' dime) but off the job since 2004 as a result of being placed on "administrative" leave for reasons still not publicly acknowledged by the agency. His dismissal in early February 2009, some five years after being benched by ICE, appears to have been carried out by agency brass to clean up one of the few remaining loose ends in the House of Death whitewash — essentially to put lipstick on a pig in hopes of staying off a new U.S. president's radar. Barack Obama was sworn into office on January 20, 2009, only a few weeks prior to ICE agent Bencomo's official ouster.

The ICE narrative is clear. The script in this case: a lone Latino federal agent, Bencomo, is to blame for the bloody deeds of a U.S. government informant. ICE management in El Paso is not responsible, nor is ICE headquarters in Washington, D.C., or the U.S. Attorney's Office in San Antonio, or officials with the Department of Justice in

Washington — all of whom were made aware of the informant's role in the first House of Death murder in August 2003 and still chose to authorize his continued use. And that's despite, as of that date, having enough evidence in hand to indict the captain of the murder machine, Heriberto Santillan Tabares. That decision to keep Lalo in the field resulted in at least 11 more victims paying a permanent visit to the House of Death.

No, the buck did not stop with the important and powerful people in the chain of command, most of them street-smart law enforcers and prosecutors. Under oath, they have claimed that they could not have anticipated that ICE informant Lalo would participate in future murders after he was given a pass on the initial House of Death murder. ICE supervisors and agents in charge and U.S. prosecutors who worked the Santillan case could not foresee the future — even if the informant, as he claims he did, told them of many past cartel murders in sordid detail, so they would understand the nature of the devil they were courting, that Santillan and the Mexican state cops on his payroll were ruthless killers who would certainly murder again. The House of Death was not unique in their world.

Rather, it was all the fault of Bencomo, a lone agent in the field and Lalo's primary contact on the front lines of the farce called the drug war. And it was Bencomo's fault because he supposedly failed to keep the bosses at ICE in the loop about the informant's participation in additional murders carried out after that first one in August 2003 was excused by those same entrenched bureaucrats — all for the sake of keeping in motion criminal cases that promised to bolster agency budgets, official careers and political fortunes.

Bencomo challenged ICE's decision to separate him from his job by filing an appeal with the U.S. Merit Systems Protection Board (MSPB), a quasi-judicial body charged with reviewing employment claims brought by federal employees. He lost that appeal in September 2009. Bencomo then petitioned for a review of that decision, according to Bernard Parker, a spokesman for the MSPB.

Bencomo's attorney, Tom Roth, did not respond to a request for comment on his client's case. I did obtain a copy of the MSPB judge's ruling in the Bencomo case through a Freedom of Information Act request, however. And it appears, based on a dissection of that ruling, that ICE was determined to make Bencomo the scapegoat for every wrong turn and decision made by the agency's command structure that enabled an ICE informant's participation in torture and multiple murders at the House of Death in Juarez.

* * *

First, we go back to some pertinent past terrain that was at the heart of Bencomo's termination from ICE. On February 12, 2004, nearly a month after the arrest of Santillan and the unearthing of the House of Death victims, Lalo traveled to the office of the Mexican General Consulate in Dallas, Texas, to provide a statement to a representative of the Mexican Attorney General's Office. As part of that statement, Lalo (then known only by his informant codename, Jesus Contreras) described a double execution in which he played a participatory role:

> Another execution that I remember was on November 23, 2003. The municipal police of Juarez seized 70 kilograms of marijuana belonging to commander Miguel Loya that was going to be transported via the Puente Libre (Free Bridge) in Ciudad Juarez. This seizure caused the deaths of "Paisa" and "El Chapo" because Santillan ordered me to have these drug mules meet him in the little Parsioneros house.

In July 2009, Lalo also described in detail the murders of Paisa and Chapo during a recorded interview I conducted with him as a *Narco News* correspondent that was later aired on Mike Levine's Expert Witness Radio show on WBAI-FM in New York City. After driving Paisa and Chapo to the House of Death at the request of Santillan, Lalo recounted on-air that he remained at the house and threatened the victims with the might of the Juarez Cartel for screwing up. A short time later, they were each shot in the head by Mexican state police commander Miguel Loya Gallegos, while 14 other state cops looked on

— one of whom handed Loya a gun with a silencer to carry out the cold-blooded murders.

The murders of Paisa and Chapo mark the second and third known homicides carried out at the House of Death in which Lalo played a direct role — either by supervising the murder, as in the case of Mexican attorney Fernando Reyes, or by delivering the victims to their assassins, as in the case of Paisa and Chapo. It would then be Lalo, an accomplice in the House of Death murders himself, who would betray the cartel's killers to U.S. law enforcers, ultimately resulting in Santillan's arrest.

As I think about these deaths, and all the other people who died around Lalo, including individuals he claims were U.S. informants — such as Abraham Guzman at the Whataburger restaurant in El Paso and Louis Padilla at the House of Death in Juarez — it seems fair to wonder whether Lalo's arrogance, self-interest, sense of self-preservation and lack of remorse guided his actions and trumped any situational loyalty he might have had at the time to what he deemed a ruthless Juarez Cartel and a hopelessly dysfunctional law enforcement agency, ICE.

In any event, Lalo claims he informed ICE of his role in the Paisa and Chapo murders carried out in November 2003 at the House of Death. Earlier, in August 2003, he also reported the murder of Mexican attorney Reyes to his ICE handlers — and the fact that he had tape-recorded and participated in the slaying. The Santillan case was of such importance to the leadership of the ICE and DOJ bureaucracies that even after being made aware of the informant's participation in murder, high-level ICE and Justice Department officials still approved Ramirez Peyro's continued use in the investigation — with the caveat that he should not participate in any more violent acts, according to Lalo, who claims he also was told to stop using a tape-recorder.

"After going through everything that happened [with the Reyes murder] they [ICE] said, 'If something like this happens again, don't record it,'" Lalo said in an interview.

ICE agent Raul Bencomo offers his take on the events in testimony he provided in the ultimately unsuccessful lawsuit filed against ICE and the U.S government by the families of the House of Death victims. Bencomo reiterates in his sworn affidavit what his fellow ICE agents testified to as well, that to his knowledge "no one at ICE or the United States Department of Justice was aware that the murders would take place prior to their occurrence." That, of course, contradicts what the informant Lalo has said, and arguably common sense — given everyone knew they were dealing with a demonstrably violent Juarez Cartel.

More from the sworn affidavit provided by Bencomo:

> We only learned about murders through interviews of Guillermo Eduardo Ramirez Peyro, a/k/a "Lalo" (hereinafter "Ramirez") after the fact. ... The Santillan [House of Death] investigation started in February 2003. I was Mr. Ramirez' handler at the time. As his handler, I was the primary person responsible for communications with him. I was removed as Mr. Ramirez' handler in later June 2003 and reinstate as his handler in mid-August 2003 [after the murder of Mexican attorney Reyes].
>
> Ramirez informed us that Reyes had been murdered by two State Judicial police officers at a house located at 3633 Parsioneros in Ciudad Juarez. ... The substance of Ramirez' statements on August 5, 2003 [when debriefed by ICE] was reported up the chain of command at the El Paso ICE office and was subsequently communicated to ICE headquarters. I was later reassigned to the source [the informant Ramirez Peyro] and instructed to continue the investigation, continue to use Ramirez as a confidential informant and work on getting Santillan arrested and into the United States. ...

The ICE and DOJ approvals authorizing the continued use of Lalo as an informant are outlined in an affidavit filed in federal court in 2006 by Assistant U.S. Attorney Juanita Fielden, who, at the time, worked for San Antonio-based U.S. Attorney Johnny Sutton.

From Assistant U.S. Attorney Fielden's sworn affidavit:

> On or about August 5, 2003, I was contacted at home by ICE GS [Group Supervisor] Curtis Compton and advised of a murder that had

taken place in Juarez, Chihuahua, Mexico in which Santillan Tabares was involved. The incident had been recorded by the CI [confidential informant Lalo]. I, in turn, contacted my supervisor, Assistant United States Attorney Margaret Leachman. She later told me that she had advised Richard Durbin, chief of the Criminal Division for the Western District of Texas, of the incident. The next morning, I spoke with my OCDETF [Organized Crime Drug Enforcement Task Force] advisor, Greg Surovic, and told him of the incident. It was sometime later that I learned that the individual murdered was identified as Ferando Reyes.

... I am aware that the El Paso ICE agents notified ICE management in Washington, D.C. and Mexico City, Mexico, of the murder which occurred on August 5, 2003, and that ICE management in El Paso and in Washington, D.C. approved the continued use of the CI and the continued investigation of Santillan-Tabares On September 4, 2003, United States District Judge Phillip Martinez, Western District of Texas, signed an order authorizing the continued interception of a cellular telephone (915-892-8888).

[That cell phone was given to Santillan by Lalo so that calls made to and from it could be secretly monitored in real time by ICE.]

The affidavit for the continued wire interception discussed the murder of Fernando Reyes on August 5, 2003. This affidavit was prepared by ICE Special Agent David Ortiz, reviewed and approved by his chain-of-command, reviewed by me and the Office of Enforcement Operations Attorney Nancy Brinkac and her supervisor and approved by Deputy Assistant Attorney General John G. Malcolm.

So, even after the ICE informant Ramirez Peyro helped to carry out a murder for the Santillan organization, DOJ and ICE officials went to bat for him and kept him on the case, even securing approval for a wiretap from a federal judge. It is not clear from Fielden's statement, however, if the judge was made aware of Ramirez Peyro's participation in the murder of Reyes prior to his approval of the wiretap order. We do know that ICE officials informed the Mexican government that the informant had only "witnessed" a murder.

What seems clear is that Lalo's reporting of the murders of Paisa and Chapo, and his role in them — only some three months after he assisted in the murder of Mexican lawyer Reyes — created a problem for ICE and the U.S. Attorney's Office overseeing the Santillan case. That problem is what led, in large part, to the eventual dismissal of Bencomo from his job as an ICE agent.

* * *

In the September 9, 2009, ruling against former ICE agent Bencomo, MSPB Administrative Judge Chizoma Ihekere concluded that the "the penalty for removal is reasonable, under the circumstances." Among those "circumstances" was Bencomo's alleged failure to report "up the chain of command" Lalo's participation in the murders of Paisa and Chapo on November 23, 2003. From Judge Ihekere's ruling, quoting an affidavit submitted by Bencomo:

> In his sworn affidavit dated April 1, 2004, the appellant [Bencomo] states the following:
>
> Yes, the CI [Lalo] called me on November 25, 2003, and told me that Santillan had murdered two more individuals. I asked the source [Lalo] if he had participated and he stated "No." I was the acting GS [group supervisor] at the time. GS [Todd] Johnson was on annual leave at the time.
>
> I then informed GS C. [Curtis] Compton that same day and was told to bring in the source and get a full debrief. The full debriefing was not conducted until December 1, 2003, because members of my group were conducting a controlled delivery [monitored sting operation] of 2,800 pounds of marijuana for the Santillan organization. The debriefing was conducted by SA [ICE special agent David] Ortiz, SA [Luis] Rico and myself. I later discovered that the source [Lalo] drove the two men to the house and inspected the burial of the bodies.

In fact, the initial debriefing of Lalo after the murders of Paisa and Chapo was actually conducted on November 25 (two days after the murders), with a follow-up debriefing conducted on December 1, 2003. Bencomo, according to the judge's ruling, claims he recalls getting a phone call from Lalo informing him of the murders, but that when questioned by ICE internal affairs he did not immediately recall the November 25, 2003, debriefing.

"The appellant [Bencomo] said that he was busier than usual on November 25, 2003, because he was the acting Group Supervisor," the judge writes in the ruling. "They did not have the manpower to conduct surveillance, and he [Bencomo] was getting ready to go on leave. He also stated that on November 25, 2003, his focus was on taking down the drugs, and he notified Compton that two men [Paisa and Chapo] had been killed."

The MSPB judge did not buy Bencomo's explanation of why he did not recall the November 25 debriefing of Lalo, however — even though Bencomo passed a polygraph indicating he was truthful in stating he did not initially remember the debriefing. The judge also took issue with the fact that there was no written report generated from the November 25 debriefing — during which the informant detailed the full extent of his participation in the murders of Chapo and Paisa. In addition, the judge deemed Bencomo "negligent in the performance of his duties" for failing to obtain the full details of the murders and to report them to Compton or other officials in the chain of command.

"[ICE supervisor] Compton testified that the appellant [Bencomo] did not contact him after the [November 25] debriefing to tell him what 913 [code for the informant Lalo] said, though he would have expected him to, given the information 913 provided that day," the judge's ruling states.

That information, communicated by Bencomo to Compton on November 25, 2003, was that two more people had been murdered at the House of Death. More from Judge Ihekere's ruling:

> ... It is undisputed that 913 [the informant Lalo] was debriefed on November 25, 2003, and that during that debriefing [unlike the December 1 debriefing], he gave specific details regarding his involvement in the murders of Chapo and Paisa. It is also undisputed that once 913 told the appellant [Bencomo] and [ICE agent] Rico [on

November 25] of his involvement, that information was neither passed up the chain of command nor memorialized in a report.

[Bencomo] claims that he was not in the room when 913 actually revealed his involvement in the murders and that he expected Rico or [ICE agent] Ortiz to generate the debriefing report. Even if [Bencomo] was on the phone during the [November 25] debriefing about what he admits was a significant event, I do not find it reasonable that he did not ask Rico what the source said when he was not in the room.

[Bencomo] knew that management wanted to be kept informed of 913's involvement in serious crimes, yet [he] failed to gather information and relay the details of the role 913 played in the murders. [Bencomo] was instructed by Compton to get the information and had previously been instructed to report such information.

... By his own testimony, he neither got the information from 913 nor did he ensure that the information was memorialized in a report. Accordingly, I find that preponderant evidence supports the agency's charges that the appellant failed to follow supervisory instructions and was careless/negligent in the performance of his duties, and the charges are sustained.

The judge in this case lays all of ICE's dysfunction at Bencomo's feet. He takes the fall for all of the mismanagement, documenting and reporting lapses related to ICE informant Lalo's participation in two additional murders at the House of Death. Yet Compton, an ICE supervisor, was made aware by Bencomo on November 25, 2003, the date of the initial debriefing of Lalo, that Santillan had murdered two more people. Bencomo reported those murders promptly to his boss, Compton, according to Judge Ihekere's ruling. Yet Compton, as Bencomo's superior, doesn't follow-up with Bencomo for the details on the November 25 debriefing. Instead, Compton blames Bencomo for not following up with him. That seems like avoidance behavior all around.

So, conveniently, other than then "acting" group supervisor Bencomo — while overseeing ICE agent Rico (who was at the November 25 debriefing and had been on the job only six months at that point) — there allegedly is no evidence, or paper trail, indicating that anyone in a supervisory position at ICE or the U.S. Attorney's Office was made aware that a U.S. government informant now had the blood of at least three victims on his hands.

Why Ramirez Peyro was approved at the highest levels of ICE and DOJ to continue going back to the House of Death in the first place after his participation in the initial murder of Mexican attorney Reyes in August 2003 is not addressed by the judge — nor are the befuddling claims by U.S. law enforcers that they could not have anticipated future murders at a House of Death operated by cartel assassins.

Also of interest is that it took an ICE internal affairs investigation to ferret out the notes that evidence Lalo's direct involvement in the slayings of Paisa and Chapo. And those notes never found their way into an official ICE report while the informant Lalo was overseeing the House of Death. Nor was the information communicated up the chain of command by Bencomo — who claims he was out of the room on a phone call when the informant Lalo communicated the details of the murders to rookie ICE agent Rico during the November 25, 2003, debriefing. And then there's ICE agent Ortiz' version of events.

"Ortiz testified that he attended a debriefing of 913 [Lalo] on December 1, 2003, and wrote the report on that debriefing, but did not even learn about the [initial] November 25, 2003, debriefing [in which the informant detailed his involvement in the murders of Paisa and Chapo] until February or March of 2004," the MSPB judge's ruling states. "Ortiz testified that he first learned about the November 25, 2003, debriefing when he began to prepare notes to turn over to OPR [internal affairs] and found Rico's notes from that day.

"Ortiz testified that the details of [Lalo's] actual involvement in the murders were not mentioned during the December 1, 2003, meeting, but Rico's notes indicated that they were discussed during the November 25, 2003, debriefing."

For that whole scenario to make sense, it would mean a greenhorn ICE agent, Rico, or at best a field agent thrust into a temporary supervisory role, Bencomo, had carte blanche control of the Santillan investigation based solely on whether they chose to file paperwork properly after a debriefing that merely confirmed what everyone should have already known by then, that they were operating an ICE informant who was a killer. That simply doesn't pass a smell test, if we consider the major investment of money, personnel and time put into the Santillan case by ICE, DOJ and U.S. prosecutors, as well as the high-stakes nature of the case. Santillan was no mere drug mule, but rather a significant player in the powerful Juarez Cartel criminal organization.

* * *

As evidence of the seriousness of the Santillan case, on February 18, 2004, the U.S. Attorney's Office in San Antonio (then headed by U.S. Attorney Johnny Sutton) announced a superseding indictment against Santillan that added five charges of murder to the original narco-trafficking charges contained in the initial indictment returned against him in December 2003.

"Allegedly, Santillan Tabares intentionally killed or aided, abetted and caused the murders of Fernando Reyes Aguado [the first House of Death victim]; Cesar Rubio (aka El Dooce); Omar Cepeda Saenz; Luis Padilla Cardona [an alleged DEA informant]; and Juan Carlos Peres Gomez," the superseding indictment states. "The bodies of the deceased were among those recovered last month [January 2004] from the backyard of a residence in Ciudad Juarez [the House of Death]."

In a distortion of justice that's hard to comprehend, the mass murder charges added to Santillan's indictment by the U.S. Attorney's Office overseen by Sutton also include the first House of Death victim, Fernando Reyes — whom ICE informant Lalo helped to assassinate. Maybe Sutton's office thought that Lalo's involvement in that first House of Death murder could somehow be kept from a jury by some evidentiary procedure or explained away as an act of necessary "minimal participation" or even technically just "witnessing a murder" and a necessary digression from ideal justice in order to preserve the informant's life at the time and the larger goal of pursuing the multiple criminal cases the informant was key to making possible.

Clearly, if we are to believe Juanita Fielden, the lead prosecutor on the House of Death case, the informant Lalo was sanctioned by the highest levels of the command chains at ICE and DOJ to continue his mission after those officials were made aware of his participation in Reyes' murder. Maybe those higher-up ICE and DOJ officials involved had become jaded by the drug war and believed Reyes was just another Mexican who would have been killed anyway by the cartel. So, it wasn't seen as a game-stopper for future criminal prosecutions and cases using the informant. Juries would buy that, right, if sufficiently frightened by cartel-horror lore? We don't know the answer, unfortunately, because all along the official position of ICE and DOJ on the House of Death has been a consistent "no comment."

If we accept that the informant's participation in the Reyes' murder can somehow be rationalized for a jury, then why not also the role the informant Lalo played in the murders of Paisa and Chapo? Yet their murders are nowhere to be found in the superseding indictment issued against Santillan and announced by Sutton in a chest-thumping press release. That's the case even though ICE agent Bencomo's MSPB ruling makes clear that in addition to him, ICE agents Ortiz and Rico and ICE Group Supervisor Compton also were made aware of the deaths of Paisa and Chapo through conversations as well as the debriefings held on November 25 and December 1, 2003 — well before the superseding indictment was issued in February 2004.

And even if those ICE agents didn't communicate details of the murders to DOJ prosecutors, which seems highly unlikely, then Sutton's office should have been aware of the statement the informant Lalo gave to the Mexican government on February 12, 2004, some six days prior to the announcement of the superseding indictment against Santillan.

"Regarding the aforementioned executions, I also saw El Paisa and Chapo [killed], and I even handed over a photograph of these subjects in which Chapo appears with a woman...," Lalo says in his statement, taken in Dallas, for the Mexican Attorney General's Office.

Lalo's February 12 statement also says, "Santillan ordered me to have these drug mules [Paisa and Chapo] meet him in the little Parsioneros house," — which is evidence that Santillan participated in those murders. In addition, both Paisa and Chapo, according to Ramirez Peyro's statement to the Mexican government, were buried in the backyard of the House of Death on Parsioneros Street.

Again, why weren't Paisa and Chapo included among Santillan's murder victims in the superseding indictment issued by Sutton's office, yet the murder of Reyes is included in the charges? One possible reason is that Sutton's office was comfortable with prosecuting the Reyes murder, because that homicide, and Lalo's participation in it, had been reported up the chain of command at ICE and DOJ and the informant's continued use in the Santillan case cleared by headquarters, so long as he didn't murder again. As crazy as that sounds, it would mean the paperwork on that murder was in order. That clearly was not the case with Lalo's handywork in the murders of Paisa and Chapo.

In any event, excluding the latter two homicides assured that the informant's role in those additional murders would not be exposed to public examination should the superseding indictment with murder charges lead to a trial. Had those two murder victims been added to the Santillan count, ICE and federal prosecutors may well have been forced to explain in open court why they continued to use the informant not only after he had participated in the initial murder of Reyes (sanctioned by leadership after the fact), but also in the subsequent murders of Paisa and Chapo.

* * *

The MSPB ruling against Bencomo sets out certain dates around the murders of Paisa and Chapo that are worth lining up, a bit like bowling pins. According to the ruling and the testimony of various ICE agents — including Bencomo — Paisa and Chapo were murdered at the House of Death on Sunday, November 23, 2003. However, it was not until two days later, on November 25, that Lalo allegedly called his ICE handler, Bencomo, to inform him that Santillan had carried out the murders. And that same day, Tuesday, November 25, according to the MSPB ruling, the informant was brought into the ICE office in El Paso to be debriefed about the murders.

The only problem with that story is that the informant himself claims things didn't go down that way. In the July 2009 interview with *Narco News* aired on Pacifica Radio in New York City, Lalo describes what happened in the wake of Paisa and Chapo's murders.

> Lalo: The next morning [Monday, November 24, 2003, after the murders of Paisa and Chapo] Santillan called me on my phone, and I'm aware ICE has this recording.
>
> And he explained to me, he said, "You know what? We made that decision to have these guys killed so now you can be in charge of the people he [Paisa] was leading. Now you take responsibility of these people and keep working with them." That was his explanation of why they decide to kill them [Paisa and Chapo].
>
> Me: Did you tell ICE about those two people [Paisa and Chapo] getting murdered? Was that reported to ICE?
>
> Lalo: ... Yes, I reported it [Paisa and Chapo's murders], but not immediately. That happened [the two murders] on a Sunday, [November 23, 2003], and I think I called on Monday [November 24] after they [ICE] listened to that call that Santillan made to me [discussing the details of the murders and why the pair were killed]. If I remember what, they just received me in the [ICE] office on Tuesday [November 25, after Santillan's November 24 call]. That's when they made the debriefing because they were busy doing something else.

Assuming Lalo's version of events is accurate, that means ICE officials knew about the murders, and their informant's involvement in them, on November 24, 2003, after monitoring the call between the informant and Santillan — a fact that Bencomo's MSPB ruling does not reflect.

If Lalo is telling the truth, then the recording of that call between him and Santillan would seem to be evidence that the ICE chain of command was well aware of the informant's participation in Paisa and Chapo's murders. So, if it exists, where is that recording, who knew about it and when, and why does the informant's version of events differ from the record in Bencomo's MSPB proceedings?

Retired DEA commander Sandalio Gonzalez, whose career suffered for telling the truth about the House of Death, had this to say about the MSPB ruling against Bencomo and the revelations by the informant: "The [MSPB] record clearly shows that the call [from Lalo about Paisa and Chapo's murders] was reported to [ICE Group Supervisor] Compton. That satisfies the requirement to report it up the chain of command. The rest is just bureaucratic paperwork." Gonzalez continued:

> Assuming what [ICE supervisor] Compton said is true [that he was notified of the murders by Bencomo], the fact is that as a supervisor he's supposed to ask questions [beyond relying solely on Bencomo's report] — particularly when he's told about the two murders while being fully aware of the informant's participation in the first murder [of Reyes]. And if the call [with Santillan] was recorded as Lalo claims, that increases the likelihood that Compton knew about the whole thing [including the informant's role in Paisa and Chapo's murders].
>
> If the call was being monitored and recorded, then there's a strong possibility that several people knew about it. Monitored to me means there was an intercept, court authorized perhaps, with people listening in real time. If so, the USAO [U.S. Attorney's Office] and the court had to be notified. Perhaps there are contract monitors out there who know about this case.

It wouldn't be the first time in the House of Death case that evidence seems to have vanished. The DEA timeline prepared on the House of Death case details events surrounding the near-fatal traffic stop on January 14, 2004, of a DEA agent and his family in Juarez by Santillan's sicarios. The timeline reveals that DEA agents from Juarez investigating that incident were allowed to review "recordings [made on

January 14, 2008] of the 8 a.m., 1 p.m., 6:45 p.m. and 6:57 p.m. conversations" between the informant Ramirez Peyro and Santillan. Other facts of note:

- The DEA timeline states that during the 8 a.m. conversation — which occurred prior to the evening traffic stop of the DEA agent and his family — Santillan requested "that the CS [the informant Lalo] bring the keys and unlock the residence [the House of Death] located at Calle Parsioneros #3633." That 8 a.m. conversation, the DEA timeline reflects, has since vanished, as has the 1 p.m. recorded call.

- "[DEA] personnel initially reviewed the recordings [including the 8 a.m. call]," the DEA timeline states. "Copies of the latter two conversations [at 6:45 p.m. and 6:57 p.m.] were obtained from ICE on Saturday, January 17. ... After repeated requests to obtain copies of the first two [recorded calls, at 8 a.m. and 1 p.m.], ICE eventually related that those recordings did not exist."

- The informant Lalo also revealed in the February 12, 2004, statement he provided to the Mexican government that Santillan had discussed the planned murders with him during phone conversations on January 13 and 14, 2004.

From Lalo's statement: "The last execution I know of was on January 13 of this year [2004]. The engineer Santillan asked me to have the house ready because he was going to have some 'grilled meat.' Later, at 10 [p.m.] in the evening [of January 13], he told me to hold off but to start early in the morning [January 14]. So then at around eight o'clock in the morning he spoke with me and told me to send someone to the house to be waiting, so I sent my buddy Jose Jaime Marquez, who went to open the door of the Parsioneros 3633 house [the House of Death]."

Within hours of that 8 a.m. phone conversation on January 14, 2004, Santillan's men brutally tortured and murdered three men, including Luis Padilla, a U.S. legal resident — and an alleged DEA informant, according to Lalo. Former DEA commander Gonzalez claims Lalo's ICE handlers were likely made aware in advance of the three murders planned and executed at the House of Death on January 14, 2004 — as a result of monitoring Lalo's communications with Santillan.

Former DEA commander Gonzalez alludes to that fact in the February 24, 2004, memo he sent to ICE's top agent in El Paso:

> Your CS [Lalo] knew on January 13, 2004, that Santillan was planning a "carne asada" for the Parsioneros house the following day, and nothing was done about it until Santillan called your CS [Lalo] on the night of the 14th to check the names of our agents. By that time, three more human beings had been tortured and killed.

At a minimum, it is clear from the available evidence that ICE had the informant's phone wired up, and that ICE officials likely were monitoring it in real time, as well as recording his conversations, including the 8 a.m. phone conversation with Santillan on January 14, 2004, which provided advance warning of the triple murder that occurred later that day at the House of Death in Juarez.

It seems beyond coincidence that the actual recording of that 8 a.m. conversation on January 14, 2004, has disappeared, as the DEA timeline reflects, while a similar bad luck appears to have been in play with the monitored phone conversation between Santillan and ICE informant Lalo on November 24, 2003, during which the murders of Paiso and Chapo at the House of Death were discussed, according to the informant.

Attorney Mark Conrad worked for years in a supervisory role in internal affairs at ICE's predecessor agency, the U.S. Customs Service, and after retiring from law enforcement represented ICE agents with employment actions against the agency. Conrad offered the following take, via email, on the Bencomo MSPB ruling and Lalo's recounting of his report to ICE of the murders of Paisa and Chapo:

> It is my understanding that the phone Lalo was using was one provided by Customs (ICE), therefore a government phone and one that probably was cloned so that it could be monitored. Any calls likely were recorded.

Regardless, there is no doubt in my mind that ICE management knew what was going on — on November 24 [2003, the day Santillan called Lalo to discuss the murders of Paisa and Chapo]. As to where the tapes are — they are gone. ...

What does not make sense to me is that if Lalo called on Monday, November 24, and he told them [ICE] about the conversation he had with Santillan that same day, why didn't ICE immediately have him come in. Any agent could have done the debriefing and alerted HQ [ICE headquarters] of this stunning development. This is not something you would delay or sit on unless you are trying to set the stage to cover your ass.

My guess is that ICE knew of the information when Lalo got the call from Santillan [on Monday, November 24, 2003]. Whoever listened would have taken the information to Compton, [Patty] Kramer [then second in charge of ICE El Paso] or [Assistant U.S. Attorney] Juanita [Fielden] immediately. The delay until the next day [November 25] for the debrief only makes sense if you are trying to cover the matter up.

My guess is that whoever got the info first (either through monitoring of the call or Lalo calling in) notified his/her superior or Compton or Kramer and it was discussed with Juanita [Fielden]. Further — if the call between Lalo and Santillan was monitored, and this info came out [the informant's participation in the murders], procedurally it would have had to be informed —immediately — to HQ [ICE headquarters] and the AUSA [Assistant U.S. Attorney] involved in the case. I believe those notifications took place.

* * *

Among the counter-charges that Bencomo raised in his MSPB case are allegations that he was being treated differently, more severely, than other ICE agents who also were made aware of the Paisa and Chapo murders. The judge in the case, however, didn't see things that way:

> ... In his closing argument, the appellant claimed that Compton, Rico, and Ortiz were treated more favorably with regard to the first two charges. I do not find that the appellant was the recipient of disparate treatment. There is no evidence that either Compton, Rico, or Ortiz

provided false statements regarding the November 25, 2003, debriefing or any false statements at all.

A lack of evidence, however, is not proof of veracity. Recall that an ICE internal affairs supervisor, Kenn Thomas, in a sworn legal deposition accused former ICE supervisor Compton — who oversaw Bencomo — of failing to "timely report" information related to the House of Death case and, in a separate matter, of making "false statements" to government investigators. Thomas also alleged that ICE "re-colored," or whitewashed, Compton's disciplinary record, which resulted in him receiving only a slap on the wrist.

The long trail of officially "re-colored" evidence that marks the House of Death is likely to continue concealing the truth so long as our judges, politicians and citizens remain distracted or disinterested — or otherwise numbed by the extent of the drug-war carnage. In such an environment, it is enough for ICE officials to set Bencomo up as the fall guy and simply move on with drug war business as usual — a path that is effective as propaganda but seriously corrupted and dysfunctional in the pursuit of justice.

Santillan is now doing time in a federal pen in Oakdale, Louisiana, after cutting a deal in April 2005 with then-U.S. Attorney Johnny Sutton's prosecution team that resulted in the murder charges against him in the superseding indictment being discarded. Perhaps that plea bargain sans homicide charges became inevitable after DEA commander Gonzalez' House of Death letter exposed the informant's murderous role in the House of Death mass murder. That letter became discoverable evidence for Santillan's defense team. Government records show Santillan, 68 years old in 2022, is slated to be released from incarceration as soon as the summer of 2023.

"I do not know how, but it seems to me that Bencomo was made the scapegoat," adds former U.S. Customs internal affairs supervisor Conrad. "...There are any number of things that do not make sense here, but ICE is hell-bent on keeping this under wraps."

Bencomo ultimately appealed his case to the U.S. Court of Appeals for the Federal Circuit, where he again was thwarted, with the appeals court affirming in February 2011 the MSPB judge's 2009 ruling against him. Bencomo's firing would mark the end of any official inquiry into the U.S. government's culpability for the House of Death bloodshed.

Dispatch 25
May 31, 2007

Rarely do we get a front-row seat in the **theater of power** when the set design is still under construction. But, occasionally, despite the best efforts of the show's producers, some of the stagehands do, quite by mistake, pull back that curtain a bit as they are at work, and the plain truth of the grand theater of illusion is revealed.

In the case of the House of Death mass murder and whitewash, which has been the subject of many critical reviews, the role of the bumbling theater-hands in this latest act happens to be played by two top DEA officials — who were charged with helping to clean up the stage in the wake of the mayhem in Juarez, Mexico.

Michele Leonhart at the time of the House of Death murders was the deputy administrator of DEA. **Mike Furgason served as** the chief of operations at DEA. They reveal in vivid detail the behind-the-scenes mechanizations that led to the House of Death coverup in public court testimony. That testimony shows the U.S. Attorney General himself, as well as a number of other high-level DOJ and DHS officials, were actively involved in the "handling" of the House of Death mass murder case after it imploded in early 2004 — when the threat to DEA agents in Juarez from paid killers working for Juarez Cartel cell leader Heriberto Santillan Tabares became palpable.

With U.S. Attorney General John Ashcroft's departure from DOJ in late 2004, the whitewashing efforts continued. His successor, Alberto Gonzales, **told me** at a press conference in San Antonio in October 2005 that he was familiar with the House of Death case. He also declined to comment on whether the fiasco was still under "investigation." Attorney General Gonzales was silent on the matter even though the internal review undertaken by a joint assessment team from DEA and ICE, resulting in the JAT report, had been completed for more than a year at that point and no known criminal investigation had been launched stemming from the JAT's (still-secret) findings.

Other DOJ officials also have been silent on the House of Death. Mark Corallo, who was the head of DOJ public affairs during Ashcroft's reign at DOJ (promoted from deputy director in September 2003), also told me in 2006 when contacted that he did not recall the House of Death case. This convenient loss of memory was advanced as an excuse by Corallo, despite the existence of court records revealing that his boss at the time, Ashcroft, was personally involved in the handling of the House of Death fiasco. And potential media coverage and public affairs were clearly a concern at the time. In addition, Corallo's name shows up in e-mails exchanged within DOJ that discuss the handling of the House of Death case (including DOJ's strategy to suppress media coverage) and the plan to retaliate against DEA El Paso's Special Agent in Charge Sandalio Gonzalez.

I also contacted another former high-level DOJ official, James Comey Jr., who served as Deputy Attorney General for two years starting in December 2003 under Ashcroft and, for a time, under Ashcroft's successor, Attorney General Alberto Gonzales. Comey grabbed the national spotlight in 2004 while acting temporarily as Attorney General during a brief Ashcroft illness. At that time, he rebuffed efforts by Gonzales, then the White House counsel, to recertify the Bush administration's controversial "War on Terror" warrantless wiretapping program. Comey, too, was a key player in DOJ's handling of the House of Death tragedy. Comey's name also shows up in the same DOJ emails in which Corallo's name appears.

After serving as the second in command of DOJ during the House of Death murders — and long before he was named FBI director by President Barack Obama in 2013 — Comey worked for a time as general counsel and senior vice president for aerospace and defense contractor Lockheed Martin. In 2007, through a Lockheed press spokesman, Comey told me that he did not wish to comment on the House of Death case.

Another key high-level official in the loop on the House of Death murders was the leader of ICE at the time, Michael Garcia, who was appointed to head the agency in 2003 by George W. Bush. The House of Death murders did not slow Garcia's career trajectory, however. In the summer of 2005, the White House named Garcia as the U.S. Attorney for the Southern District of New York. That was only a year and a half after a dozen bodies were unearthed at the House of Death in Juarez, victims sent to their deaths with the help of an ICE informant, Guillermo Eduardo "Lalo" Ramirez Peyro.

In 2008, Garcia joined a global law firm, Kirkland & Ellis LLP, after George W. Bush's second term ended and the Republicans were swept from office with the election of Barack Obama. And in 2016, Garcia was nominated by New York's Democrat governor at the time, Andrew Cuomo, and approved by the state's senate as an associate judge on the state of New York Court of Appeals.

After President Donald Trump unceremoniously fired FBI Director James Comey, Garcia was reportedly among the candidates interviewed for the post, which ultimately was awarded to Christopher Wray.

But you don't have to rely solely on the word of the public officials involved, or my word, to understand the careerist turf-war/revolving-door dynamics that led to the House of Death mass murder and subsequent efforts to erase it from history. The evidence to support the truth of the House of Death tragedy is out there and includes government documents and court pleadings.

Among those documents are transcripts of the 2006 court testimonies of DEA Deputy Administrator Leonhart (who later became the top gun at DEA) and DEA Chief of Operations Furgason. Their testimonies are part of the court record in an employment discrimination case filed by former DEA commander and House of Death whistleblower Sandalio Gonzalez — a case he won via a jury verdict. At the time, no one knew what the future held for Leonhart.

Ultimately, though, it didn't turn out well for her or the agency she was leading. In May 2015, after the House Oversight Committee on a bipartisan basis issued a statement of no confidence in Leonhart, she stepped down from her post as head of DEA. Under Leonhart's leadership, the agency was tarnished by revelations of its agents in Latin America having sex parties with prostitutes — bashes allegedly underwritten by narco-traffickers where DEA agents were provided "money, expensive gifts, and weapons from drug cartel members," a DOJ Office of Inspector General's report found.

Excerpts from Leonhart and Furgason's 2006 testimony made under oath during trial in former DEA commander Gonzalez' civil lawsuit in Miami, are reproduced below, with context provided as needed and denoted in [brackets].

* * *

United States District Court, Southern District of Florida, Miami

Sandalio Gonzalez v. Alberto Gonzales, Attorney General, U.S. Department of Justice — JURY TRIAL: December 4, 2006

For the government: Lawrence Rosen, U.S. Department of Justice

Mr. Rosen — questioning DEA Deputy Administrator Michele Leonhart]:

Q: Good afternoon, Ms. [Michele] Leonhart.

A: Good afternoon.

Q: Tell the jury, please, what position you currently hold within the DEA.

A: I'm the deputy administrator of the Drug Enforcement Administration.

Q: And to obtain that position, did it require the President of the United States to nominate you and the senate to confirm that nomination?

A: Yes, it did.

Q: Would you explain for the jury, please, the confirmation process that you engaged in?

A: After the president [George W. Bush] announced his intent to nominate me, there's a background process. There's interviews, and then the Senate meets to review that and votes on my nomination.

Q: How long have you been with the DEA?

A: It will be 26 years at the end of the month.

Q: ... Okay. Now, did you at some point in time get some information about events in Ciudad Juarez [the House of Death]?

A: Yes.

Q: And please tell the jury what your role became when you attempted to determine what was happening there?

A: Because I'm the deputy administrator, when there are critical incidents or serious matters, I'm briefed very often by the chief of operations. And it was brought to my attention that we had an agent and his family pulled over by a Mexican police officer and some other individuals [on January 14, 2004], and I was also advised that we believed that those people had been to his [the DEA agent's] home earlier.

Q: Okay. Did you begin to learn of other information and events down there as time went forward or went on?

A: Yes, because a car stopped in Mexico of our agents and his family, and this visit to his house, was pretty irregular and concerning, I was kept apprised for the next day or two on other events that started to be uncovered.

Q: And those other events which we haven't gone into in any great detail here, but they were horrible events.

A: Yes.

[Those events involved the torture and slaying of at least a dozen people by Mexican cops and other killers affiliated with the Juarez Cartel. Most of those victims were murdered with some assistance from ICE informant Lalo, whose job was to oversee the House of Death and ensure the bodies were buried in the backyard.]

Q ... Okay. But when you learned of what was going on, did you go to Customs [meaning ICE], your equal in Customs, and bring to their attention what was going on down there?

A: Yes, I did.

Q: And did they deny what was going on?

A: I told them what I had found out. He [the ICE official] said that that's not the story that he had. He didn't seem to express the same concern that we had. I tried to explain that this is, you know, a life-or-death situation. We had a family and an agent at risk. We needed to get to the bottom of this. And we stressed — I stressed that we needed to get together, and we offered to give him a briefing on everything we had learned and urged him to come to our office to meet with me and the chief of operations [Mike Furgason].

Q: And when you say he, you are referring to someone within the Customs Service?

[Again, the government's attorney in the case, Rosen, is referring to ICE. The U.S. Customs Service was dissolved over the course of 2002 and its special agents in early 2003 were blended into the then newly formed ICE. The court testimony took place in December 2006.]

A: It would be my counterpart at the Customs Service or ICE, the number two person for that agency.

Q: Okay. So, were you doing all you could to enlist the involvement and raise the concerns of this other agency ... about this event?

A: Yes, not only at my level, but also at the chief of operations level.

Q: Okay. Now, did there come a time in which the Office of the Attorney General, in fact, the Attorney General of the United States himself [John Ashcroft at the time], wanted to know what was going on with this matter?

A: Yes.

Q: And was there a plan in place with the acknowledged approval of the Attorney General on how to handle the investigation of what events occurred in Ciudad Juarez?

A: Yes. We notified the Attorney General of the United States and the Deputy Attorney General of the United States [then James Comey] of what we had learned and the events and our concerns. We told [them] we had talked to Customs [ICE] and let them know what we had found out. Our administrator [DEA's Karen Tandy] had also contacted the U.S. Attorney's Office [Johnny Sutton in San Antonio], and we thought the best thing we could do is get the agencies together, put an independent review team together to go down and find the facts [what became the JAT team] because the person I was talking to [at ICE] said he had a different set of facts and didn't see it the way that we saw it.

Q: Who was the point person assigned within the DEA to oversee this investigation of the Juarez matter?

A: Mike Furgason, our chief of operations, was in charge of that team.

Q: Okay. And similarly, did Customs [ICE] have a counterpart to Mike Furgason that would oversee the matter for them?

A: Yes, that was John Clark.

Q: Okay. So was the investigation into this matter, was this being handled at the highest levels of our government?

A: Absolutely.

Q: Is the — is the Attorney General the highest law enforcement person within the federal government?

A: Yes, he is.

Q: And did the Attorney General approve of how customs and the DEA was going to handle this matter?

A: Yes, he was very concerned for our employees. He was very concerned to get to the bottom of what had happened, and he approved our plan.

Q: Did you consider this a delicate situation?

A: Absolutely.

Q: And why?

A: I felt it's life or death. We have had an agent kidnapped and murdered in Mexico [Enrique Camarena in Guadalajara in 1985] and we didn't [want to] see that happen.

DEA agent Enrique "Kiki" Camarena was abducted in early February 1985 shortly after leaving the U.S. consulate in Guadalajara, Mexico. His body was found several weeks later, partially decomposed, wrapped in a plastic death shroud and buried in a shallow grave some 70 miles north of the Mexican city.

One of the alleged architects of Camarena's kidnapping, brutal torture and ultimate death, Rafael Caro Quintero, was released on August 9, 2013, from a Mexican prison, by order of a Mexican federal court, after having served 28 years of a 40-year-sentence for the crime. His release caused an outcry among U.S. law enforcers and officials, who contend his freedom is an affront to justice and to the memory of Camarena. (He was re-arrested in Mexico in 2022.)

Narco News as well as a number of mainstream publications — among them Fox News and *The El Paso Times* in the U.S., and *Proceso* and *El Pais* in Mexico — published reports raising the specter of CIA involvement or acquiescence in Camarena's death. Evidence points to that to some degree, given Caro Quintero was a suspected CIA cooperator linked to covert drug- and gun-running operations, and the CIA somehow had tapes of Camarena's torture interrogation, which surfaced later. *Proceso*'s coverage went so far as to allege the CIA ordered Camarena's murder. CIA officials released a statement to the media claiming that "it's ridiculous to suggest that the CIA had anything to do with the murder of a U.S. federal agent or the escape of his killer [Caro Quintero]."

DOJ attorney Rosen continues his questioning of DEA Deputy Administrator Leonhard:

Q: Go ahead. I'm sorry.

A: We had five employees [DEA agents] and their families in the Ciudad Juarez area, and we didn't know why our agent had been stopped by the [Mexican] police. We also didn't know why suspicious people had shown up at his house while his wife was home. We had to get to the bottom of that.

Q: Was it also made delicate by the fact that you had another agency involved, one that you had no control over?

A: Yes.

Q: Was it a concern of yours at all that a foreign government was involved in this matter, the country of Mexico?

A: Absolutely.

Q: Now it's many years after the investigation. Was the Drug Enforcement Administration in any way responsible for causing or even previously knowing what happened in Ciudad Juarez, any employees of the DEA?

A: No. ...

* * *

Direct Examination of DEA Chief of Operations Mike Furgason by DOJ Attorney Lawrence Rosen:

Q: Mr. Furgason, good late morning to you, sir.

A: Good morning.

Q: Could you tell us how many years you worked with the Drug Enforcement Administration prior to your current employment.

A: With the DEA, I was with the DEA 22 years.

Q: ... We have been discussing a matter concerning the event in the city of Ciudad Juarez in Mexico. And at the time of that event, what position did you hold within the Drug Enforcement Administration?

A: I was the chief of operations for the DEA.

Q: And who did you report to, your first-line supervisor?

A: First-line supervisor was the deputy administrator, who was Michele Leonhart.

Q: Now, with respect to this Ciudad Juarez matter, was there a joint management review of the events there being coordinated by you for the DEA?

A: Yes. I commissioned a joint — myself, along with my counterpart from the Immigration Customs Service [ICE], the former Customs Service, John Clark commissioned a joint team [the joint-assessment team, or JAT] to go to Juarez/El Paso and Mexico City on a fact-finding mission.

Q: What time period was that, sir?

A: It was in February of 2004.

Q: Now, who requested that you undertake this task?

A: I — well, I did it — it was my own thought process, along with my counterpart, John Clark [at ICE].

Q: Was the deputy administrator and the administrator [at DEA] involved in any way in deciding to have this joint effort between the DEA and Customs [ICE]?

A: No. I mean I recommended to them. Obviously, I wouldn't have done it unilaterally. I recommended it to the deputy and administrator [of DEA] it should be done, and they agreed, and I sent a team down.

Q: Now, what role was Mr. Sandy [Sandalio] Gonzalez, who at that time clearly we all know was the [DEA] special agent in charge in El Paso, what role, if any, was Mr. Gonzalez supposed to have in this joint assessment team matter?

A: Well, I called Sandy before the team arrived and told Sandy that they would be coming and to facilitate the process, host them and accommodate them, and then also make himself, along with any DEA personnel under his command, available for interviews.

Q: What role was Mr. Gonzalez supposed to have in determining who was at fault in this matter?

A: I mean there was — who was at fault in El Paso?

Q: Yes, in the Juarez, the whole Juarez matter.

A: That was going to be left up to the joint assessment team to render, to go out, gather facts, present them back to each agency, the DEA and ICE, the leadership back in Washington, so we could make a decision back in Washington what further action should be undertaken.

Q: Was there a — well, let me back up a moment. The team that you had go down and find out what was going on out of this incident, were they — were all of them from outside the El Paso and Mexico office?

A: Yes. I mean I selected the two from the DEA, and the selections I made, they were from outside. One was from Boston, one was from — well, they were assigned in Boston and Washington at the time, but both had prior Southwest border experience as [DEA] supervisors. So, I selected them from the DEA side and ICE did the same thing.

Q: Was there a thought process or reason why you wanted people who were not in that area to conduct this investigation?

A: Well, yes, because, you have to understand, as this — the initial issue of the agents being pulled over by the Juarez police, who we later found out to be the Juarez police, and the evacuation of the [Juarez DEA] office happened January 14 [2004], and several weeks had passed, and the information that was coming back to me, because I'm being asked what was going on by the Attorney General of the United States of America [again, then, John Ashcroft], was not sufficient to make decisions or even provide information.

For whatever reason, there was disagreements that were going on in the El Paso office between the agencies [ICE and DEA], as well as in ... our Mexico offices. So, I got with [ICE's] Clark and said, we have to send someone down there that people will talk to. So, we sent a joint team or a bipartisan team to go down, gather facts, and bring back that information to us in hopes that by doing that we could bring — we could put together a whole story, because ICE people would talk to ICE people, and DEA people would talk to DEA people.

Q: Go ahead, sir. I'm sorry.

A: And I just wanted to say too, that those teams went out jointly. So, if they were going to interview Sandy [Gonzalez], it would have been a DEA representative and ICE representative. I didn't want, nor did Clark, want any innuendo or any idea to come back, well, ICE just interviewed ICE, and they created a story to satisfy. So, we had people from each agency that participated in this fact-finding team when they did the 40-some interviews.

[That JAT report, to this day, still remains a closely guarded secret within DEA and ICE, despite multiple Freedom of Information Act requests filed seeking its release.]

Q: And those 44 interviews were of Customs, or ICE individuals, El Paso DEA individuals, and Mexican officials, is that true?

A: Right. As well as Assistant United States Attorneys.

Q: Right. And just so that we were all comfortable, we have been using the term Customs here throughout the trial, and that's fine. [What] did ICE stand for –

A: Immigration and Customs Enforcement.

Q: And that's a result of the change, the [Department of] Homeland Security, and the division of the agencies, but for the purposes of our trial, ICE is the same as Customs, is that correct?

A: That's correct.

Q: Okay. So, as I understand it, Mr. Gonzalez was supposed to cooperate in the interview that was going to be taken of him. And with respect to this joint assessment team, did Mr. Gonzalez have any other purpose or role other than to be interviewed and to be a good host?

A: No, I mean, no.

Q: Now, and you had direct communication with Mr. Gonzalez on that matter?

A: Before they [the JAT team] arrived, yes.

Q: ... After the 24th [of February 2004], after he [Gonzalez] sent the letter [the House of Death letter to his counterpart at ICE], did he contact you, or as far as you know, anyone else, to say, "By the way, I've sent this letter, and this is what I've done?"

A: No.

[The letter referred to by DOJ attorney Lawrence Rosen is the one Gonzalez sent in late February 2004 to his counterpart at ICE, a copy of which also was provided to U.S. Attorney Johnny Sutton. The letter, among other things, outlined ICE's dubious role in the murders due to its handling of its informant, former Mexican cop Guillermo Eduardo "Lalo" Ramirez Peyro, whom the U.S. government subsequently, unsuccessfully, tried to deport back to Mexico, where Lalo claims he would be murdered by the Juarez Cartel he betrayed to assist ICE.]

The questioning of DEA Chief of Operations Mike Furgason by DOJ attorney Rosen continues:

Q: Did it come as a surprise when you found out about this letter?

A: Yes.

Q: By the way, close in time, did you have a meeting with the Attorney General of the United States [Ashcroft] concerning the Ciudad Juarez matter?

A: Yes, I did.

Q: Now, what was your reaction, sir, when you found out about this letter?

A: I was a little surprised. I mean, the way I found out about it, I was contacted initially about it by the United States Attorney's Office in San Antonio [Sutton's office] who asked if I knew about this letter. I said, "No, I was not, I wasn't aware of it." And then of course it wasn't long after that I was contacted by the Department of Justice, by the Deputy Attorney General's office [Comey's office], and asked if I knew about the letter, and I said, "No, I wasn't." And I was a little disappointed in the way I found out. And, frankly, I was a little disappointed that it was written.

Q: Was it an embarrassment to you?

A: Well, yeah. I mean because the day before I had briefed the Attorney General and Deputy Attorney General that we had a fact-finding team [the JAT] that had just returned. They were preparing a report, and as soon as the report was finished, I would come back and brief them [Ashcroft and Comey] on what was, you know, found and provide them a copy of the report. And I might add, too, that while I was briefing the Attorney General, John Clark, my counterpart [at ICE], was briefing the heads of Homeland Security, I think [Tom] Ridge at the time and Asa Hutcheson [later elected governor of Arkansas, but then head of DHS' Directorate of Border and Transportation Security and the former head of the DEA].

So, it was at the highest levels of these particular departments we were briefing them because it was a serious incident down in Juarez that could have potential ramifications between our governments [Mexico and the United States, given most of the murder victims were Mexican citizens], and they needed to know what was accurate. So, it was somewhat embarrassing as I left their office that I find out that a letter had been written sort of outlining a lot of the facts that the team had uncovered.

[The fact that the DEA's Chief of Operations at the time, Furgason, concedes Gonzalez' letter denouncing ICE's handling of the House of Death case was accurate and articulated many of the same facts the JAT was uncovering, speaks to the veracity of Gonzalez' allegations in his missive dated February 24, 2004.]

DOJ's Rosen continues his questioning of DEA's Furgason:

Q: What was Karen Tandy, the administrator of DEA, what was her reaction when she found out about this letter?

A: She was upset.

Q: Now, despite the letter having been sent, you still had a job to do with regard to this, correct?

A: Yes, that's correct.

Q: What impact did you find that Mr. Gonzalez' letter had on what you were attempting to do?

A: Well, it — well, the trust factor between myself and the — my ICE counterparts, that actually we had lost a little ground there because they thought we were trying to, forgive the saying, but back-door them, so to speak. In other words, let information out before we completed [the report]. And so, we had to regain some ground there. And we were also involved in some negotiations of agreements between the two agencies that had expired with the creation of the new ICE, the new agency. So, it set those back as well. So, there was a break or a disruption in the trust I think would be the best way to capture it.

That trust, however, as the reporting has shown, had already been shattered long before Gonzalez' letter. ICE did not inform DEA or the Mexican government of the extent of their informant's participation in the House of Death murders until after the DEA agent and his family were stopped and nearly killed (and after at least a dozen other people had already been murdered). And even then, U.S. prosecutor Fielden and ICE officials prevented DEA officials from getting access to the informant for days.

DEA wanted to use the informant to lure one of the major players in the murders, Mexican State Police Commander Miguel Loya Gallegos, into a setting where he could be arrested. As a result of the stonewalling, Loya and several of his underlings escaped and their whereabouts are not known to this day.

DOJ attorney Rosen's questioning of DEA Chief of Operations Mike Furguson continues:

Q: By the way, did the joint assessment team ultimately get to the bottom of what happened down there?

A: Yes. I mean they — I mean what I was trying to find out, could I reopen an office in a safe manner in Mexico, and was there a real threat on our agents or were they targeted. And the bottom line on that was they came back and said, "No, it was just — it was an accident that the agent had been pulled over. It was a mistaken identity." The other thing that it did was it allowed myself, and I assume Clark [at ICE], because I did understand that they [ICE] initiated an office of internal investigation or internal affairs investigation over at ICE based on those facts [in the JAT report]. And I took the report that was provided to me and forwarded it to my internal inspections for review as well to see if there was anything wrong going on, on the part of any DEA personnel.

Q: You mentioned, sir, that there were 44 interviews [conducted for the JAT report] and those were interviews [of] the team of people in Mexico, people in El Paso, the U.S. Attorney's Office, and so forth?

A: Right.

Q: Did Mr. Gonzalez participate in those interviews of other people with your JAT team?

A: Not other than him being interviewed himself, not to my knowledge. He was not a participant in any other interview with the JAT team.

Q: Was he receiving the reports of the JAT team?

A: Not to my knowledge, no. I mean written reports, I mean he may have — I don't know if he was getting verbal reports, you know, because they were there, but he did not receive any written reports. I didn't receive the final written [JAT] report until late March [2004].

[And, again, to this day, no one outside the DOJ and DHS inner circles of power has seen that JAT report.]

Q: And is the final written report what you would rely upon in assessing the situation?

A: Right. I mean I was getting updates every evening from the team leader, you know, over the phone. But they still had to assemble themselves and go through all that information that they had collected and come up with some conclusions. And that didn't happen until the end of March.

Q: By the way, do you know whether or not Customs [ICE] is addressing the problem with their agents that came out of this incident?

A: I'm aware that they had initiated an internal investigation and that certain people down there, supervisors, were moved. I don't know the outcome or the disciplinary action, if any. I left the position.

To date, other than DEA commander and whistleblower Sandalio Gonzalez, a Latino agent pressured into early retirement; and the informant's direct handler, Raul Bencomo, a Latino ICE agent put on administrative leave and later terminated by the agency, no federal agent, supervisor or U.S prosecutor has been fired, let alone prosecuted criminally, as a result of the House of Death mass murder.

* * *

The testimony continues: Cross-Examination of DEA Deputy Administrator Michele Leonhart by Richard Diaz, attorney for Sandalio Gonzalez:

Q Good morning, Ms. Leonhart.

A Good morning.

Q: ...Okay. Now, you also said that there were problems with — after this Juarez matter, which is in early 2004, you said that there were issues or problems with residual or collateral effects, joint investigations with other agencies, FBI or Customs, which is now called ICE, I think, lack of trust and things of that nature. Do you remember that testimony?

A: Yes.

Q: All right. Historically there has been — there have been problems with these inner-agency cooperations. There's been competition between the DEA and Customs [ICE]. There's been fights over confidential informants and who gets to use whose informants in different investigations, correct?

A: Everyone has relayed that the relationship prior to this incident between the DEA and ICE in El Paso was good.

Q: Well, you would agree with me, would you not, that the entity responsible for whatever happened after that was not the DEA. It was ICE?

A: ICE was responsible, yes.

Q: Okay. So, if they are now complaining that the relationship is soured, it's not Sandy's fault. He didn't have one of his agents controlling an informant that was participating in murders in Mexico. Right, it's not his fault? He reacted to it. He didn't cause it, did he?

A: ICE caused the incident.

Q: And if they don't like the consequences, it's not Mr. Gonzalez' fault, is it? He didn't cause it.

A: Mr. Gonzalez, by writing the letter [to his counterpart at ICE], it was at an inappropriate time. It was inflammable. It was nothing new. It was information that we already knew and had relayed to the highest levels of the DOJ, Department of Justice and ICE. [Again, an admission that Gonzalez' letter was on the money, yet the whitewash continues.] It was unnecessary. And it caused friction, distrust amongst the agencies, and it's been harder for our new SAC to work there because of it.

And again, no one at ICE, DHS, DEA or DOJ, has to date been held liable criminally in the House of Death mass murder. Former El Paso DEA commander Gonzalez, however, suggests in a complaint he filed in September 2004 with the U.S. Office of Special Counsel (OSC) that some government officials might well be criminally culpable for their actions in the House of Death case. Ironically, he filed that complaint because of retaliation he faced as a consequence of his truth-telling in the House of Death mass murder. For that effort, he was ordered to remain silent by his superiors, who eventually forced him into early retirement from DEA.

It's worth revisiting Gonzalez' comments from that OSC complaint.

"I believe that I'm being punished for speaking the truth about a serious matter of public concern that is not publicly known," Gonzalez writes in the complaint, obtained through a Freedom of Information Act request. "When I made this known to the United States Attorney for the Western District of Texas [Johnny Sutton], rather than take corrective action, he attacked my professionalism.

"... And, indirectly criticized my integrity, ironically for refusing to participate in a coverup, which may even constitute the criminal offense of obstruction of justice, misprision of a felony, or, to a lesser extent, a federal agency's negligence resulting in multiple homicides."

* * *

The testimony in former DEA commander Gonzalez' civil whistleblower-retaliation trial continues: Examination of Sandalio Gonzalez by his attorney, Richard Diaz:

Q: Okay. With regard to Mr. Furgason, he would have been the chief of operations when this Juarez matter arose. Did you get any direction or signal from him as to what your responsibilities on the Juarez [House of Death] matter should be?

A: Yes, I spoke to Mike. We — when that matter was developing, well, after the discovery, after the events of January 14th, 2004, [when the DEA agent and his family were stopped] — we had to determine if there was a threat against the agent and his wife and all the other agents. So, I had a lot of communication with headquarters and with Larry Holifield [head of DEA's Mexico City office at the time] in coordinating this. And during one particular conversation, Mike Furgason asked me what I was doing in that regard.

And I explained to him that my role up to that point was strictly a support role. I was supporting the Mexico City [DEA] office [headed by Holifield] or the Juarez office [also overseen by Holifield] in what they were doing at the time, which was they had evacuated the city, or the office [in Juarez], and I had put their agents, five agents, I think it was, and their support personnel, in our training room and provided them with equipment and computers so that they could work from there and prepare or continue their investigation of the threat.

Mr. Furgason asked me if I had contacted the — my counterpart at ICE or Customs [El Paso's Special Agent in Charge John Gaudioso]. And I told him no, that I had been leaving that up to the Mexico City office because the Mexico City office had flown in an assistant agent in charge ... to conduct an inquiry, so I was kind of leaving it alone and letting Mexico handle that.

And Mr. Furgason said, "Well, Sandy, the ICE SAC [Gaudioso] is your domestic counterpart, and, you know, you have every right to contact him and ask him what's going on, and, you know, find out." So, I asked him, do you want me to get involved in this. And he said, "Yes, get involved." And I did.

Q: And is that why you got involved, and is that why you wrote the letter?

A: Absolutely, yes.

MR. Diaz: Thank you, sir. ...

In weighing this testimony, please keep in mind that the jury came back with a verdict in Gonzalez' favor, finding that DEA did discriminate against him. Gonzalez in July 2007 walked away with $385,000 settlement from the DOJ. But also remember the bigger picture of the House of Death mass murder — a portrait colored with questions over:

• The U.S. law enforcement's role in the bloodshed.

• The mainstream media's lack of attention to the subsequent whitewashing of U.S. law enforcement's role.

• The racism embedded in a system that too often renders victims of color invisible and ultimately disposable under our laws.

• And Congress' continuing diligent disinterest in exercising oversight in this matter.

Dispatch 26

October 23, 2007

The cronies suckling the government teat are anything but subtle when they feed.

On October 22, 2007, within a week of President George W. Bush unveiling his administration's $1.4 billion Plan Mexico, which Congress later approved to the tune of $1.6 billion over three years, the head of the DEA, Karen Tandy, announced she was stepping down. Plan Mexico, also known as the Merida Initiative, provided Central America and Mexico — the latter by far the largest recipient of the largesse — with a Christmas list of combat training and equipment, including communications gear, all to to beef up militarization of the drug war.

And where was Tandy — heiress to the Tandy/Radio Shack fortune — headed after stepping down from the top role at DEA? To a major communications equipment manufacturer, of course: Motorola. She accepted a job offer as the senior vice president of the Fortune 100 company's Global Government Relations and Public Policy Division.

"Ms. Tandy will serve as Motorola's top public policy spokesperson on issues related to global telecom policy, trade, regulation, spectrum allocation, and country relations," PRNewswire reported in the fall of 2007. Following Tandy's announcement, much of the national press gushed, swallowing the DEA's talking points wholesale, such as this tidbit from the Associated Press: "Under Tandy, the DEA said it eliminated more than 65 percent of the nation's illicit methamphetamine labs."

When you read a statement like that, you have to assume DEA knows precisely how many meth labs exist — like they file taxes or something — and that it's a fixed number. If that's not the case, then somebody is selling us bad pork. But given that Plan Mexico ultimately passed easily through the bowels of Congress, despite being bad policy with the digestive impact of an undercooked chorizo taco, you have to give Tandy credit for avoiding the negative and seizing the day. Plan Mexico's $1.6 billion in funding will buy a lot of chorizo and telecommunications equipment for the bi-national effort targeting dastardly drug cartels.

With Tandy serving in a key "spectrum allocation" role with Motorola, the telecom needs of the drug war were sure to be sated. After all, Motorola has a track record of serving the **communications needs** of federal law enforcement agencies, and Tandy has a record of heading a federal law enforcement agency with a big presence in Mexico. It was a marriage made in heaven — or at least in a backroom in Washington — it seemed. But given the reality of the Mexican government's corrupt alliance with narco-traffickers, you also have to wonder if some of the weapons, radios and other equipment provided under the Plan Mexico pact **might be diverted** to increase the efficiencies of contraband-drug production and transportation.

ICE informant and House of Death killer Guillermo Eduardo "Lalo" Ramirez Peyro described the tight relationship between the Mexican government and its narco-trafficking industry as follows while under oath in **immigration court proceedings**:

> During the three years of working [an] investigation [as a U.S. government informant infiltrating the Juarez Cartel], I recorded and I showed that, that the [Mexican] police are under the order and to service the people from the cartel.
>
> ... I would record the conversations that I would have with [Juarez Cartel cell leader] Santillan, and he would explain to me the arrangements that they would have with militaries with high executives, high-level government people [in Mexico].
>
> ... Well, the [Juarez] Cartel had arrangements with people that were close to President Fox [Mexican President Felipe Calderon's predecessor]. He explained to me that President Fox took, took the position to arrange, consult with the cartel from Juarez to — which

means that he was going to attack the enemy [rival] cartels being from Tijuana and from the Gulf, and then the cartel from Juarez would be operating with this court [protection], you know — without the government being ... on top of them. ...

But then it doesn't seem that Tandy while DEA administrator paid too much attention to the cozy relationship between the Mexican government (at all levels) and the "drug cartels." At least that might explain why she worked to silence El Paso DEA commander Sandalio Gonzalez, who sought to expose the homicidal role played by the informant Lalo and his employer, ICE, in the House of Death murders — which led to the near assassination of a DEA agent and his family.

After Gonzalez revealed those connections in an **internal memo** sent in late February 2004 that landed on the desk of U.S. Attorney Johnny Sutton (a **dear friend** of President Bush), Tandy sprang into action at Sutton's request. After all, Bush, Sutton and Tandy are all from Texas, and these Texans stand together when danger threatens — particularly when it is an extreme danger like the truth.

On March 5, 2004, DEA Administrator Tandy sent **an e-mail** to high-ranking members of the Justice Department, including U.S. Attorney Johnny Sutton, the top prosecutor in the Western District of Texas where the House of Death case played out. In that email, Tandy says she apologized to Sutton for Gonzalez' memo exposing ICE informant Lalo's role in multiple homicides in Mexico. That revelation was threatening to Sutton's pending headline-grabbing drug cases against narco-trafficker Heriberto Santillan Tabares and cigarette-smuggler Jorge Abraham — both cases in which the informant Lalo played a central role. Tandy then wrote that she "agreed on a no comment to the press."

More from Tandy's **March 5, 2004, email:**

Mike Furgason, chief of operations, notified the El Paso SAC [Gonzalez] last night that he is not to speak to the press other than a no comment, that he is to desist writing anything regarding the Juarez matter and related case, and defer to the joint management and threat assessment teams out of HQ — and he is to relay these directions to the rest of his El Paso Division. The SAC, who reports to Michele [Leonhart], will be brought in next week for performance discussions to further address this officially.

The end result of Tandy's truth-suppression strategy was that Gonzalez was given a black mark on his employment record, never again considered for a promotion and eventually forced to retire. Tandy in 2005 provided a deposition during the discovery stage in Gonzalez' whistleblower/discrimination lawsuit in Miami and was scheduled to testify at his trial in early December 2006. A day before the start of the trial, however, citing health complications due to a surgery the prior month, she sent word to Gonzalez' attorney that she would be unavailable to take the stand under oath.

On another front in the House of Death case, avoiding public scrutiny is the mode as well. The internal probe examining the players and decisions that led to the House of Death murders and near assassination of a DEA agent — conducted by "joint management and threat assessment teams" from ICE and DEA — resulted in the JAT report. To this day that report remains a controversial document that DEA and ICE have failed to make public for various shifting reasons — ranging from national security to it can't be found.

The House of Death was not Tandy's first trip to the coverup rodeo. She also has the distinction of heading DEA during the time that the infamous "Kent memo" was drafted in December 2004 by a DOJ trial attorney Thomas Kent, who at the time was assigned to the wiretap unit of the Justice Department's Narcotic and Dangerous Drugs Section. That memo revealed a disturbing set of allegations linking DEA agents in Bogota, Colombia, to narco-traffickers. Kent's memorandum contains some of the most serious charges ever raised at the time (2004) against U.S. antinarcotics officers: that DEA agents on the front lines of the drug war in Colombia are on drug traffickers' payrolls, complicit in the murders of informants who knew too much, and directly involved in helping Colombia's infamous rightwing paramilitary death squads to launder drug money.

In the memo, Kent says his claims are supported by a number of DEA agents in Florida whom the agency muzzled and retaliated against after they also tried to expose the corruption. And just like DEA Special Agent in Charge Gonzalez, then-DOJ attorney Kent was silenced (transferred to another job) and the whole affair again covered up by DEA — despite documented evidence that has surfaced since then lending credence to Kent's allegations.

Ironically, the individual to whom Kent wrote the memo — Justice Department Narcotic and Dangerous Drugs Section Chief Jodi L. Avergun, subsequently became Tandy's chief of staff at DEA. But then, why rain on Tandy's retirement. She was a great public servant in the eyes of many who benefited from her term in power and who, like so many other political appointees in the past, is simply cashing in on her connections. In her case, she landed an executive post with a Chicago-based company, Motorola, which sells phones to the U.S. feds, Mexicans and other global trading partners. And maybe even the Colombians to facilitate communications in the war on the cocaine cartels?

Tandy's online LinkedIn profile indicates she served in an executive role at Motorola for seven years, until 2014. She then moved into the consulting world, focused on government affairs, of course, as a principal with KPT Consulting LLC in Washington, D.C. She also serves as executive vice president of a telehealth firm, NLW Partners, which specializes addiction-recovery technology.

And so, with addiction in mind — to power, money and the revolving door — it seems appropriate to conclude here with a nod to the continuing escalation of the drug war and its spin-off benefits. From the mouth of Tandy herself — excerpted from a September 16, 2003, speech she made at her DEA swearing-in ceremony:

> We will hunt down the drug trade no matter where it seeks to hide and no matter where it spreads with a singular focus on achieving maximum impact of reducing our country's drug supply. President Bush and the American people expect real results, and we will hold ourselves

accountable at DEA for measuring our true impact in reducing the drug supply and drug use, rather than simply the collection of empty statistics....

To say nothing of empty promises....

Dispatch 27
May 17, 2009

Johnny Sutton stepped down from his U.S. Attorney post effective Sunday, at midnight, on April 19, 2009.

Sutton's resignation came three months after newly elected President Barack Obama took office on January 20 — and a little more than five years after the last of a dozen decaying corpses were dug up on February 6, 2004, in the backyard of the House of Death in Juarez, Mexico. All of those homicides took place on Sutton's watch and with the help of an ICE informant who was a key to multiple criminal cases being pursued at the time by his office.

Sutton's resignation did garner a bit of press in Texas but went largely unnoticed by the national media — which helped to hype Sutton's career in the wake of the sentences meted out to two Border Patrol agents, Ignacio Ramos and Jose Alonso Compean. They were prosecuted by Sutton's office, and each was sentenced to more than a decade in prison for attempting to cover up their roles in shooting a dope smuggler in the posterior in 2005. President Bush on January 19, 2009, a day prior to leaving office, **commuted the sentences** of Ramos and Compean, though he did not pardon them for the crime, and the pair was released from prison after serving about two years. Jump forward in the future from there and you'll discover another pertinent but little-noticed story: President Donald Trump in late December 2020, just prior to leaving office, issued a full **pardon to Ramos and Compean.**

Sutton's departure from the U.S. Attorney post based in San Antonio in the spring of 2009 provided an opportunity for the Texas media to revisit that case, and to once again give Sutton a soap box to defend his prosecution of the Border Patrol agents as being just — although resulting in sentences that he agrees were too harsh but beyond his control. That same media, however, was silent about another case marked by the fingerprints of Sutton, the one this book is devoted to, the House of Death mass murder that cost the lives of at least a dozen people in the borderlands. The bodies of the House of Death victims, discovered in early 2004 in shallow graves in the rocky dirt behind a stucco house in Juarez, were tortured, killed and buried with the help of an ICE informant who played a key role in the mass murder. By the time of Sutton's resignation, however, the victims were little more than forgotten bones in a zone of barren ground that forms the border between Mexico and the U.S. Those bones, and likely more not yet discovered, are what remain of a long-forgotten sacrifice to the hypocrisy of the drug war.

So, Sutton, with his resignation in early 2009, **was now moving onto another chapter** in his career and, for him, that meant stepping through the government revolving door. "Serving as United States Attorney has been one of the greatest honors of my career, and I will be forever grateful to President Bush for giving me the opportunity to fight for justice on behalf of the American people," Sutton said in prepared remarks announcing his resignation.

Thus, Sutton, with his political future intact thanks to the effective whitewashing of the House of Death, was allowed to project an image in a servant media as a tough-on-crime prosecutor who was willing to take the heat for a "just" prosecution of criminal law enforcers like Compean and Ramos. He is that rare conservative whose principled approach to justice is even respected by liberals. We've heard that narrative before, no?

The script was set in motion, then, played perfectly by Sutton who, according to the *Austin American-Statesman*, in 2009 landed a job in the far more lucrative private sector, though he declined to disclose specific details then. He also told the same newspaper that he planned to continue using the mainstream media to manipulate reality to his benefit — well, he colored it in more heroic terms designed to play to his base.

From an April 14, 2009, story in the *Austin American-Statesman*: "The [Ramos and Compean] case was an amazing tidal wave of misinformation," said Sutton, who noted that his critics were mostly right-leaning. "I want to be a conservative voice of reason in the media."

Sutton then added, according to the *Statesman*: "I don't mind a good knife fight."

Sutton certainly has proven that point — though I wouldn't recommend turning your back on the man in such a fight.

* * *

What happens to your career in America when you oversee a federal investigation in which an informant, paid by the government and with the knowledge of federal agents and prosecutors working for you, is allowed to assist in the torture and murder of a dozen people? You later land a high-paying job defending well-heeled corporate clients against the government, right?

And when the facts of the U.S. government's role in those heinous crimes are pointed out to you in a letter from a DEA commander, what course of action best advances your career? It certainly has to be orchestrating the retaliation against the whistleblower to silence him. And then, with the assistance of your bosses and their underlings, the government's role in the murders has to be whitewashed, right?

Well, if you think that scenario is backward, think again. This is America!

DEA Special Agent in Charge Sandy Gonzalez stresses that U.S. Attorney Johnny Sutton orchestrated the retaliation he faced for writing his House of Death letter. Sutton wanted to bury the letter because it was "discovery material" (evidence) that threatened to compromise a career-boosting death-sentence case against a major narco-trafficker. Consequently, Gonzalez says, that means Sutton is implicated in the coverup of a U.S. government informant's participation in mass murder.

Sutton has declined numerous requests from me to be interviewed about the House of Death case.

In his whistleblower complaint to the U.S. Office of Special Counsel, filed in September 2004, Gonzalez lists the following three "whistleblower disclosures" related to the House of Death case:

- Murder.
- Gross mismanagement of a criminal case.
- Obstructing an investigation of a threat against the lives of a federal agent and his family.

I obtained hundreds of pages of documents related to the House of Death case through a Freedom of Information Act (FOIA) request lodged with the U.S. Merit Systems Protection Board, where Gonzalez filed a whistleblower retaliation case. Those FOIA records shine even more light on the House of Death, showing that a number of high-ranking officials — including then DEA Administrator Karen Tandy — were aware of the informant's complicity in the murders in Juarez.

Other documents surfaced in federal court in Miami, as part of an employment discrimination case Gonzalez filed and won against the Department of Justice. Those records include a sworn pre-trial deposition provided by Tandy herself. In the deposition, Tandy admits that sometime prior to early March 2004 the U.S. Attorney General (then John Ashcroft) and the Deputy Attorney General (then James B. Comey) were "personally briefed" on the "issues with ICE" — that is, the role ICE agents and their informant played in the House of Death murders.

To date, however, no one has been prosecuted or sanctioned criminally in the U.S. for those brutal slayings; not the informant who participated in them, not the ICE agents or U.S. prosecutor who were aware of the informant's participation in the homicides yet continued to use him to make a drug case; not even Santillan, the narco-trafficker accused of ordering the House of Death murders. In fact, in the case of Santillan, there was no trial, assuring that the whole bloody affair would not be exposed to the glare of courtroom scrutiny. Rather, U.S. Attorney Sutton cut a plea deal with Santillan in which all murder charges against him were dropped.

But with Sutton's resignation from his U.S. Attorney post in the spring of 2009, that was all behind him. His next move was to reunite with John Ashcroft, who served as Attorney General from February 2001 to February 2005 — leaving office within a year of the House of Death bodies being dug up. Ashcroft by 2009 was running his own very successful consulting firm and related law practice. So, it was a natural fit for Sutton and Ashcroft to reunite and inflict more of their brand of justice on the American people. The Texas Lawyer Blog, the *San Antonio Express News*, the *Wall Street Journal* and more reported that Sutton planned to go into business with his former boss and three other former U.S. Attorneys, all of whom had been enlisted to expand the law firm attached to Ashcroft's consulting company, the Ashcroft Group — which primarily feeds off of U.S. government contracts.

One publication, the Litigation Daily blog, had this to say in 2009 about the Ashcroft Law Firm: "The Litigation Daily caught up with Ashcroft on Thursday.... He told us that the [law] firm will represent mainly individuals and organizations facing government investigations and regulatory enforcement actions."

The *Austin American Statesman* quoted Ashcroft as saying Sutton and the other new attorney hires at the Ashcroft Group also would help to advance the affiliated law firm's mission of serving as an "interface between corporate America and government." Among the Ashcroft Group's past consulting clients, the *Statesman* reported, are medical-equipment maker Zimmer Holdings Inc., which reached an out-of-court settlement with the U.S. Justice Department after being accused of offering kickbacks to physicians who used its products. Ashcroft's firm was hired by the U.S. Attorney's Office in New Jersey to monitor the execution of the settlement.

"Ashcroft was criticized for the deal," the *Austin American Statesman* reported, "because he was given the business — which according to a 2007 Securities and Exchange Commission filing was worth between $28 million and $52 million — by then-New Jersey U.S. Attorney Christopher Christie, who had worked for Ashcroft at the Justice Department."

U.S. Attorney Christopher "Chris" Christie would later serve from 2010-2018 as New Jersey Gov. Christie. In 2016, he led Donald Trump's presidential transition team, for a time — from the spring of 2016 to just after election day that year, when Trump demoted him to vice chairman. Christie was replaced by Vice President Mike Pence. And three of Trump's children (Don Jr., Eric and Ivanka) and Ivanka's husband, Jared Kushner, were named to the transition team's executive committee.

And it seems another Ashcroft underling, former DOJ Director of Public Affairs Mark Corallo, who was included in the DOJ e-mail chain that was part of the media damage-control for the House of Death murders, also is in the Ashcroft Group mix. He was serving as the firm's PR spokesman at the time former U.S. Attorney Sutton was hired, according to the *Wall Street Journal*.

"The new [Ashcroft law] offices are in Boston, St. Louis, Austin [Sutton's home base with the firm] and Dallas, said spokesman Mark Corallo," the *Wall Street Journal* reported in April 2009. "The lawyers will do corporate compliance work [i.e., using their insider connections to win DOJ and other lucrative government contracts], as well as represent white collar clients."

Corallo later served as PR spokesman for President Trump's legal team. He stepped down from the post, however, in the summer of 2017, after only two months on the job. *Politico* reported at the time that, according to its sources, Corallo was frustrated with infighting on Trump's legal team, then dealing with special counsel Robert Mueller's Russia probe, and also was "concerned about whether he was being told the truth about various matters."

Concerns about the truth? Really? Or is it really more about careerism and maintaining access to the revolving door that allows long-time insiders to move freely between high-powered government and highly compensated corporate executive roles?

Here's some truth, as I've come to find it in my reporting on the House of Death and the federal government generally over decades. These long-running relationships among well-known powerbrokers tell us that the country's law enforcement and "justice" bureaucracies aren't run by some all-knowing dystopian "deep state." That tripe is for those who want to spread disinformation or avoid the hard work of learning how power and reality work in this nation.

The root of the problem as I have come to see it is that too many of our democratic institutions have been infected by entrenched good 'ol boy networks that have their own internal caste systems and systemic treachery. They operate with impunity to ensure self-preservation — screw up; you move up. And these largely white-male good 'ol boy networks also maintain power and build fortunes through a seemingly unfettered access to the revolving door that connects government and private-sector power centers. Ultimately, they feed off the taxpayers in the bargain.

* * *

The "revolving door" pattern of political appointees and career law enforcers moving to lucrative private sector jobs after their government service ends is well-documented across the federal government. And usually the new private-sector jobs these former high-powered government officials land tend to be with corporations and firms that depend on the U.S. government for revenue in some way or are regulated by the feds and need an insider's help to navigate troubled waters. That pretty much describes the private-sector careers, post-government, of Ashcroft, Sutton, Corallo, former DEA head Karen Tandy and former Deputy Attorney General James Comey.

They are simply using their government connections to make hay once back in the private sector. That is the norm, not the exception, in Washington, D.C., and America. Sutton and all those in officialdom benefiting from that revolving door, but who turned a blind eye to the

House of Death, or even helped to enable the carnage, however, should keep in mind that they cannot control destiny. The House of Death is not going away, even if it has failed, to date, to capture the national media spotlight.

It is like a worm in the wood, gnawing away day and night at the fetid foundation of the phony drug war on which many law enforcers, prosecutors and other enablers — including Ashcroft, Sutton, Corallo, Comey, Tandy and more — have built their careers. One day, as sure as the sun unravels the dark, it will all come crashing down on them. And all the rotting corpses buried under that foundation will be, at long last, exposed to the light of day.

And then Sutton, who says he doesn't mind "a good knife fight," and all those who fell in line behind him to whitewash the House of Death, will realize that no one can win a knife fight with the dead.

Dispatch 28

June 1, 2013

President Barack Obama in mid-2013 was on the cusp of nominating former George W. Bush-era Deputy Attorney General **James Comey** as the next director of the FBI. By then, the House of Death mass murder was nine years in the rearview mirror.

In the run-up to Comey's nomination, multiple mainstream media outlets published **fawning reports highlighting** Comey's supposed independence and upstanding moral character. The effect was to congeal public opinion and the necessary Senate confirmation vote around Comey, **then 52**.

Fast-forward to September 4, 2013, and Comey was **sworn in** as the new director of the FBI. At the time, no one foresaw **Comey's future**, which would include providing a major October-surprise boost to then-presidential candidate Donald Trump's campaign — arguably **helping to elevate Trump to the presidency**. That boost came at the expense of Trump's rival, former Secretary of State Hillary Clinton, and was the result of Comey's decision to send a very public letter to Congress on October 28, 2016 — only 11 days before the presidential election.

The letter served as a highly unusual public notice that the FBI was reopening an investigation into email correspondence involving Hillary Clinton after a stash of new Clinton emails surfaced on a computer as part of a separate FBI probe. The emails had become a flashpoint in the 2016 election because they supposedly contained borderline classified information and were sent using a private email server — as opposed to the supposedly better-protected White House email system. Comey explained his decision to notify Congress in **a letter to FBI employees** shortly after he sent his notice to the U.S. Congress:

> This morning I sent a letter to Congress in connection with the Secretary Clinton email investigation. Yesterday, the investigative team

briefed me on their recommendation with respect to seeking access to emails that have recently been found in an unrelated case. Because those emails appear to be pertinent to our investigation, I agreed that we should take appropriate steps to obtain and review them.

Of course, we don't ordinarily tell Congress about ongoing investigations, but here I feel an obligation to do so, given that I testified repeatedly in recent months that our investigation was completed.

Then, on Sunday, November 6, 2016, only two days before the presidential election, Comey sent **a second letter to Congress** indicating that Clinton had not broken any laws and no charges were warranted. By then, however, the damage was done, and Trump went on to squeak out an election victory. Ironically, Trump's win would **truncate Comey's tenure as FBI director**. Trump canned Comey in the spring of 2017, less than five months after the presidential inauguration on January 20 — cutting short Comey's expected **10-year tenure** as FBI director by some six years.

As a pretext, Trump said publicly he fired Comey over his handling of the Clinton email investigation — primarily because he didn't prosecute her and "lock her up." Comey's termination also came within two months of him confirming publicly that he had authorized an investigation into the Kremlin's interference in the 2016 U.S. presidential election and any links the Russian government had to the Trump campaign.

"While I greatly appreciate you informing me, on three separate occasions, that I am not under investigation, I nevertheless concur with the judgment of the Department of Justice that you are not able to effectively lead the Bureau," **Trump wrote in a letter directed to Comey, dated May 9, 2017.**

Comey's firing would be among the first of many moves to come in Trump's presidency in which he sought to defang corruption investigations while also consolidating power. And Comey proved to be an easy marker to take off the board. **The White House Office of the**

Press Secretary released the following statement, also on May 9, 2017, in the wake of Comey's termination as head of the FBI:

> Today, President Donald J. Trump informed FBI Director James Comey that he has been terminated and removed from office. President Trump acted based on the clear recommendations of both Deputy Attorney General Rod Rosenstein and Attorney General Jeff Sessions. "The FBI is one of our Nation's most cherished and respected institutions and today will mark a new beginning for our crown jewel of law enforcement," said President Trump.

In 2013, however, when Comey was under consideration for the FBI post, his past ethical challenges with the House of Death mass murder case should have offered a clue to Comey' future performance as FBI director. Clearly, no one was paying attention then. In fact, in 2013, according to media reports, Comey was deemed the ideal pick as FBI director because he was a Republican who also was admired by Democrats for his "principled stand" against the George W. Bush Administration's warrantless surveillance program. Comey ultimately signed_off on the highly classified program, however, as did other top DOJ leaders who previously had threatened to resign over it, including Ashcroft. After some unspecified technical changes to the spying program were adopted by the Bush administration, the threatened resignations were averted, and the surveillance program moved forward, with Comey's blessing.

So, was Comey really the guy in the white hat that the commercial media — always enamored of power and not so much principle — painted him to be prior to the Clinton email debacle? The giant British lender HSBC Holdings Plc must think so. The bank brought Comey on board in March 2013, providing him annual compensation of some $190,000, to serve on its board and as a member of the bank's "Financial System Vulnerabilities Committee." The lender in late 2012 admitted in a little-noticed settlement with DOJ that its U.S. and Mexican subsidiaries, because of lax oversight, or worse, were essentially used as money-laundering machines for Mexican and Colombian narco-traffickers. As part of the deal, dubbed a "deferred prosecution agreement," HSBC received a slap on the wrist from the U.S. Department of Justice, accepting enhanced regulatory oversight and a $1.3 billion fine — still chump change, given its $16.2 billion profit a year earlier.

"HSBC is being held accountable for stunning failures of oversight — and worse — that led the bank to permit narcotics traffickers and others to launder hundreds of millions of dollars through HSBC subsidiaries, and to facilitate hundreds of millions more in transactions with sanctioned countries," said Assistant Attorney General [Lanny A.] Breuer in a December 2012 press release announcing the HSBC settlement. "The record of dysfunction that prevailed at HSBC for many years was astonishing."

After stepping down in 2005 from his post as deputy attorney general at DOJ, Comey cashed in on that experience, and the connections he had cultivated, and initially walked through the revolving door to a job in the private sector — as an executive and legal counsel at Lockheed Martin, a position he held from 2005-2010. He later served as the general counsel for Bridgewater Associates LP, a global hedge fund, leaving that job just prior to being retained to serve on HSBC's board as part of its Financial Systems Vulnerability Committee. The committee was established to help the bank improve its legal compliance. So, in some senses, it could be argued Comey was collecting a consulting fee and profiting off of his former employer's prosecution of the lender.

There is a troubling story in Comey's history related to his role in the House of Death mass murdered, however. Still, there was little likelihood that the facts of that case would be a factor in his rise to the top law enforcement post in the nation because the House of Death itself had been buried by DOJ, ICE and largely by the commercial media. So, Comey's integrity, or lack of it, in his handling of the House of Death mass murder would have no effect on the PR steamroller that cleared the path for his anointment as director of the FBI — where his later actions and "moral character" helped to boost Donald Trump to the presidency in 2016. In other words, this one really mattered.

DEA commander Sandalio Gonzalez was forced out of the agency after attempting to raise alarms inside DOJ, DEA and ICE via a letter he addressed to his ICE counterpart. And Comey could have done something to stop that retaliation and the whitewashing of the House of Death mass murder — enabled by a U.S. government informant whose use was approved by Comey's DOJ. At the time of the House of Death case, Comey was the second-highest ranking official at DOJ as deputy attorney general — overseeing the day-to-day operations of the Justice Department. Comey served in that role for two years, starting in December 2003. The House of Death murders played out between August 2003 and mid-January 2004, with the subsequent whitewashing and coverup efforts continuing through the balance of his term at DOJ.

So, Comey was the operational head of DOJ when Gonzalez' February 2004 letter set off alarm bells inside the bureaucracy. The letter itemized the dangers posed by a "homicidal maniac" ICE informant, whose actions resulted in the "unnecessary loss of human life in the Republic of Mexico and endangered the lives of special agents of the Drug Enforcement Administration and their immediate families assigned to the DEA Office in Ciudad Juarez, Chihuahua, Mexico." The effort to expose and address the House of Death atrocities backfired on Gonzalez, in part, however, because Comey and other top DOJ officials went along with the plan to silence him and to disappear the needless death caused by a U.S. government informant in Juarez, Mexico.

Recall that Gonzalez' letter made its way to then-U.S. Attorney Johnny Sutton, who, rather than ordering an investigation of the serious charges contained in the letter, instead complained to his superiors at DOJ headquarters in Washington. Among Sutton's superiors was then-Deputy Attorney General Comey. The fact that Comey played an enabling role in the House of Death coverup, through his silence and acquiescence, should have been a big deal during the 2013 nomination process for the top FBI job, given one of the FBI's jobs is to handle informants during criminal investigations, and to also deal with the intricacies and sensitivities of law enforcement operations carried out on foreign soil. I did attempt to contact Comey to ask him about his role in the House of Death case but, through a spokesman, he declined to comment.

The allegation that Comey played a role in helping to whitewash a U.S. government informant's participatory role in the House of Death murders is not based on a flimsy six-degrees-of-separation conspiracy theory. There is a long paper trail illuminating the facts, which was uncovered in my reporting for *Narco News* over the course of many years but, again, largely ignored to this day by commercial media. "The situation is perplexing, for it appears that both White House staff and mainstream media have ignored the indisputable facts," former DEA Special Agent in Charge (SAC) Gonzalez said. "The House of Death murder coverup is a total joint fiasco by the departments of Justice and Homeland Security...."

After U.S. Attorney Sutton ran DEA commander Gonzalez' February 2004 letter up the DOJ chain of command, then-Associate Deputy Attorney General Catherin O'Neil, on March 4, 2004, responded with an email titled: "Possible press involving the DEA (Juarez) ICE Informant issue." That email was sent to then-Attorney General John Ashcroft's chief of staff, David Ayers; to one of his counsels, Jeff Taylor; and to then-Deputy Attorney General James B. Comey. The DEA Administrator at the time, Karen Tandy, also was included in the email.

The following day, March 5, DEA Administrator Tandy sent off another email to O'Neil, Ayers, Taylor and Comey as well as others within DEA — including Michele Leonhart, then-deputy administrator and later DEA administrator. That email later showed up as an exhibit in a whistleblower/discrimination federal court case filed by Gonzalez, a case he ultimately won.

It's worth stressing again that Comey, who went on to become the head of the FBI, also was getting these emails as an individual with immense power — serving as the No. 2 person at DOJ, appointed by **President George W Bush.** The emails, obtained via a Freedom of Information Act request, paint a picture of an effort to circle the wagons and accomplish the following:

• Prevent the media from getting information about Gonzalez' internal letter and the details of the government's handling of the House of Death mass murder generally.

• Prevent access to the ICE informant and ensuring his activities, including his role in the House of Death murders, remain shielded from public scrutiny.

• Prevent any leaks about the DEA agent and his family who were nearly assassinated by the same Juarez Cartel cell that had given ICE informant Guillermo Eduardo "Lalo" Ramirez Peyro the job of preparing the House of Death for murder and cleaning up after those murders.

• Silence and retaliate against the whistleblower, former DEA commander Gonzalez, who penned an internal letter that exposed the whole sordid House of Death mess.

In the **initial email on March 4**, the tone is set by this statement from then-Associate Deputy Attorney General Catherin O'Neil:

> We just heard from Johnny Sutton that the DEA SAC in El Paso [Special Agent in Charge Gonzalez] wrote a rather lengthy and inflammatory letter to the ICE SAC [Giovanni Gaudioso] regarding the "mishandling of the [House of Death] investigation that has resulted in unnecessary loss of human life in the Republic of Mexico and endangered the lives of (DEA agents)." ... [U.S. Attorney Sutton] was not sure who was talking, but we are certainly concerned that there may be press and there may be inquiries here in DC as well.

The next day, March 5, 2004, in the **email penned by then-DEA administrator Tandy,** she discusses the decision to stonewall the media and kicks off the plan to retaliate against DEA commander Gonzalez for sending what she clearly saw as a disruptive missive. "I apologized to Johnny Sutton last night [for Gonzalez' letter] and he and I agreed on a no comment to the press," Tandy wrote. "The SAC [DEA commander Gonzalez], who reports to Michele [Leonhart], will be brought in next week for performance discussions to further address this officially."

So, within a bit more than a week of Gonzalez' February 24, 2004, letter, which blew the whistle on U.S. Attorney Sutton's office and ICE's role in the House of Death murders, a coverup had already been put in motion — with Comey right in the middle of it.

DEA El Paso commander Gonzalez was not brought in for "performance discussions" the following week as Tandy threatened in her email. He was, however, the target of another threat in early May 2004 via a letter from a DEA attorney, according to Gonzalez' complaint filed with the **U.S. Office of Special Counsel**. "The DEA attorney threatened me with a negative performance rating if I did not retire by June 30, 2004," Gonzalez states in the OSC complaint. "

Gonzalez refused to retire on June 30. So, the threat made in the letter from the DEA attorney was carried out at his annual job-performance review in late August 2004, when Gonzalez received a negative job-performance rating for exercising "extreme poor judgment'" in writing the House of Death letter. He was later denied promotions and was subsequently pressured into retiring from DEA.

Gonzalez filed a discrimination lawsuit against DOJ based, in part, on the retaliation he suffered after exposing the U.S. government's role in the House of Death mass murder. And he was vindicated, with DOJ **agreeing to settle the case** in 2007, paying Gonzalez and his attorney a total of $385,000. Also, as part of that discrimination litigation, both the administrator of DEA, then **Karen Tandy**, as well Deputy DEA Administrator **Michele Leonhart** were each compelled to testify under oath about the House of Death case.

Following are some **excerpts from those sworn testimonies** that show **Comey was fully** aware of the bloody **events surrounding** the House of Death murders and the plan to circle the wagons at DOJ to ensure the informant's role in those brutal murders was not exposed to the sanitizing light of public sunshine.

JURY TRIAL: December 7, 2006 — DEA Deputy Administrator Michele Leonhart questioned under oath:

Q: And was there a plan in place with the acknowledged approval of the Attorney General [then John Ashcroft] on how to handle the investigation of what events occurred in Ciudad Juarez?

A: Yes. We notified the Attorney General of the United States and the Deputy Attorney General of the United States [James Comey] of what we had learned and the events and our concerns. We told him that we had talked to customs [ICE] and let them know what we had found out.

Our administrator [then Karen Tandy] had also contacted the U.S. Attorney's Office [Sutton in San Antonio], and we thought the best thing we could do is get the agencies together, put an independent review team together to go down and find the facts because the person I was talking to said he had a different set of facts and didn't see it the way that we saw it.

Again, that independent review team produced the internal JAT report, which was buried by DOJ and Homeland Security as part of the House of Death whitewash. Following is an excerpt from then-DEA Administrator Tandy's **August 23, 2005, deposition,** in the Gonzalez whistleblower/discrimination lawsuit, which was filed in federal court in Miami.

Tandy is **being questioned** by former DEA agent Gonzalez' attorney, Richard Diaz.

Diaz: Okay. And how did you learn of that (Gonzalez' February 24, 2004, letter to Sutton)?

Tandy: The letter?

Diaz: Yes.

Tandy: I believe I was notified about the letter by the Deputy Attorney General's office [James Comey's office].

Diaz: ... And when you said utter loss or lack of confidence, based on the letter, what in particular in the letter caused you to have that utter lack of confidence [in DEA commander Gonzalez]?

Tandy: The letter was inexcusable.

Diaz: Why?

Tandy: It was like tossing a hand grenade into the middle of a firefight. There was a substantial issue between DEA and the Immigration and Customs Enforcement agency, known as ICE, over ICE's use of an informant. And the jeopardy that DEA agents and others had been placed in as a result of ICE's handling of an informant that DEA had previously blackballed.

Mr. Gonzalez was very well aware at the time he sent that letter that this was a very sensitive, very delicate situation between DEA and ICE. It was such a significant issue for these two agencies, that I went personally to brief the Attorney General [then John Ashcroft] and the Deputy Attorney General [James Comey] over the issues with ICE, that I spoke to the U.S. Attorney [Sutton] about my concerns about the issues of ICE's handling of this informant along with [the] U.S. Attorney's AUSA [Assistant U.S. Attorney Juanita Fielden], that I met with DEA — personally met with in El Paso, the DEA agents, employees and their families, who had been evacuated from [Juarez] Mexico as a result of this issue.

... We had requested, DEA headquarters had requested, an interagency ICE and DEA headquarters review team to go into Mexico and El Paso to review what had happened in this debacle, and that team [the JAT, or joint-assessment team, including ICE and DEA investigators] had been hand-selected by DEA and that team had been on the ground, and was still in the course of conducting their joint review for a report jointly to DEA and ICE and ultimately to the Attorney General.

Diaz: Based on your recollection of the letter, do you believe that anything that Mr. Gonzalez wrote in the [February 24, 2004] letter was untruthful?

Tandy: I don't have a recollection either way. It was such colossally poor, fatal judgment on Sandy's [Gonzalez'] part, to get in the middle of what he knew was a sensitive, established, ongoing process to deal with the issues.

Diaz: Were you aware of the matters that were raised in the letter [which exposed the role of ICE agents, U.S. prosecutors and a U.S. informant in the House of Death mass murder] before you became aware of the letter [Gonzalez' letter] itself?

Tandy: Absolutely. I had already briefed the Attorney General and Deputy Attorney General on the issues, the underlying issues with ICE's handling of this informant [Ramirez Peyro], along with the AUSA, [Assistant U.S. Attorney Juanita Fielden, who worked under U.S. Attorney Sutton and was the federal prosecutor directly overseeing the House of Death case].

Remember Tandy sent an e-mail on March 5, 2004, to a number of high-ranking Department of Justice officials — including Comey — concerning Gonzalez' letter, indicating that she only recently became aware of it. In the e-mail, Tandy describes Gonzalez' letter as "inexcusable" and indicates that she "apologized to Johnny Sutton ... and he and I agreed on a no comment to the press." Her testimony in Gonzalez' civil case continues:

Diaz: ... When you say that Mr. Gonzalez exercised poor judgment in sending the letter, what would have been — once Mr. Gonzalez became aware of this issue, what, in your estimation, would have been the proper course of action for him to take? ... Nothing at all or something different, and if so, what differently?

Tandy: This was being handled at the highest level of the Department of Justice and at the highest executive levels of ICE and DEA, at headquarters' levels. Mr. Gonzalez knew that that is how this was being handled. He knew that that was the process that was sensitive and important to this agency.

From there, DEA commander Gonzalez was given a negative performance review, hurting his post-retirement employment opportunities, and ultimately retired from the agency. Plea deals were cut with the major targets of the ICE investigations that utilized the informant Ramirez Peyro.

One of those devil's bargains resulted in all murder charges being dropped against the House of Death boss, Heriberto Santillan Tabares. And the informant Ramirez Peyro was jailed in isolation for years after being put into the deportation pipeline — which, if successful, would have been a death sentence, according to Ramirez Peyro. Finally, the only internal review of the House of Death mass murder and near assassination of a DEA agent and his family, the JAT report, was buried and to this day has not been released publicly.

***

If you, kind reader, knew little or nothing about the House of Death case prior to reading about it here and were not aware of the extent of the coverup — nor the fact that it went to the highest levels of the Department of Justice, including to Comey — it's because you've likely only seen sporadic mainstream media accounts of the case that tend to sanitize and disappear the coverup. Remember, it is that same commercial media that manufactured consent for Comey's ascent to the FBI's top job.

Unfortunately, there seems little chance the mainstream media collectively — and specifically its major agenda-setting publications — absent a major nudge, will do anything at this late stage to delve deeper into the House of Death mass murder and subsequent efforts to keep the U.S. government's role in it under wraps. Any examination of the carnage, even at this late stage, should include a hard look at the role played by then-Deputy Attorney General Comey — whose later missteps as head of the FBI helped to elect Donald Trump as president.

The mainstream media also is unlikely to use its considerable legal resources and muscle to force the release of the long-buried JAT report. Because, to date, the national media — with its reliance on protecting sources with power in order to retain access to them — essentially have helped to provide cover for the coverup. That's a hard truth to accept for me as a journalist, but that doesn't make it any less true.

And neither Congress nor the White House are likely to take action at this point either, so long after the House of Death carnage, regardless of which party is in power. And they have not to date. In our existing hyper-partisan era, there's just too much political downside to investigating the U.S. government's role in the House of Death mass murder. It's better to let sleeping dogs lie.

So, the die was cast, and James Comey ascended to one of the most powerful posts in the nation as FBI director, a position where he made calls daily on civil rights, life and death, and ultimately presidential elections. And he was placed in that powerful position without any examination of his arguably pivotal role in the House of Death tragedy, which retired DEA commander Gonzalez describes as one of "the darkest chapters in the history of U.S. federal law enforcement."

The Prodigal Son

Dispatch 29

September 3, 2014

Guillermo Eduardo "Lalo" Ramirez Peyro had spent a long few days visiting family in California and was now fighting off sleep behind the wheel of a cherry red Ferrari. Transporting the exotic coupe — a $200,000 612 Scaglietti — back to the Big Apple was to be the highlight of the Christmas vacation out West. But in reality, the vehicle's cramped quarters and the tense silence of his girlfriend, Kelly Schroer, ensured that the last leg of the journey would be an unpleasant ride for both of them.

Ramirez Peyro recalls that the couple was heading toward the southwestern border of Missouri when Schroer's phone began to vibrate.

"I saw the 1111111 [on the screen]..., and I knew it was the cops," says Ramirez Peyro, a tall, fair-skinned Mexican with black hair and hazel eyes. "I said, 'Hey, Kelly, the police are calling you.' She said, 'No, I don't want to answer.'

"And then they called once again, and she did not want to answer. And I didn't even force her to call or not call or speak," continues Ramirez Peyro.

The pair would continue driving west on Interstate 44 for a few more miles without speaking. Schroer, a strawberry blonde from Ramirez Peyro's recently adopted hometown of Buffalo, considered her boyfriend too controlling. He, in turn, didn't trust her.

They first met the prior summer, 2013, in a bar in Buffalo, and their relationship was troubled from early on. Within a few months of dating, Schroer accused Ramirez Peyro of harassing and physically abusing her, a complaint that led a New York court to issue a "stay-away" order of protection against Ramirez Peyro that fall. Two weeks before the couple was to leave on their cross-country journey in December 2013, police in the Buffalo suburb of Tonawanda picked up Ramirez Peyro for violating the order. He was soon let go, and a few days later Schroer signed an affidavit, prepared by Ramirez Peyro's attorney in Buffalo, stating that the allegations of harassment and abuse she made "are not true."

"He never physically hit or abused or hurt me, and I want to be able to spend time with him without there being a violation of a court order," Schroer wrote in an affidavit.

Now, alone in the cramped Ferrari, whatever peace the two arrived at then was gone as Ramirez Peyro exited the highway and pulled the sports car into the parking lot of a La Quinta Inn. An exhausted Ramirez Peyro hit the bed in room No. 365 around 11 p.m. and was soon out cold. An hour and a half later he awoke to a pounding on the door. Schroer was gone. Again, the loud knock.

Ramirez Peyro pulled himself together, slipped out of bed and opened the door. In front of him were several Joplin, Missouri, police officers with their guns drawn. While he had been asleep, Schroer had gathered up her possessions and the keys to the Ferrari and quietly run off. At a nearby Quality Inn, Schroer checked into a room and immediately called the front desk to ask the attendant to flag down a pair of officers she'd seen conversing in their patrol cars in an adjacent lot.

Once the officers arrived, Schroer breathlessly launched into a story that seemed nearly too surreal to believe. Ramirez Peyro, she told the patrolmen, was an extremely dangerous man holding her against her will.

"He has cartel contacts in the U.S. that will kill my family, and I'm afraid what's going to happen now. He's going to have them killed," Schroer told the cops, according to the probable-cause statement prepared by the Joplin Police Department.

Schroer then handed one of the patrolmen her smartphone on which the cops could read for themselves an article from *Narco News* with the headline, "House of Death Informant, a Confessed Killer, Soon to Be Released from Jail." The press coverage discussed how Ramirez Peyro had once been a police officer in Mexico before becoming a top lieutenant for the powerful Juarez Cartel. In that role Ramirez Peyro had overseen multiple murders in a home just across the El Paso border that had a history so gruesome it had earned the name the "House of Death." And the story didn't end there.

Lalo — fast asleep in room No. 365 of the adjacent La Quinta — of course was more complicated than that. According to the articles, while working for the cartel, Lalo had also been an informant for ICE. He later embarrassed the American government when it became known that one of its own undercover operatives had been involved in the grisly murders inside the notorious House of Death.

***

Dressed in an orange jumpsuit, his limbs shackled, former ICE informant Lalo, now in his early 40s, enters the Newton County courthouse in Neosho, Missouri, located just south of Joplin. Lalo labors to lower his six-foot-two-inch frame into a chair next to his public defender. It's late July 2014, and he's in court for a hearing regarding the charges of kidnapping and violating a protection order that have kept him an involuntary guest of the Newton County jail since his arrest on December 28, 2013

Lalo's hair is longer than it was in his mugshot, and his body is thinner, a result, he says, of the crummy prison cuisine. As the lawyers debate his case before the judge, Lalo sits expressionless, occasionally looking down at his attorney's notes.

In April 2014, the court reduced his bond from $250,000 to $125,000. Around the same time, some individuals that Lalo says he does not know offered to provide the funds necessary to secure his release. The inmate refused the offer, fearing they might be with the cartel. For now, anyway, it seems he could be safer in jail than out on the streets. Lalo says he's heard from inmates associated with the Latino gang MS-13 that his old associates in the Juarez Cartel have placed a $500,000 bounty on his head. Retired U.S. Customs supervisory agent Mark Conrad says a $500,000 hit seems a bit high, likely exaggerated by street talk. "Heck, for $10,000, they could get the job done," he adds.

And the cartel's not his only adversary. Lalo believes the charges he's currently facing are drummed up in order for the U.S. government to finally deport him because it no longer has a use for him.

"I'm absolutely going to be killed by the Juarez cartel or the Mexican government, which is basically the same thing," says Lalo, speaking by phone during a jailhouse interview.

That the cartel would want him dead is not all that surprising to Lalo. They've tried to execute him before. But that the U.S. would now be aiding it by seeking to deport him to a certain death is something he never foresaw back in 2000 when he crossed into the United States to El Paso seeking to offer information and intelligence on drug trafficking and other crimes to federal agents.

"When I start getting relationship with people working in the drug trade, and start helping them, I didn't really like it or trust them," Lalo said, attempting to explain why he decided to go to work for Uncle Sam.

But his covert job did prove to be a lucrative venture, at least initially, earning him tens of thousands of dollars per case. His work for ICE — which included counterfeit credit-card, illegal-cigarette and drug-smuggling investigations — resulted in the arrest of more than 50 people and the seizure of some 660 kilos of cocaine and in excess of 20,000 pounds of marijuana over the next four years, court records assert.

His work was deemed so valuable that even after he was caught in late June 2003 smuggling 100 pounds of marijuana by car into New Mexico, a U.S. prosecutor in El Paso intervened to get the charges dismissed, so that Lalo could continue his clandestine informant work.

DEA was not so confident in Lalo's veracity, however, and deactivated him as an informant after the arrest in New Mexico. Yes, for a time, Lalo was helping DEA too, after they initially had targeted him for investigation — only to discover he was an ICE informant and decided to enlist his services as well.

"Confidential informants are liars 99 percent of the time," former DEA deep undercover agent Mike Levine says. "Dealing with them is like going through the looking glass."

It was in 2001, however, long before his untimely arrest in New Mexico, that Lalo made a connection with a major player in Juarez — a sociopath named Humberto Santillan Tabares — that would lead him to make an offer. Would ICE want his help bringing down the Juarez cartel?

By 2003 Lalo had wormed his way into Santillan's confidence and into a position of importance within the cartel cell the Santillan controlled. One of Lalo's primary jobs was to oversee a house at 3633 Parsioneros Street — which, on the surface, was a middle-class home in a quiet neighborhood in Juarez. But it served a sinister purpose for Santillan and his assassins, which included more than a dozen Mexican state cops.

In late November 2003, Lalo brought two of his underlings to the Parsioneros house, per Santillan's orders, because they had screwed up and lost a load of marijuana to a police bust in Juarez. With some 15 Mexican state cops present at the house, the duo were ordered to lift their shirts over their heads, forced to the floor, and then the commander of the state police — whose drugs they had lost — pumped bullets into them using a gun with a silencer, so as not to disturb the neighbors.

This was not the last time, or even the first time, that Lalo was called on by his cartel bosses to play a role in murder. The House of Death on Parsioneros was the site of at least a half a dozen grizzly murders over a six-month period ending in early 2004. It also served as a burial site for bodies, whose souls were tortured and murdered elsewhere. A dozen corpses were eventually found in the narcofosa — each covered with lime and dumped into shallow, rock-caked holes in the fenced-in backyard of the house, which is nestled along a U-shaped street in a middle-class neighborhood in Juarez.

* * *

Kelly Schroer declined to talk with me about the kidnapping charges facing her now ex-boyfriend, Lalo. Her brother, Jeff, was a bit more willing.

"She's having a tough time dealing with this case," Jeff Schroer said by phone from suburban Buffalo.

"Did he [Lalo] tell you about the restraining [protective] order and that seven or eight felonies are waiting for him in Tonawanda [New York]?" Jeff Schroer asks. "All the violations, beating her up a few times; he broke her ribs; stalking. I don't even know, but there's a whole shit ton of detectives up here waiting to get their hands on him too."

The Erie County District Attorney's Office in New York confirms that a case against Lalo for "harassment, unlawful imprisonment and criminal contempt" was presented to a grand jury there in February 2014, a little more than a month after Lalo was taken into custody in Joplin, but no charges were then brought against Lalo, though the DA's office said at the time that the case remained open.

"They had talked about transferring the charges [in Missouri] to New York because that's where the events originated at," says Newton County Sheriff's Office Capt. Richard Leavens, who oversees the jail where Lalo is being held. "[The prosecutor's office in Erie County, New York] had been in contact with our prosecutor's office, but I don't know where that stands now. We've not heard anything further on this."

If a hostile reception awaits Lalo upon his return to Buffalo, if he somehow beats the rap in Missouri, that's not how it started out for him. Buffalo was supposed to be his second chance, a place where he could build a new life and leave the cartel world behind him. He landed a job as a long-haul truck driver there, which provided him with a low profile and an unpredictable schedule — all the better for staying off the radar. But Lalo had driven in the fast lane of the narco-trafficking business for years and shaking the excitement of that edge, and the glitzy lifestyle it afforded, would prove tough. So, when a cousin asked Lalo if he would do him a favor and fly out to California and retrieve a Ferrari he owned, the former cartel member jumped at the chance.

Lalo first asked a friend in Buffalo to accompany him on the trek, but the pal, a businessman who asked not to be named, said he told Lalo he was "nuts." For starters, driving a Ferrari — with Mexican plates — through a well-known drug route like Interstate 44 was bound to attract the wrong kind of attention. And if the cops didn't stop the car, the snow along the way likely would. The Ferrari rides only three inches off the ground.

The friend insists that Lalo asked Schroer to accompany him only as an "afterthought." He says he doesn't understand how Lalo can remain in jail in Missouri some eight months after his arrest.

"How can they keep him incarcerated so long over a hearsay case, where she [Schroer] could have stopped anywhere along the line?" Lalo's friend asked. "He didn't intend to kidnap her. That's ridiculous."

The point of bringing the Ferrari to New York, Lalo says, was so that he and one of his cousins from Mexico could attend the NFL Super Bowl in New Jersey in February 2014. Lalo also told me during one interview while he was jailed that "the other reason" for the trip was for him and his cousin to "meet in New York with people ... from China" to grease the wheels for a potential future meeting in Mexico where they could hopefully persuade them to get involved in a construction business. "I cannot go there [Mexico] which is why we initially were going to meet there in New York," Lalo said in the interview.

Joplin Police Department's Lieutenant Matt Stewart says the Ferrari was towed after Lalo's arrest, but no charges were brought against him in relation to the vehicle. Lalo says his cousin ultimately reclaimed the Ferrari.

In her statement to Joplin police, Kelly Schroer told authorities that Lalo had prohibited her from contacting her family during their trip to California. But according to a police report in New York, Kelly and her brother were in touch during the journey. Just eight hours prior to Lalo's arrest in Joplin, Jeff Schroer filed a report with police in their hometown of Tonawanda stating that he was "concerned about his sister's welfare" because his phone calls with his sister were "very short" and the text messages he received appeared to be written by someone who "speaks little English." Jeff told police he believed his sister was "being held against her will" by her boyfriend with connections to the "Mexican drug trade."

The Tonawanda police then contacted ICE. The agents responding indicated that "there are no restraints" on Lalo's ability to travel. The ICE agents asked to be made aware of any charges that might be brought against him, however, and also to be kept apprised of any developments.

Lalo contends that Schroer's kidnapping allegations are "all lies," pointing out that he has photos of them together, smiling and embracing during the trip. He too notes that she could have escaped at any time or brought her concern to authorities prior to them arriving in Joplin. Lalo believes the affidavit she signed, denying that she had ever been abused or threatened by him, also is more proof that she accompanied him of her own free will.

During the court hearing on July 21, 2014, Lalo's public defender, Kathleen Byrnes, makes another argument.

"The prosecution has filed [charges] in the case, but there are no facts alleged concerning what particular crimes were committed in Missouri," Byrnes tells the judge. "The probable cause statement refers to things that may or may not have occurred in other parts of the U.S."

Byrnes continues: "There is nothing to show why the state thinks there was a kidnapping. Ms. Schroer said they were on their way back to New York. She desired to go there, and there does not appear to be any acts in the allegations that occurred in Missouri. What did my client do in Missouri that constitutes kidnapping?"

The hearing ends with Judge Timothy Perigo, a middle-aged magistrate with close-cropped hair, stating that he will draft an order spelling out what the state needs to disclose. "The prosecution will not be required to answer interrogatories [from the defense], but they should give the defense some more specificity on the charges."

* * *

Once the bodies at the House of Death were dug up in early 2004, the Mexican media, and later the U.S. mainstream media, were all over the blood-pornography angle of the story — for a news cycle or two, before the story largely disappeared from the headlines. But that spate of news coverage, coupled with Lalo's assist in arresting Juarez Cartel operative Santillan, meant that his cover was blown, and he was a marked man in the cartel's eyes, he says.

The rest of the story we know by now. He was put into protective custody in San Antonio, Texas, working a job as a shopping-center security guard while living with his ex-wife and kids — also put into protective custody because of the threat to their lives. Lalo didn't last long there, and in late August of 2004 he made a trip to El Paso in an effort to reunite with his then-girlfriend. While there, the cartel sent a hitman to finish off Lalo at a Whataburger fast-food restaurant, after becoming aware of a money-drop Lalo had arranged — from the supposed sale of property he still controlled in Juarez, a federal agent close to the case says. Lalo insists he was assisting with a legit ICE sting operation that went south.

Regardless, ever wary, Lalo instead sent a friend to pick up the cash at the drop site — the Whataburger's parking lot. He claims that "friend" was an FBI informant (Abraham Guzman), and the cartel wound up killing the wrong man — by pumping four bullets into the chest and face of Lalo's buddy, Guzman, while he was sitting in his car at the burger joint. ICE then swept up Lalo under what his attorney in Buffalo describes as the pretense of protecting him from would-be assassins.

Over the next six years, they moved Lalo from prison to prison, in Texas, Minnesota and finally New York — while pressing deportation proceedings against him. Lalo eventually prevailed, arguing successfully in immigration court that he would be murdered with the Mexican government's acquiescence if sent back to Mexico. He was released in April 2010 and allowed to stay in the country with temporary immigration status. From that point forward, until his arrest in Missouri in late 2013, Lalo earned a living initially as an employee of a Target retail outlet and later by driving truck around the country, even operating under his real name — yet somehow able to stay one step ahead of the cartel that he is convinced wants him dead.

In fact, Lalo in July 2013, only months before his arrest in Missouri, filed a $125 million lawsuit against a group of federal prosecutors and federal agents as well as several county sheriffs and detention-facility officials alleging they acted in a conspiracy to violate his constitutional rights by keeping him imprisoned against his will for years without charges — while seeking to return him to Mexico and a gruesome death. The case, filed in U.S. District Court for the Western District of New York, is sealed, and its ultimate outcome is unknown — though it appears to have not survived Lalo's escapades.

The lawsuit named some 35 defendants as actors in the alleged conspiracy to violate Ramirez Peyro's constitutional rights. They include past and present employees of ICE, the Department of Homeland Security, the U.S. Marshals Service and various county sheriffs in Texas and Minnesota. In addition, the litigation accuses some of the most powerful U.S. prosecutors in Texas of being party to the alleged conspiracy.

Ramirez Peyro, in his pleadings, claims those U.S. prosecutors, with the assistance of the other defendants, as part of a "meeting of the minds," conspired to imprison him for nearly six years in furtherance of a coverup designed to conceal their complicity in the House of Death murders. Among those named in the lawsuit are former Western District of Texas U.S. Attorney Johnny Sutton as well as **Margaret Leachman**, at the time the Criminal Division chief in the Western District; **Richard Durbin**, then first Assistant U.S. Attorney in the Western District; and Juanita Fielden, then Assistant U.S. Attorney in the Western District's El Paso division.

Although the litigation was cloaked from public inspection, through sources, I was able to inspect pleadings from the case. The lawsuit was filed under seal, in large part, to assure that Ramirez Peyro's location was not revealed, given his life was deemed to be in jeopardy. That issue was made moot with Lalo's arrest in Newton County, Missouri, however.

In addition to the ongoing threat from the Juarez Cartel, "about 16 people are now out of prison that Lalo helped to put in prison," says **Steve Cohen**, the Buffalo-area attorney who replaced South Texas attorney Jodi Goodwin as Ramirez Peyro's lawyer. Cohen declined to comment directly on the litigation, given it is sealed. He stressed, however, that, "Mr. [Ramirez] Peyro put his life on the line for the United States of America time after time. He is directly responsible for approximately 50 criminal convictions of upper-echelon cartel members, as well as the removal of huge quantities of drugs from the streets of this country...."

I did once again contact Sutton for comment on the House of Death case in the fall of 2013, after he joined former Attorney General Ashcroft's law firm at its then-new office in Austin. Sutton did not respond. Daryl Fields, spokesman for Sutton's former employer, the U.S. Attorney's Office for the Western District of Texas in San Antonio, also was contacted about the allegations raised in Ramirez Peyro's pleadings.

"We have no comment," Fields replied in an email.

Likewise, an effort was made in 2014 to seek a comment about the House of Death case from former Attorney General John Ashcroft, or someone at his law firm, where Sutton was still employed at the time. No one ever responded to the inquiry — made through an assistant with his law firm, the Ashcroft Group.

After all, the mainstream media has given them a pass on their role in the carnage, so why would they willingly sow new seeds with me and my pen?

* * *

Lalo said in a 2014 jailhouse phone interview from Missouri that he believed a major reason he was locked up in Newton County — at the time for the better part of a year on what he described as trumped-up charges — was because of that then-sealed lawsuit against Sutton, et. al., and the damage it could do to some powerful former and current U.S. officials if it were to go to trial.

ICE spokesperson Danielle Bennett says she's not familiar with Lalo's kidnapping case in Missouri but sees no merit in his claim. "When a local authority has someone on criminal charges, that's not an influence that we would have," she says. "If he's got criminal charges, it would be the local authority that is setting the limits for keeping him in their custody."

Cohen, the Buffalo attorney serving as Lalo's lawyer, says he is certain that "the U.S. Attorney's Office and the Department of Justice are well aware of Lalo and the particular embarrassing facts and events he is witness too, and will do all they can to marginalize him."

Retired DEA El Paso commander and House of Death whistleblower Sandalio Gonzalez echoed Lalo's take: "I think they [DOJ and ICE] would have reason to do whatever they could to prevent that lawsuit ever seeing light of day from a trial."

If there was a plot afoot against Lalo, however, the prosecutor handling his case in Missouri insisted he had not been read in on it.

"No one from federal government has contacted me about the guy [Lalo]," said Newton County Prosecuting Attorney Jake Skouby.

Joplin Police Department's Lt. Mathew Stewart, adds that officers with his department work with federal law enforcers from the FBI, ATF, DEA and ICE on various task forces, "and they are aware of [Lalo's] case and have talked about it ... but as far as I'm aware, they [ICE or the other agencies] haven't done anything with it."

Regardless, Lalo remains convinced that something is not right in Newton County when it comes to the justice he is now confronting. "They are trying to portray me as a kidnapper, which is not true," he says. "In my mind, I knew from the beginning from what my public defender told me. She said, 'Oh we got a big case here. They will make it a high-profile case because of who you are ... that you were a member of a cartel.'"

Lalo stresses that he was working for the U.S. government and that the only ties he has to the cartel "is they want to kill me."

Prosecutor Skouby says it's not unusual for a felony case to take close to a year to play out in the Newton County court system. "This [case] is really more intrigue than I'm used to dealing with. I'll tell you that," Skouby says. "Basically, I-44 runs through my district, and that's how I caught this case. That's it."

Sheriff's Office Captain Leavens has dealt with plenty of dangerous people, including "mass murderers and militia people," at the Newton County jail in the past, he says. Lalo, though, is in a category all by himself. "I've not seen anything quite like this," Leavens adds. "I've been here 25 years just about now, and I've never dealt with anything of this type of circumstance. ..."

All of the intrigue came to an end in April 2015 when, after spending nearly a year-and-a-half in the Newton County pokey, the kidnapping charge against Ramirez Peyro was dropped. He pleaded guilty to a misdemeanor charge of violating a court-protection order.

Under the terms of the plea deal, the *Joplin Globe* reported, he was sentenced to a year in jail but was released after being given credit for the time he had served. "We didn't have one of the elements we needed to prove kidnapping, that he took her for the purpose of doing her harm or to terrorize her," prosecutor Skouby said at the time.

Dispatch 30

July 9, 2020

The House of Death informant known as Jesus Contreras, SA-913-EP and Lalo, and later by his legal name, Guillermo Eduardo Ramirez Peyro — a moniker revealed after he was deactivated by ICE in early 2004 and later exposed in media reports — once again found himself back in the slammer in the spring of 2020.

His run-in with the law, the FBI specifically, played out during the onslaught of the coronavirus pandemic in the U.S. He was arrested and jailed on federal charges in Miami accusing him of conspiring to possess and distribute cocaine.

If convicted, Ramirez Peyro, born in 1971, and on the cusp of 50 when busted, faces up to 10 years in prison — or more if the charges against him are expanded. He was caught up in an FBI sting in the spring of 2020 that involved ironically, an informant, as well as audio and video surveillance, which the criminal complaint alleges prove Ramirez Peyro's intent to purchase and distribute at least five kilos of cocaine.

The federal criminal complaint against Ramirez Peyro, filed in U.S. District Court for the Southern District of Florida, contends he arranged multiple meetings with an FBI informant seeking to purchase a large quantity of cocaine. In at least one of those meetings, an accomplice, referred to in the initial pleadings only as "Pollo," also was present. "Ramirez Peyro indicated he wished to purchase five kilograms of cocaine from the confidential source for approximately $120,000," the criminal complaint alleges. "That meeting was audio- and video-recorded."

Between late March and mid-April of 2020, U.S. government court pleadings allege Ramirez Peyro met with the FBI informant several times at locations in the greater Miami area, including a Dunkin' Donuts shop, and provided the individual with a total of $20,000 as a down-payment on the cocaine contraband.

The federal judge's **detention order** explains more:

> At that hearing, the court heard evidence that, on or about March 23, 2020, [Ramirez Peyro] met with a law enforcement confidential source ("CS") in Miramar, Florida, and discussed purchasing multiple kilograms of cocaine from the CS [an informant]. ... [Ramirez Peyro] subsequently made a down payment of $13,500 to the CS for the future cocaine purchase.
>
> On or about March 24, 2020, [Ramirez Peyro] and an additional co-conspirator met the CS in Miramar, Florida. During the meeting, [Ramirez Peyro] and the co-conspirator provided the CS with an additional $6,500.00 down-payment for the future cocaine purchase. That meeting was recorded with audio and video. On or about April 16, 2020, [Ramirez Peyro] and the CS again met in Miramar, Florida. During the meeting, the CS and [Ramirez Peyro] discussed the specifics of the cocaine transaction that they scheduled to occur the following day. That meeting was audio- and video-recorded.
>
> ... On or about April 17, 2020 ... [Ramirez Peyro] and the CS met at a Hilton Garden Inn in Miramar, and [Ramirez Peyro] showed the CS a bag full of money for the cocaine that he [Ramirez Peyro] had in the trunk of the car he was driving.
>
> After seeing the money, the CS told [Ramirez Peyro] the cocaine was located at a different location in Miramar. As [Ramirez Peyro] was driving to pick up the cocaine, he was stopped by Miramar Police Department. Miramar Police Department subsequently recovered $50,000 from the car. That was the same money [Ramirez Peyro] had shown to the CS, and that [Ramirez Peyro] intended to use to purchase the five kilograms of cocaine from the CS. A K-9 sniff test was conducted on the money, and the K-9 gave a positive indication for the presence of narcotics.

Trace amounts of cocaine can be found on a majority of U.S. currency, however, media reports over time show. It's evidence of the prevalence of cocaine use in the U.S., which does not produce cocaine. Cocaine and its cousin, crack cocaine, are derived from the coca plant, an indigenous species that grows in the mountainous Andean region of South American. Some 95 percent of the cocaine entering the U.S. originates in Colombia, Peru and Bolivia, according to the White House Office of National Drug Control Policy.

Of note in the court pleadings is that there was no cocaine found on Ramirez Peyro or in his vehicle when he was arrested. Key to helping to decipher what is up here, however, is the following excerpt from judge's detention order:

> [Ramirez Peyro] was in possession of a Mexican passport and Puerto Rican drivers' license, and a U.S. work authorization card. The government also proffered that [he] was a member of the former Juarez cartel, currently known as the Sinaloa cartel. Evidence was also presented that [Ramirez Peyro] had an immigration detainer on him, has connections to Mexico, has connections to the Mexican cartels, and has no connections to Miami.

Despite a lack of cocaine in a cocaine case, the FBI's evidence was enough of a ham sandwich for a grand jury, and the former ICE informant was indicted, arrested, arraigned and then jailed without bond. The **"immigration detainer"** in place for Ramirez Peyro is a legal tool used by ICE to establish a claim on individuals it deems deportable. Consequently, in the event Ramirez Peyro somehow beats the criminal charges, or even if he doesn't and serves time, when he is released from federal custody, Ramirez Peyro will get turned over to ICE, his old employer, to potentially face deportation proceedings once again.

"Having considered the evidence and arguments of counsel presented at the hearing, the court finds, by a preponderance of the evidence, that the defendant poses a reasonable risk of flight if allowed to be out on bond," states the judge's **detention order** lodged in U.S. District Court in Miami on April 24, 2020. The judge based that decision on the following factors, according to his ruling:

Ramirez Peyro faces a long mandatory-minimum sentence if convicted. There is considerable evidence against him:

- He is a Mexican citizen who has strong connections "to Mexico and to the Mexican cartels."
- He faces an immigration detainer.
- Ramirez Peyro was carrying "multiple identification documents" when arrested, including a Mexican passport and Puerto Rican drivers' license.
- And Ramirez Peyro "lacks connections in the Miami area."

To make matters worse for Ramirez Peyro, in early June 2021 federal prosecutors in Miami issued **a superseding indictment** in his case accusing him of multiple counts of money laundering. So, even if he beats the cocaine charges, he is up against another wall with the alleged financial crimes.

The enhanced indictment includes a chart listing some 15 separate wire transfers and check transactions in Miami-Dade and Broward counties that the FBI and federal prosecutors allege are, per the indictment, "the proceeds of a specified unlawful activity." If convicted, the indictment calls for those proceeds — about $1.5 million in total — to be "forfeited to the United States."

How Ramirez Peyro might have come into such a treasure, given his last known payroll job was as a truck driver, is not clear at this point, assuming the federal charges withstand legal scrutiny. What is clear is that it is not the only mystery surrounding the former ICE informant's return to the public spotlight via a criminal prosecution.

The Mexican passport — the fact that Ramirez Peyro even had one, given his supposed fear of being tortured and murdered there by the "cartels" — well, that's a bit hard to explain. Might Ramirez Peyro still be working for a U.S. agency?

That's a possibility I can't discount. Although there may be another explanation. Ramirez Peyro also may have benefited from the changing tide in the war for drugs and fell in with a group that found his unique talents of use. In fact, in the pleadings in his criminal case, the government contends Ramirez Peyro is "a member of the former Juarez cartel, currently known as the Sinaloa Cartel" — the latter steered for many years by the now-jailed Joaquin "Chapo" Guzman Loera and, as of the start of 2022, also by his still quite free partner, Ismael "El Mayo" Zambada.

It's possible that Ramirez Peyro has been given a new lease on life, and his past gig as a U.S. informant targeting the Juarez Cartel overlooked, at least for now, by the Sinaloa Cartel leadership because he is somehow deemed valuable to them or their associates. And the Sinaloa Cartel leadership has allegedly welcomed and worked with U.S. government assets and informants in similar positions in the past, court pleadings contend.

Jesus Vicente Zambada Niebla, the son of El Mayo, was arrested by DEA agents at a hotel in Mexico in March 2009 and a year later extradited to the U.S. He inked a plea bargain in April 2013 and agreed to tell the U.S. government everything he knew about his alleged partners in crime, their operations and enablers. The plea agreement promised to reward Zambada Niebla for his cooperation by shaving decades off his prison sentence — assuming he had gone to trial and lost. Zambada Niebla ended up getting a **15-year sentence from the judge.**

In his pleadings, however, prior to inking a plea deal, Zambada Niebla made a shocking claim, alleging that he essentially was a cooperating source for the U.S. government. His allegation was **laid out originally** in a two-page court filing in March 2011 with the U.S. District Court for the Northern District of Illinois in Chicago. More detailed and disturbing allegations were advanced by Zambada Niebla — who at the time was being held in solitary confinement in a jail cell in Chicago — in motions filed in July 2011 in federal court. Those pleadings spell out the supposed cooperative relationship between the U.S. Department of Justice and its various agencies, including DEA and the FBI, and the leaders of the "Sinaloa Cartel" — including Zambada Niebla, born in 1975 and then in his mid-30s.

That alleged relationship was cultivated through a Mexican attorney, Humberto Loya Castro, whom Zambada Niebla claims is a Sinaloa Cartel member and "a close confidante of Joaquin Guzman Loera (Chapo)." From Zambada Niebla's court pleadings, filed on July 29, 2011:

> [Humberto] Loya Castro was indicted along with Chapo and Mayo [Zambada Niebla's father] in 1995 in the Southern District of California and charged with participation in a massive narcotics trafficking conspiracy (Case No. 95CR0973). That case was dismissed on the prosecution's own motion in 2008 after Loya [Castro] became an informant for the United States government and had provided information for a period of over 10 years.
>
> Sometime prior to 2004 [when George W. Bush was president and within the time frame of the House of Death mass murder] and continuing through the time period covered in the indictment, the United States government entered into an agreement with Loya and the leadership of the Sinaloa Cartel, including Mayo and Chapo.
>
> Under that agreement, the Sinaloa Cartel, through Loya, was to provide information accumulated by Mayo [Ismael Zambada], Chapo [Guzman], and others, against rival Mexican drug trafficking organizations [such as the Juarez Cartel] to the United States government. In return, the United States government agreed to dismiss the prosecution of the pending case against Loya, not to interfere with his drug trafficking activities and those of the Sinaloa Cartel, to not actively prosecute him, Chapo, Mayo, and the leadership of the Sinaloa Cartel, and to not apprehend them. The defendant [Zambada Niebla] is alleged to be a high-ranking member of the Sinaloa Cartel.
>
> ... United States government agents in Mexico, including but not limited to the DEA and ICE, were told by Loya that Mayo and Chapo and other alleged members of the Sinaloa Cartel, and Mr. Zambada Niebla, were providing information to the United States government under the agreement with Loya, who would then pass along the information to the agents.
>
> The protection extended to the Sinaloa leadership, according to the court filings, included being "informed by agents of the DEA through

Loya that United States government agents and/or Mexican authorities were conducting investigations near the home territories of cartel leaders so that the cartel leaders could take appropriate actions to evade investigators."

U.S. prosecutors, of course, deny that any such immunity or cooperation arrangement was in place between U.S. agencies and Zambada Niebla, or the broader leadership of the Sinaloa Cartel. And they claim Zambada Niebla has no evidence to prove the existence of such a pact. At the same time U.S. prosecutors invoked national security via the Classified Information Procedures Act (also called CIPA) in Zambada Niebla's trial in an attempt to assure certain sensitive information and communications — or arguably embarrassing revelations — were not made available to his attorneys or the public.

For those who doubt that there is any chance that the leadership of the Sinaloa Cartel and individuals like Ramirez Peyro or Loya Castro might develop, in effect, a quid pro quo relationship with U.S. law enforcers or intelligence agencies, or both, then a little history lesson is in order. That is precisely the role **Manuel Noriega, former military leader of Panama, played for the CIA and DEA** in the 1980s, prior to falling from grace and being arrested in the wake of the U.S. military invasion of Panama in 1989.

In 1987, then-**DEA administrator Jack Lawn penned a letter** to Noriega that stated, in part: "The DEA has long welcomed our close association and we stand ready to proceed jointly against international drug traffickers whenever the opportunity arises." In early 1988 — after Noriega was indicted in the U.S. — Congress and Justice Department officials accused DEA of giving the Panamanian dictator a free pass on his narco-trafficking activities during the period they were using him to help make cases against other narco-traffickers, the *New York Times* reported at the time.

A July 1999 appeals-court ruling in the Noriega criminal case also reveals that the CIA had an intimate relationship with the Panamanian dictator. However, the appeals-court ruling let stand the trial court's decision to conceal the nature of that relationship. CIPA also was invoked in Noriega's trial. From the appellate court ruling:

> The government objected to any disclosure of the purposes for which the United States had paid Noriega. In pre-trial proceedings, the government offered to stipulate that Noriega had received approximately $320,000 from the United States Army and the Central Intelligence Agency. Noriega insisted that the actual figure approached $10,000,000, and that he should be allowed to disclose the tasks he had performed for the United States.
>
> The district court held that information about the content of the discrete operations in which Noriega had engaged in exchange for the alleged payments was irrelevant to his defense.

If a quid pro quo relationship did exist between the Sinaloa Cartel leadership and key law enforcement and intelligence agencies in the U.S., as alleged in Zambada Niebla's court pleadings, would that be any different than U.S. war strategy elsewhere on the planet where a divide-and-conquer strategy is employed? Support the Sinaloa Cartel and its loyal soldiers in their blood battle with rival organized criminal groups, like the Juarez Cartel, and then clean-up the Sinaloa Cartel leadership afterward. It makes some strategic sense, if it were really a hot war and not a corrupt business — where contracts and markets are controlled by bullets.

Recall that one federal agent familiar with Ramirez Peyro's work, who asked not to be named, said far from being murdered by the cartels, "if [Lalo] goes back to Mexico, he's going to be the next one of the cartel leaders." Ramirez Peyro does understand how the drug business works, is comfortable with its corruption, and has proven adept at playing on both sides of the border. And he can be seen as doing essentially what Mexican attorney Loya Castro did, and apparently what Sinaloa Cartel leader Zambada Niebla believed he was doing — cooperating openly with the U.S. government to hurt the Juarez Cartel.

As in the past, the House of Death informant may find a way to continue to play both sides at the same time to his favor — without anyone realizing it but him. How that would look is anyone's guess, but he's already done it once before, with ICE and the House of Death. His life, it seems, has always been suspended on a precarious bridge — one linking the myriad dysfunctional U.S. law enforcement bureaucracies (often mired in turf wars and racism) to the always-spinning web of criminal cells, cartels and sicarios hardened by decades of street wars and the treacherous politics of doing business under the Mexican government's long shadow.

Why would that change now?

Only time will tell if the jig is finally up for Guillermo Eduardo "Lalo" Ramirez Peyro.

* * *

In mid-June 2021, nearly a year after he was indicted, an **order of recusal** was lodged by the judge in his case, Donald L. Graham. Ramirez Peyro's case was reassigned to Chief Judge K. Michael Moore. Then, some two weeks later, on June 29, the new judge held a telephone hearing on sealed motions that had been filed in mid-June asking the court to **seal pleadings in the case and issue a "protective order."** Pleadings filed after that point — in July and August 2021— were, in fact, sealed by the judge's order "until further notice," according to the **court docket** for the case.

Because the pleadings are sealed, the public is not allowed to know even why they have been sealed, much less their contents. Only the judge and the parties to the case are allowed that knowledge.

In late September 2021, there was yet another twist. The court docket shows a "paperless order" calling for the case to be referred to a magistrate judge "to take all necessary and proper actions ... regarding the change of plea by defendant Guillermo Eduardo Ramierz Peyro." The court docket also indicated that a "change of plea hearing" for Ramirez Peyro was set for October 5, 2021.

Lalo had pled "not guilty" at his arraignment hearing on January 29, 2021, after the first indictment against him, and he pled "not guilty" again at a June 3, 2021, arraignment hearing following the superseding indictment issued against him. At the October 5 hearing, however, Ramirez Peyro entered a guilty plea as part of a deal reached with prosecutors. Finally, on January 4, 2022, a judgement was entered in his case. In the wake of his plea bargain, Lalo was convicted on one count of "conspiracy to engage in money laundering," and the other 18 counts of alleged cocaine trafficking and money laundering were dismissed, the judgement shows.

Lalo was sentenced to 78 months in federal prison plus 3 years supervised release by the U.S. District judge in Miami hearing his case — Judge Moore. The court ordered that he serve his term in a federal prison located somewhere in southern Florida, "or as close as possible," the judgement signed by the judge states. As part of the terms of his eventual supervised release from federal prison, he also agreed to "cooperate" with any deportation proceedings initiated by ICE.

A later search of online records available through the Federal Bureau of Prisons showed Lao was doing time at a medium-security prison in Arizona, called FCI Tucson. His scheduled release date is Oct. 30, 2025, according to the BOP website.

Many pleadings are still sealed in Lalo's case, but a couple of public motions filed around a sealed pre-sentencing report reveal an interesting detail that seems important to Lalo's fate in prison and beyond, if he makes it that far. Federal prosecutors claim Lalo stole $190,000 from a "Colombian Cartel." In a counter motion filed by Lalo, however, he disputes he took the money, arguing instead it was one of his partners in crime, an individual named Carlos Rodriguez de la O, who stole the money. Rodriquez de la O, of course, claims Lalo stole the loot, according to prosecutors.

"Some member of the conspiracy stole approximately $190,000. ...It is currently unclear who exactly took the money, or whether [Ramirez Peyro] and Rodriguez de la O split the money," pleadings filed by prosecutors state in a reply to Ramirez Peyro's motion protesting the allegation.

Whatever the reality is with the missing "cartel" money, it appears Ramirez Peyro also was working with one or more co-conspirators based in Mexico. Court pleadings filed by prosecutors contend that one of those co-conspirators was "his uncle" and that Ramirez Peyro admitted he "handled business for his uncle in the United States" — although Lalo disputes that allegation as well, and the uncle is not identified by name in the court filings.

More from pleadings filed by U.S. prosecutors in the case:

In October 2018, two law enforcement sources met with a co-conspirator of [Ramirez Peyro] in Mexico City. The sources represented themselves as drug traffickers from Miami. The [law enforcement] sources explained that they needed help cleaning money from the sale of drugs in the United States. [Ramirez Peyro's co-conspirator in the Mexico City] said that he could help the sources and that he would send [Ramirez Peyro], who handles [the co-conspirator's] business in the United States. Between January 25, 2019, and January 28, 2019, [Ramirez Peyro] and [yet] another co-conspirator [Rodriquez de la O] came to Miami to meet with the [law enforcement] sources several times. During the meetings in Miami, [Ramirez Peyro] and [Rodriquez de la O] agreed to move the money for the sources ....

The Defendant [Ramirez Peyro] admitted to receiving hundreds of thousands of dollars in bags full of cash along with Rodriguez de la O and sending that money back to the drug dealers/sources through either wires or checks, for a 6 percent fee. Those wires were commonly sent in several separate wires, instead of one large wire.

Also in the court pleadings, the identity of another of Ramirez Peyro's alleged co-conspirators is surfaced. In those pleadings, Ramirez Peyro denies U.S. prosecutors' claim that he handled business in the United States for an individual named "Fernando Peyro de la O." Unfortunately, that is the only information provided in the pleadings about the individual.

An investigative report published by Univision in mid-2022, however, identifies Ramirez Peyro as Fernando Peyro de la O's relative (a cousin). It's not clear, though, if Peyro de la O is the same relative federal prosecutors identified (or misidentified) in their pleadings as being Ramirez Peyro's "uncle," or if they are separate individuals.

In any event, in an interview I conducted with Ramirez Peyro some six years before he was busted by the FBI in Miami, he confided that he was in communications with one of his cousins in Mexico who had ties to the construction business. That's the cousin who asked him to fly out to California and retrieve — and drive back to the East Coast — a Ferrari he owned, so they could attend the NFL Super Bowl in New Jersey in February 2014.

The **Univision report** alleges that Fernando Peyro de la O, 52, is trained as a civil engineer and now owns construction companies in Mexico. The report also alleges that he is a close friend of Catholic **prelate Norberto Rivera Carrera**, 80, who was elevated to cardinal in 1998 and served as the archbishop of Mexico City from 1995-2017 before retiring from the post. The news report also notes that Peyro de la O and Rivera — both of whom are originally from Durango, Mexico — deny being close now. Univision's report, based on leaked clandestine video recordings made by an alleged U.S. government informant, also alleges that Peyro de la O is on the FBI's radar for alleged money-laundering activities that may also implicate Rivera. Both Peryo de la O and Rivera claim such allegations are without merit.

Regardless of where this high-intrigue case involving Mexican semi-royalty leads, if anywhere, it seems clear former ICE informant Ramirez Peyro got a dose of his own medicine with his arrest in Miami as part of an FBI drug and money-laundering case. This time he was the one being stung by an undercover U.S. law-enforcement operation utilizing informants.

To make matters worse for Ramirez Peyro, a story circulating in prison claiming he stole hundreds of thousands of dollars from a Colombian drug cartel can only make him a high-value target for retribution — on top of his already very public past role as a high-paid "snitch" for ICE. Ironically, as you may recall, one of Lalo's first cartel jobs in Mexico was coordinating the transport of cocaine shipments from Colombia into Mexico, allegedly with the help of the Mexican Navy, according to his 2005 immigration-court testimony.

Ramirez Peyro's attorney, Christian Dunham, a public defender, declined to speak with media about the case shortly after Lalo's arrest. I later sent an email query to Dunham and to the prosecutors handling Lalo's case seeking comment, but they did not respond.

Lalo's plea deal precluding a public trial is not a big surprise in the scheme of the U.S. justice system. After all, Lalo's boss at the House of Death, Santillan, also accepted a plea bargain that accomplished the same ends — lessoning his jail time and keeping the former ICE informant Ramirez Peyro off the stand in a jury trial. The darker secrets of the drug war are best kept under wraps, it seems.

In this case, arguably, Lalo's big mistake was not so much committing a drug-war crime, but rather doing so while not on the payroll of U.S. law enforcement. Whether Ramirez Peyro will ever again work for the U.S. government or for a drug cartel, or end up being murdered in prison or elsewhere, remains an open question. The drug war exists in our prison system too, even as it continues to be waged on the streets of the Americas. For those wrapped up in it, there is no escaping its embrace.

So, once again, secrets in the drug war compound and congeal around the past and future of the former ICE informant Guillermo Eduardo Ramirez Peyro. Anything seems possible in Lalo's world. After all, the war for drugs, so far, has no expiration date, nor is justice its master.

Closing the Door

Dispatch 31

The Past is Always Present

Following the inner-workings of the Mexican narco-trafficking business is like playing in a three-card Monte tournament in a dark back alley of a very tough neighborhood. It's very difficult, likely impossible, to predict where the right card will fall at any given time, and that is by design. The illusive outlaws of the narco-trafficking shadowlands have attained folk-hero status in Mexico and beyond for that very reason. But another factor in the difficulty of following the cards is the reality that the alliances in the narco-trafficking business are constantly shifting, because so much is at stake — power, money and life itself.

Elements of the Mexican government are very active participants in the narco-trafficking trade. Corrupt politicians and law enforcement at all levels (federal, state and local) have thrown the force of law behind the criminal trade — whether that be police operating in the border plazas of Nuevo Laredo, Tijuana and Juarez, or the Mexican military special-forces defectors who gave rise to the ruthless Los Zetas paramilitary drug gang earlier in this century. On the U.S. side, it is not so different, especially along the border. Stories of U.S. law enforcement profiting off of or being complicit in the drug trade are nothing new — if you're willing to look.

The allure of the narco-trafficking business seems to cross all lines, even borders. It offers untold riches if you are willing to spill blood — and risk your own life in the bargain. Getting behind the scenes in this game is no easy task. That's because the corruption seems to be woven into the very fabric of national drug policies and mainstream media coverage in the United States and south of the border.

So, it is no wonder that the most successful narco-traffickers manage to evade for decades or longer the very governments supposedly charged with apprehending them in the so-called drug war. They have far more to fear within their own ranks and from their rivals, it would appear, than they do from any government — given the ease with which government players can be turned with promises of silver and threats of lead.

To the extent that these mythic outlaws can build alliances to reduce the risk of internecine fighting, their potential for greater control of the multibillion-dollar illegal drug trade expands. At best, though, it has to be assumed that such alliances are held together with very weak glue, given lethal treachery, slithering deceit and paranoid distrust are always part of the mixture. And even if some cartel leaders, or even entire cartels, are taken down occasionally by law enforcers, they are simply replaced by new ones — sowing yet more dragon's teeth in the borderlands.

All of this makes one wonder where the line is between the law and corruption in the war for drugs — if such a line even exists anymore. All I know is only a fool believes he can pick a winning card in a game of three-card Monte — because, as we all should know by now, the game is fixed. It has no end. And the only card you can count on being dealt if you play in that dark alley long enough is the one that marks your death.

Conditions along the border today are different now compared with 2003, when the first House of Death murder occurred, yet they remain dire for most poor immigrants fleeing violence and desperation. The House of Death's shadow still extends across both sides of the border.

As I have reflected on the House of Death mass murder, and the why of it all, I have come to agree with what former DEA commander and House of Death whistleblower Sandalio Gonzalez said to me when I first started reporting on this drug-war horror story. "If this had been a city on the Canadian border, these murders would not have happened," Gonzalez told me, shortly after he was forced to retire from the DEA. "Our government would not allow Canadian citizens to be tortured and murdered.

"But, in the House of Death case, they did let it happen, because it was El Paso and Juarez and a bunch of Mexicans that they don't give a shit about."

That assumes a double standard exists in the U.S. justice system — one defined by evidence, due process and truth on one side; and privilege, racism and raw power on the other. But then that is not a new proposition. We fought a civil war over slavery, the ultimate racist system, yet its systemic stench still lingers in our halls of justice.

In many ways, a cold war continues to this day in this nation over the often-camouflaged legacy and remaining vestiges of slavery and its racist legacy. The corrupt drug war is simply one more front of that larger cold war, as I have come to see it. And like all battlelines, it tends to flare up from time to time and get hot. Even when relatively quiet, however, murder never sleeps in that world — as the House of Death reveals.

The whitewashing of the U.S. government's role in the House of Death mass murder continues to this day, even as the murder toll in Mexico continues to climb and the flow of drugs north across the U.S./Mexico border — and the river of guns and cash heading south — remain largely unimpeded. The only tangible accomplishments of the war on drugs to date, the best I can see, has been arresting a seemingly endless parade of "cartel kingpins," who are as replaceable as strawmen; garnering breathless newspaper headlines; and boosting the careers of too many law enforcers and political appointees who have become callous to the escalation of carnage and death in Mexico. It's a callousness, some argue, rooted in racism and political oppression.

In fact, John Ehrlichman, a Watergate co-conspirator and former domestic policy adviser for Richard Nixon — the U.S. president who launched the war on drugs in 1971 — said the following in a 2016 interview with *Harper*'s magazine:

> You want to know what this was really all about? ...The Nixon campaign in 1968, and the Nixon White House after that, had two enemies: the antiwar left and black people. You understand what I'm

saying? We knew we couldn't make it illegal to be either against the war or black, but by getting the public to associate the hippies with marijuana and blacks with heroin, and then criminalizing both heavily, we could disrupt those communities. We could arrest their leaders, raid their homes, break up their meetings, and vilify them night after night on the evening news. Did we know we were lying about the drugs? Of course we did.

Still, history shows us that there is often a reckoning for double standards, including racism. The South didn't win the Civil War, even if some folks today are in denial about that. Yet that cruel war — still the bloodiest in our history — reminds us that reckonings delayed for too long can come at great price to all of us and our society.

Take this book as a warning, then — one that hopefully nudges us to do more to end the extreme injustices faced by so many of our fellow human beings daily because of the corrupt "war for drugs." Absent that pressure from us together to reduce the harm, to "defund murder," there is reason to believe that some with power above us, out of sheer callousness and racism, frankly, will continue to amplify the carnage.

As evidence of that callousness and racism, I return to early October 2006, when the informant Guillermo Eduardo "Lalo" Ramirez Peyro and I communicated for the first time. He was responding to written questions I had submitted to him through his attorney while he was being held in isolation in a prison cell in Minnesota battling the U.S. government's efforts to deport him back to Mexico.

"What else would you like to convey to the readers about your situation that has not been addressed to date?" I asked as a concluding query. The informant's response was chilling, even considering the blood on his own hands from the House of Death mass murder.

"It has been said that there are investigations into the house at Parsioneros Street, but curiously, no one, not one of these investigators, has ever talked to me," Ramirez Peyro replied. "ICE is trying to deport me to a sure death — not necessarily to cover up the fact that they don't care about the lives lost [at the House of Death], but rather to confirm that theory. They DON'T care about the lives lost, and that is something even darker than we know within the U.S. government."

There is no neat conclusion to this book. It's a chronicle of a war that is seemingly perpetual — a war that begets more war because the chess game simply resets from time to time.

"I know this is wishful thinking, but just going at it through enforcement alone ... I think it's been shown that it really doesn't work," former DEA commander Gonzalez said in capturing the heart of it in an interview with *Reason* magazine. "We're successful in putting people behind bars, but then other people take their place right away. It's a never-ending cycle."

The drug war, launched half a century ago when Richard Nixon was president, is now our nation's longest-running, unsuccessful bloody war. And the only conclusion it offers us is more violence and death — absent an expansive social movement that pushes our society to stem the bloodshed.

* * *

Author and drug-war journalist Charles Bowden sent an email to me about half a decade after the House of Death mass murder and subsequent disappearance of Mexican state police comandante Miguel Loya Gallegos, the House of Death's lead executioner. That was some four years prior to Bowden's death in 2014. At the time, Bowden relayed to me that his sources were informing him that cartel-loyal police commander Loya was still very much alive and active in the drug business.

"I asked. Here is what I was told," Bowden wrote in email correspondence. "Loya went to Sinaloa [home base of the Sinaloa Cartel]. May still be there. One guy in his unit was recently seen in El Paso at a nice restaurant, which I am told means the unit [Loya's unit] is still functioning. And the way I was told convinces me it is functioning: Given the blown [House of Death] operation, they would all be dead. So, if one is alive, the unit is alive."

Former ICE informant Guillermo Eduardo Ramirez Peyro, in an interview, confirmed that survival is not an unlikely outcome for someone with the skillset of Miguel Loya Gallegos.

"... He [Loya] was dependable and could handle a fight, and the bosses appreciated that," Ramirez Peyro said. "So, they might have just put him in another city as a strong man. He could not work in law enforcement.... Well, you never know. A lot of Mexican [police] commanders have warrants [against them] in other states. Mexico is a magical land."

Dispatches: Document and Article Sourcing

References by chapter as well as other related content can be found at https://houseofdeath.org.

To contact the author, email warfordrugs@gmail.com.